Drawing on examples from both original staging practices and contemporary performance, leading critics in Shakespeare and Performance studies explore the ways in which Shakespeare is brought to life in the theatre. Each chapter takes an element of dramaturgy or stagecraft – costume, fighting, openings, sound – and unpacks the ways in which these theatrical practicalities make meaning in performance.

Firing debate about how Shakespeare can be studied in performance, the book contains contributions by:

- Carol Chillington Rutter
- Peter Holland
- Paul Prescott
- John Russell Brown
- Rob Conkie
- Robert Shaughnessy
- P.A. Skantze
- Christie Carson
- Sarah Werner
- Farah Karim-Cooper
- Margaret Jane Kidnie

Stuart Hampton-Reeves is the Head of the British Shakespeare Association and a Professor at the University of Central Lancashire, where he is Head of the Graduate Research School.

Bridget Escolme is Senior Lecturer in the Department of Drama at Queen Mary, University of London.

Shakespeare and the Making of Theatre

Edited by

Stuart Hampton-Reeves

and

Bridget Escolme

 macmillan
international
HIGHER EDUCATION

 RED GLOBE
PRESS

First published 2012 by
RED GLOBE PRESS

Red Globe Press in the UK is an imprint of Springer Nature Limited, registered in England, company number 785998, of 4 Crinan Street, London, N1 9XW.

Red Globe Press® is a registered trademark in the United States, the United Kingdom, Europe and other countries.

ISBN 978–0–230–21868–0   ISBN 978–1–137–28493–8 (eBook)

A catalogue record for this book is available from the British Library.

A catalog record for this book is available from the Library of Congress.

Contents

Illustrations

Notes on Contributors

John Russell Brown is a visiting Professor of English at University College London and a theatre director. For 12 years he was the National Theatre's Associate Director in charge of the script department and new writing. He has edited *The Oxford Illustrated History of Theatre* (2001) and plays by Webster and Shakespeare, and directed old and new plays in England and North America.

Christie Carson is Senior Lecturer in the Department of English at Royal Holloway, University of London. She is the co-editor, with Jacky Bratton, of *The Cambridge King Lear CD-ROM: Text and Performance Archive* (2000), and most recently edited *Shakespeare's Globe: A Theatrical Experiment* (with Farah Karim-Cooper, 2008) and *Shakespeare in Stages: New Theatre Histories* (with Christine Dymkowski, 2010).

Rob Conkie is a Lecturer in Theatre and Drama at La Trobe University, Melbourne, Australia. His research brings together practical and theoretical approaches to Shakespeare in performance. He is the author of *The Globe Theatre Project: Shakespeare and Authenticity* (2006) and of articles in *Shakespeare, Shakespeare Survey, Shakespeare Bulletin* and other journals and edited collections with and without Shakespeare in the title.

Bridget Escolme is a Senior Lecturer in the Department of Drama at Queen Mary, University of London. Her publications include *Talking to the Audience: Shakespeare, Performance, Self* (2005) and *Antony and Cleopatra* (Palgrave Shakespeare Handbooks series, 2006). She has worked as a performer and a dramaturge in the UK and USA.

Stuart Hampton-Reeves is Professor of Research-informed Teaching at the University of Central Lancashire. He is the author of books on *Othello* (2010), *Measure for Measure* (2007) and the *Henry VI* plays in performance (2007) and editor, with Bridget Escolme, of the Palgrave series *Shakespeare in Practice*.

Peter Holland is McMeel Family Professor in Shakespeare Studies in the Department of Film, Television, and Theatre at the University of Notre Dame. He is editor of *Shakespeare Survey* and the series *Redefining British Theatre History*. He has written widely on Shakespeare and performance, including *English Shakespeares: Shakespeare on the English Stage in the*

1990s (1997), and often works with the National Theatre and the Royal Shakespeare Company.

Farah Karim-Cooper is Head of Courses and Research at Shakespeare's Globe Theatre, London and author of *Cosmetics in Shakespearean and Renaissance Drama* (2006). She is co-editor of *Shakespeare's Globe: A Theatrical Experiment* (with Christie Carson, 2008) and, together with Tiffany Stern, *Shakespeare's Theatre and the Effects of Performance* (2012).

Margaret Jane Kidnie is Professor of English at the University of Western Ontario, and author of *Shakespeare and the Problem of Adaptation* (2008). She is also the editor of *The Humorous Magistrate,* and Thomas Heywood's *A Woman Killed with Kindness.*

Paul Prescott is Associate Professor of English at the University of Warwick and Academic Associate of the RSC-Warwick Centre for Teaching Shakespeare. He has acted and taught Shakespeare in the UK, Japan, America, Australia and China, and is currently completing *Reviewing Shakespeare*, a history of Shakespearean theatre criticism.

Carol Chillington Rutter, Professor of English and Comparative Literary Studies at the University of Warwick, writes the annual review of Shakespeare performance in England for *Shakespeare Survey* and is author of several books on performance, most recently *Enter the Body: Women and Representation on Shakespeare's Stage* (2000) and *Shakespeare and Child's Play: Lost Boys on Stage and Screen* (2007). An award-winning teacher and named a National Teaching Fellow in 2010, from 2006 to 2010 she was Director of the CAPITAL Centre at the University of Warwick, a collaboration with the Royal Shakespeare Company to bring creativity and performance into university teaching and learning.

Robert Shaughnessy is Professor of Theatre at the University of Kent. He has published widely in the fields of Shakespeare and performance, and his books include *The Shakespeare Effect: A History of Twentieth-Century Performance* (2002) and *The Routledge Guide to William Shakespeare* (2010).

P.A. Skantze, Reader in Performance Practices in the Department of Drama, Theatre and Performance at Roehampton University, directs, writes for and teaches theatre and performance in London and in Italy. Her many publications include *Stillness in Motion in the Seventeenth-Century Theatre* (3rd edn 2007) and 'Unaccommodated Woman: Mabou 'Mines': *Lear*, the Universal, and the Particular in Performance', in *Shakespeare Re-Dressed: Cross-Gender Casting in Contemporary Performance* (ed. James C. Bulman, 2008). Together with Matthew Fink she runs the performance group Four Second Decay, who have performed in Europe, the UK, and the USA.

Sarah Werner is the Undergraduate Program Director at the Folger Shakespeare Library, Washington, DC. She is the author of *Shakespeare and Feminist Performance: Ideology on Stage* (2001) and the editor of *New Directions in Renaissance Drama and Performance Studies*; she is also Associate Editor of *Shakespeare Quarterly*, for whom she has guest-edited a special issue on performance.

Preface: Shakespeare in Practice

The essays in this book historicize, analyse and theorize the material text of performance, approaching Shakespeare as a maker of theatre. They engage with the material stuff of theatre production and explore models for close reading of theatre texts.

At the centre of this book is a set of things that must be taken into account by theatre practitioners making a performance of a Shakespeare play. Entering and exiting, beginning and ending, pausing, fighting, wearing clothes, picking up, using and putting down props, making noise, addressing or ignoring the audience, producing visual patterns and effects: these are all things that actors must do and, in today's theatrical culture, directors and ensembles will make decisions about how they do them and designers will render all these doings coherent through an overall scenographic vision.

Most of these things happen doubly, in the world of the fiction and the world of the theatre – the character comes in, picks up a lost hand-kerchief and leaves; the actor enters, picks up a prop and exits the stage. In the daylit or candlelit playhouses for which these plays were written, or on modern open stages, performed on or even built with these conditions in mind, some of this double action has a fascinating illogic to it: the actor addresses the audience but it seems to be Hamlet doing so, quite consciously, a fictional figure who cannot know three thousand people have paid to see him. Other elements are part of dramaturgical and aesthetic plans that characters have no knowledge of. The production company must decide how and why these things are happening in the fictional world of the play – and how and why they should happen dramaturgically, aesthetically and practically.

This book asks questions about how performers engage with these material things and to what effect, how audiences receive them and how meaning is produced in this dialogic process. Almost the first thing a theatre company does with a Shakespeare script is dismantle it. The text is split into parts for the actors to learn – quite literally in Shakespeare's time; by an actor with her highlighter pen today. Action scenes are given to fight directors, scene descriptions to set designers, sound cues to musical directors. The 'master copy' becomes altered through the process of rehearsal. Lines are cut and rearranged, some-times whole characters removed or conflated to fit the company's resources. Blocking and other stage actions are recorded on the script, along with information about technical cues and other performance notes. In its reassembly, Shakespeare's script is inscribed with annotations which capture this activity. This, the 'prompt book', becomes the new text which represents the product of the company's deconstruction and reconstruction of Shakespeare's play.

This textual fragmentation, the first step towards making theatre out of Shakespeare, is one that Shakespeare himself might have recognized, although the textual fragmentation he would have been used to might look bizarre or radical now. He parodies the process in *A Midsummer Night's Dream*, when Quince's company assemble in the forest to start rehearsals for their play *Pyramus and Thisbe*. Quince, the putative director, hands out the parts as individual scrolls, literally taking apart the text into its individual elements. None of the players are given a whole play to read; they are expected to know only their part and their cues. As Margaret Jane Kidnie observes in the introduction to her chapter, the company then have to work together to solve some of the staging problems that the text presents them with. They need a wall for the lovers to speak through. How will they represent moonshine? As the company worry about their audience, they decide to add a prologue too, further altering the text. The final text of *Pyramus and Thisbe* only fully emerges in Act 5, when the company present their play to an onstage audience, whose interjections become part of the play for the offstage audience. By weaving together *Pyramus and Thisbe* with audience comment, Shakespeare recognizes that the final version of the play is not the one prepared in rehearsal, but the one that is received and commented on by the audience, whose responses, usually silent in real theatre, are here given voice as part of the new play of *Pyramus and Thisbe* that emerges as the result of the labours of actors, directors, designers and audience.

As this performance of *Pyramus and Thisbe* demonstrates, Shakespeare-performance is not simply a recitation of a static series of words, but a multi-voiced, multi-authored, collaborative work of theatre which depends upon the many negotiations, innovations and interpretations of all involved in the process of making theatre out of text, from first rehearsal through to actual performance. The concept of a play-text as a 'work' by a single author, with a finite number of interpretable meanings, has been challenged by scholarly traditions of the twentieth and twenty-first centuries as far removed from one another as Critical Theory and the History of the Book. The very nouns that describe the Shakespeare scholar's object of study – drama, play, work, text, performance text – have been contested and will mean different things within different critical discourses. And nowhere is the Shakespearean text more infinitely multivalent, more transitory and unfixed, than in Performance Criticism, where text becomes 'performance text'. If we call a play edition a performance text, suggesting either that it is what will enable performance as its final and most significant end or that it is a record of a past performance, we are at least acknowledging that in this case, performance is the *raison d'être* for text, not simply a by-product of it. If we watch a performance using the tools offered by semiotics, naming and analysing the theatrical sign systems of coming and going, clothes and things, sounds and visuals that make sense of the text, we confer on matter other than the written word the power to make meaning.

This book started life as a series of conversations between academics who work with Shakespeare's plays in workshops and rehearsal rooms. We talked about how some of the insights of working with Shakespeare in practice could be brought into critical writing about Shakespeare's texts. We also talked in depth about contemporary performances and how they worked with and through the plays to create a work of art that is both a part of and separate from Shakespeare's own work. In providing studies of the way we make theatre with Shakespeare, and the way Shakespeare makes theatre with his plays, we offer a critical practice that follows the logic of the rehearsal room, and borrows from that process both its rigour and its creative freedom. We have aimed to take the text apart in a way that resembles theatre work.

Rather than focus on one play, we have encouraged our contributors to look at a number of plays, so that their insights and their methods can be applied to any of Shakespeare's works. Peter Holland and Paul Prescott analyse how plays open and how they end with reference to *Antony and Cleopatra* and *Hamlet*, but their analysis can, and should, be applied to all Shakespeare's plays. All of Shakespeare's plays require props (Farah Karim-Cooper) and costumes (Bridget Escolme), all have their own unique soundscapes (P.A. Skantze) and silences (Robert Shaughnessy), their own visual scores (Christie Carson), all have their exits and their entrances (Rob Conkie), and all performances must negotiate the text (Margaret Jane Kidnie). Not all plays have severed heads (Carol Chillington Rutter) or fight scenes (Stuart Hampton-Reeves), but the body is a central part of all Shakespeare performance, and all performances depend, ultimately, on audiences (Sarah Werner), who have the power (as *Pyramus and Thisbe*'s audience realize) to change performance through their own engagement with it.

Many of our contributors also refer directly to contemporary performers and practitioners to illustrate how Shakespeare's actors continue
to make unique works of theatre out of their engagement with
Shakespeare. Again, this is a method that can be applied to any performance, and we encourage readers to use these methods in their critical
and creative engagement with Shakespeare-performance. One of our
agendas in this book is to move the focus of criticism from one which
always stands between the text and its performance, to one which can
move around the different locations of theatrical making, from behind
the stage to the audience. We approach Shakespeare-performance as a
work of art in its own right, a product of a series of creative collaborations as well as a negotiation with theatrical memories and traditions.
The study of Shakespeare in performance is limitless. There are 37 plays
to study in the Shakespeare canon, but there are thousands of plays in
the Shakespeare-performance canon.

Each chapter in this book presents different ways of approaching
Shakespeare and the making of theatre. Some historicize, going back to
what we know about original practices to help us understand the way
Shakespeare makes theatre; some theorize, offering critical reflections
on modern Shakespeare-performance. Many do both, and in doing
so offer rich models for new researchers and students. In this sense,
the critical approach exemplified here is an ensemble one, just like a
theatre company. We wanted this book to feel like an ensemble work.
It has grown out of seminars, conferences and post-show discussions.
The authors bring different perspectives to the study of Shakespeare
in performance, and as editors we have tried to work like directors to
bring these contributors together to produce a multi-faceted analysis of
Shakespeare and the making of theatre.

This collection is also a forerunner for a series of monographs which
will explore in greater depth and detail a Performance Studies approach
to studying Shakespeare. This series, called *Shakespeare in Practice*,
follows the challenge given to the authors of this book: to address
Shakespeare performance thematically, in ways which can be modelled
for all of Shakespeare's plays, drawing on a range of plays and engaging
as much as possible with contemporary performance.

The series takes its name from an international network of scholars
who have met informally and online over the last few years to develop a
way forward for the study of Shakespeare in performance. We would like
to acknowledge the support and help of the people in this network. We
do not claim to represent their views, as the network has produced some
lively and robust debate, but we are indebted to them for their work in

developing the concepts and attitudes which shape this collection. In particular, we want to acknowledge the significant contributions made by Christian Billing and John Russell Brown. We are also grateful to our editors at Palgrave, Kate Haines and Jenna Steventon.

Stuart Hampton-Reeves
Bridget Escolme

1
Textual Clues and Performance Choices

Margaret Jane Kidnie

The scene of Bottom's transformation in *A Midsummer Night's Dream* begins with a rehearsal of *Pyramus and Thisbe* that stages many of the sorts of creative decisions that typically arise during the early stages of theatrical production, issues of interpretation that contributors to this volume explore in depth in separate chapters. The actors are particularly concerned to find a good fit between their play and the audience before whom they will perform. Lion's costume is modified to entertain rather than frighten the ladies, and the casement of the court's great chamber window is considered as a possible source of actual moonshine before the actors decide to assemble properties ('a bush of thorns and a lantern') to stand in place of moonshine. When they finally get down to rehearsing their parts, Peter Quince choreographs Bottom's exits and entrances into and out of a nearby bush, and instructs Flute on the importance of silence. The process is guided throughout by clues to performance found by the actors in their parts.

Their preparations, however, begin with a rather different, no less textually attentive, type of actorly reading. Bottom enters the rehearsal space to complain that the text needs modification, since '[t]here are things in this comedy of Pyramus and Thisbe that will never please' (3.1.8–9). His specific concern is that Pyramus' suicide by sword might affront the audience. Starveling's suggestion is simply to cut both sword and death. Bottom's less drastic solution, taken up by Quince, is to remedy the perceived failings of the script by composing a pre-show sequence that explains 'we will do no harm with our swords, and that Pyramus is not killed indeed' (3.1.16–17). By introducing a prologue to the action, the actors simultaneously compensate for perceived deficiencies in the text (their play needs some introductory explanation), and begin to develop a particular interpretation of the script, an

1

interpretation they further reinforce by adding a few new lines to Lion's part that serve to reveal the actor beneath the costume.

While modern theatre practitioners may not wish to replicate the mechanicals' literal-minded approach to dramatic presentation, the process by which they get their play on its feet is familiar. The actors closely read a script and their parts, and out of those words on the page develop a live show. This model of how actors create theatre is commonly described through the metaphor of the text as the blueprint for performance.[1] If spectators perceive that a production makes extensive or substantial enough changes to the underlying blueprint, the performance might seem to shade into adaptation – related to, but somehow not quite, the play they came to see. This impulse to measure the play-as-enacted against the play-as-written arises from a perception that text (like a 'blueprint') is designed to allow theatre practitioners (the play's 'construction workers') to realize the playwright's (or 'architect's') intentions. However, and as actors and directors quickly discover, Shakespeare's 'blueprints' frequently resist ready assembly.

Editorial choices and theatrical opportunity

The instability of Shakespeare's texts is not a new concept, but its consequences for actors are worth reviewing in the context of uncovering textual clues and making performance choices. There are a number of different respects in which these scripts are indeterminate or ambiguous. Scholars and theatre practitioners have long known, for instance, that certain of the plays exist in multiple versions. To take some obvious examples, Lear's final line as printed in the First Quarto ('Break, heart, I prithee break') is transferred to Kent in the First Folio, the First Folio instead adding in its place lines that suggest he may believe Cordelia is still alive (TLN 3282–5; 5.3.285–7);[2] the First Folio, but not the First

---

[1] Kent Cartwright, for example, suggests that 'the theatrically oriented critic explores the text as a blueprint for performance (independent of any particular performances)' (29), while Edward L. Rocklin includes 'the script that functions as the performance's blueprint' among eight 'constitutive elements of drama' (139). The director Richard Eyre praises the *RSC Shakespeare*, edited by Jonathan Bate and Eric Rasmussen, for providing an 'invaluable guide' to the plays 'as they were intended to be read: blueprints for live performance', a review which also ran under the headline 'Blueprints for performance' (*Sunday Telegraph* 26 April 2007).
[2] References to the First Folio are based on the through-line numbers (TLN) in Charlton Hinman's facsimile edition of the First Folio published by Norton (1968).

Quarto, version of *A Midsummer Night's Dream* brings Egeus on stage in Act 5 after Hermia's marriage to Lysander, so potentially offering closure to the tensions between daughter and father with which the play opened; and the 'How all occasions' soliloquy printed in the Second Quarto of *Hamlet* (4.4.22–56) is not printed in the First Folio.[3] The Quarto and First Folio *Othello*, printed within a year of each other, contain hundreds of variant readings, many of which seem relatively minor but which cumulatively contribute to alternative conceptions of racialized identity politics (Marcus, 2004). Any company wishing to stage these plays has to choose among the available textual options (or at least choose a modern edition which makes these choices on its behalf), the actors thus not only realizing, but also in part assembling, their 'blueprint' for performance.

Textual choices remain even when only a single version of a play survives from Shakespeare's day. In the scene of Bianca's music lesson in *The Taming of the Shrew* as printed in the First Folio, for example, two consecutive speeches are assigned to Hortensio:

> HORTENSIO. I must beleeue my master, else I promise you,
> I should be arguing still vpon that doubt,
> But let it rest, now *Litio* to you:
> Good master take it not vnkindly pray
> That I haue beene thus pleasant with you both.
>
> HORTENSIO. You may go walk, and giue me leaue a while,
> My Lessons make no musicke in three parts.
>
> (TLN 1347–53; 3.1.52–8)

The context of the action, along with conventions of dialogue that render doubled speech prefixes within a single speech redundant, make it clear that an error has been introduced, and editors and actors therefore usually reassign the first speech to Bianca. *Shrew* may not exist in parallel versions (if one sets aside for the moment the uncertain relation between Shakespeare's comedy and the anonymous *The Taming of A Shrew*), but the single text nonetheless generates multiple readings – the reading as printed, and the reading as emended. To take a slightly different example of a textual glitch that might likewise seem in need of correction, the First Quarto of *Much Ado about Nothing* twice provides an entrance for Innogen,

---

[3] For discussions of the interpretive significance of these alternative textual versions, see Clayton, 1983: 134–5; Hodgdon, 1986; Werstine.

Leonato's wife (at the beginning of the first and second acts), but this character never speaks and is never spoken to, or of, by any onstage character.

Error, however, can be treacherous to identify. Entrances for Innogen may have been printed in the quarto by mistake (and they are omitted from the First Folio version), but the quarto reading remains tempting, especially since the silent onstage presence of Hero's mother potentially provides a rich staging opportunity for modern performance.[4] To return to the scene discussed above from *Shrew*, Hortensio's doubled speech prefix has seemed to 'contaminate' the three preceding lines, editors assuming they are also wrongly assigned. In the First Folio, Lucentio says, 'In time I may beleeue, yet I mistrust', to which Bianca replies, 'Mistrust it not, for sure Aeacides / Was Aiax cald so from his grandfather' (TLN 1344–6; 3.1.49–51). As Margaret Maurer explains, these speeches are playable as they are assigned in the First Folio, but modern editions typically reverse the speech prefixes, so 'diminish[ing] Bianca's sauciness' and preventing the realization that '[h]er wit is more than a match for the men's' (Maurer, 2001: 190; see also Maurer, 1998, and with Gaines, 2010). This is perhaps precisely why the emendation recommends itself – it provides continuity with the character of Bianca as dramatized in the early scenes, constructing her as the docile, and so desirable, foil to her sister. A perception of error, in other words, is shaped in this instance by underlying critical and cultural assumptions about dramatic character and the sort of language appropriate to young, unmarried women. Another moment that has led to suspicions of error is found in both the Second Quarto and First Folio versions of *Romeo and Juliet*, when Romeo comments on the sunrise as he leaves the Capulet bower. Friar Laurence immediately enters the stage in a new scene, cued to deliver a very slightly variant version of the same four lines just spoken by Romeo (TLN 999–1009; 2.2.1–4). The question here for performance, as with Innogen's entrance and the assignment of Bianca's lines in the music lesson, is whether to correct the reading, and if so, how. Who, if not both characters, should comment on the sunrise? While one might argue that the lines seem more appropriate to either Romeo or Friar Laurence, such preferences, as with emendations made to Bianca's part in the music lesson, are never objective.[5]

---

[4] Stanley Wells discusses these entrances as evidence of an author 'in process of composition' (1980: 7).

[5] Competing bibliographical and literary arguments for assigning the lines on the sunrise either to Romeo or Friar Laurence are presented in Wells and Taylor 295.

These are the sorts of complexities over which editors, typically required to provide a text for readers that is consistent with itself, ago-nize. One or other version of *Hamlet* is presented, or else the separate versions are conflated into a single text; doubled speech prefixes are reassigned; and 'ghost' characters such as Hero's mother are allowed to remain in the text or, more frequently, they are omitted. In most edi-tions, these editorial decisions are discussed in the introduction or else accompanied by an explanatory note. Sometimes an editor can adduce a bibliographical cause for a textual glitch – the repetition of the lines in *Romeo and Juliet*, for example, might result from either Shakespeare in the process of composition, or his actors in the process of rehearsal, moving a wordy speech to the other side of the scene break, the com-positors in the printing-house not noticing the signs of alteration and so setting the speech twice. Often, however, such explanations are not available, or are contested, and then editors – or actors standing in place of editors – simply have to decide whether and how to amend the text.

Audience expectations and the spectre of adaptation

Shakespeare's texts are filled with such examples, and therefore fre-quently invite of editors and actors an interventionist readerly col-laboration. These sorts of complexities, however, are typically glossed over by injunctions to think of a Shakespeare play as a blueprint for performance. The blueprint model is a useful pedagogical tool, since it makes the study of a 400–year-old author seem less intimidating by implying that everything one needs for performance is right there on the page. Less helpfully, and as W.B. Worthen's 1997 landmark analysis of the network of ideological assumptions from which modern perform-ance claims 'Shakespearean' authority demonstrates, it also functions to control or limit the perceived excesses of performance by privileging certain kinds of 'fit' between text and performance.

From such a perspective, interpretive nuances brought to Shakespeare's plays by actors can seem to carry a far greater potential for disruption than variants between extant quarto and folio versions or seeming glitches within individual early editions.[6] However, debates about theatrical interpretation – what constitutes 'enough' or 'too much' actorly input – have proven extremely resistant to either theoretical

---

[6] This is the thrust of Michael D. Friedman's argument that Shakespeare's texts do not change all that much from one version or edition to another (39).

or practical resolution. Not only can no text provide (nor would any theatre company want it to provide) instructions about every detail of performance, but printed stage directions can be variously realized. Even the seemingly explicit, if horrific, direction, '*Enter the Empresse sonnes, with Lauinia, her handes cut off, & her tongue cut out, and rauisht*' (*Titus Andronicus* 1600, sig. E1) is open to a wide variety of stagings. At this moment in the Deborah Warner Royal Shakespeare Company (RSC) production of 1987, for example, Chiron and Demetrius entered, laughing and crawling on their elbows, followed by Lavinia; it was only when Lavinia entered behind them that the audience realized that the men were imitating and mocking their victim's anguished movements (Dessen, 1988: 223). The quarto stage direction is fulfilled, but in a manner that many readers probably would not immediately intuit from close study of the text. As Marco de Marinis explains, 'It is never possible to go "backward" from the theatrical transcoding (or performance) of a given stage direction to the stage direction itself ... the stage directions within a dramatic text do not constitute a "score," since they are not expressed in a notational language' (28–9). Nelson Goodman therefore argued that the only way to guarantee preservation of the work through time (to prevent, as he characterizes it, the potential transformation of Beethoven's *Fifth Symphony* into *Three Blind Mice*) is to define 'accuracy', both textually and theatrically, in terms of word-perfect repetition of the dialogue (186–7). However, this approach brings its own problems for performance since it deliberately excludes actorly interpretation from consideration of what constitutes the work of art. An actor – or a robot – could stand on a stage and deliver every word of dialogue in a monotone, and the performance would count, using Goodman's terminology, as a 'correct copy'. One intuitively feels that Goodman's definition of accuracy fails to address the issues that matter most to actors and spectators. Factors such as costuming, lighting and sets, playing space, voice intonation and actor physique — although impossible to regulate by means of a script – are frequently more defining of a particular performance than the omission or transposition of passages of text, or the substitution of one word for another, textual alterations that many spectators would not object to (or perhaps even notice).[7]

An escape from this ontological impasse has so far proven elusive. Once one introduces interpretation to a definition of the dramatic work

---

[7] Music theorists, in particular, have sharply resisted Goodman's discussion of the identification of the work in performance; see Robinson 217.

of art, a firm correspondence between performance and text can no longer be guaranteed, or even defined. What counts as 'excessive' or 'wrong-headed' actorly input becomes a matter for debate, since there are no aesthetic or philosophical grounds – beyond the objective assessment of whether or not every word in the script was delivered – from which to argue that any one performance more fully realizes the play than another. The play, or perhaps more precisely, one's *expectation* of the play in performance, is not contained within the pages of a book. That said, it frequently remains the case that spectators who consider a particular staging to stand at a distance from their own interpretation of the action will appeal to 'the text' or the author to argue that performance betrays his or its instructions. R.A. Foakes sets out a version of this position when he comments that 'the less a production depends on the text and the more the text is refashioned, the less it has to do with Shakespeare' (2006: 52). Jay L. Halio, in a volume designed as an introduction for spectators wishing to engage with modern performance, also encourages a sort of hierarchical or unidirectional understanding of the relation between text and performance by explaining that the touchstone of successful performance is 'Shakespeare's original'. He argues that even when the dialogue is not altered, 'the visual aspects of a production ... can so distract or distort that we find the connections between Shakespeare's original and the current production too distant – so far removed, in fact, that we are compelled to reject the production altogether' (1988: 29–30). However, once one accepts both that cutting or rearranging words and lines will not necessarily impact negatively on the drama, and that interpretation is an indispensable part of what constitutes the play in performance, there no longer remains an indisputable point beyond which one can insist that actors have gone too far, whether in terms of innovative design choices or alterations to the dialogue.

This brings us back to the issue of textual clues, both in terms of what constitutes a clue, and what an actor might choose to do with it. As other chapters in this volume demonstrate, clues to staging can be found in a play's text(s). However, as the mechanicals' rehearsal implies, it is sometimes less than obvious precisely how such clues might be acted upon. Starveling's suggestion that unwelcome actor–audience tensions prompted by the sight of Pyramus' sword might be handled simply by cutting the text (and so the 'clue' to the sword it contains) is not an entirely impractical response. Merely because a textual clue exists does not mean that it will, or must, appear in performance. It is also the case that what is considered a clue can change over time. Hamlet's abrupt opening line – 'A little more than kin and less than

kind' (1.2.65) – in response to Claudius' address to him in court seemed
so inappropriate to eighteenth-century sensibility that it was assumed
it must be an aside. The line was accordingly marked as such by Lewis
Theobald in his edition of 1740, and his stage direction survived well
into the twentieth century. More recent thinking about Hamlet, however, has felt comfortable with the idea that the prince would dare to
provoke his new king and father to his face in such a public forum, and
so the editorial aside, along with the textual clue that seemed to require
it, has largely disappeared from the page.

Another example of how reader expectations can shape perceptions of what constitutes a clue to performance is found in the closing
moments of *The Taming of the Shrew*. The First Folio text prints '*Exit
Petruchio*' after Petruccio's triumphant rhyming couplet, ''Twas I wonne
the wager, though you hit the white, / And being a winner, God giue
you good night' (TLN 2745–7; 5.2.190–1.1). No cue to exit is provided
for the rest of the onstage actors. This is not unusual: surviving early
modern manuscript playbooks carefully mark entrances for actors, but
less consistently note their exits. The convention seems to have been
that playwrights and bookkeepers expected professional actors to know
when they were no longer needed in a scene, and as a consequence,
exits were recorded sporadically.[8] What seems unusual about the final
scene of *Shrew* is not that an exeunt is missing from the First Folio, but
that the First Folio so clearly marks an exit for Petruccio, and Petruccio
alone. One might consider this an important textual clue, but so firmly
have assumptions about marriage, gender politics and the endings of
romantic comedies dominated thinking about the play that the first
modern edition even to make visible Petruccio's solitary exit was not
published until 2010 (Hodgdon, 2010: 5.2.193.1).[9] In their different
ways, these two examples suggest the potential benefits of searching for
clues to performance in the earliest available texts; they also demonstrate how clues come in and out of focus as theatrical conventions and
cultural circumstances change over time.

Actors are therefore less constrained by the play-as-book than the
practice of looking for clues or the metaphor of the blueprint might

---

[8] As Antony Hammond explains, playbooks are 'much more casual' about
recording exits than entrances: 'after all, once the actor was on stage, there
wasn't much the prompter could do to get him off again' (79).
[9] See also Hodgdon's discussion of editorial and theatrical stagings of this
moment (2010: 306–8).

imply. Or to come at it from the audience's perspective, spectators should not be too dogmatic about what seems to them a textually justified – or unwarranted – stage moment. Performance choices are often inspired by clues discerned in Shakespeare's text(s), but textual clues, because they are only discerned as clues in the first place by means of readerly interpretation, cannot regulate performance choices. A nice example of the problem is provided by Alan C. Dessen, who has studied early modern scripts for clues they might offer to original staging practices. A scene in the anonymous *Two Noble Ladies* involves two soldiers drowning a female character in the river; unexpectedly, they themselves are 'hurried headlong to the streame' where they both 'must drowne and die' (ll.1.170–1). As Dessen comments, repeated verbal references to the stream, the tide and to drowning seem to offer strong clues to the onstage representation of water. Unusually, however, a marked-up manuscript survives from the period, its marginalia suggesting how the action was probably staged:

> [A]t line 1166 ('what strange noise is this?') the marginal signal reads: '*Enter two Tritons with silver trumpets*'; next to the subsequent lines we find: '*The Tritons seize the soldiers*' and '*The Tritons drag them in sounding their trumpets.*' Whatever our modern expectations, the original effect was keyed not to an on-stage river but to Tritons and trumpets. The sense of headlong, precipitate action, of drowning in a swelling tide, is conveyed not by the direct representation of water or immersion but by signals in the dialogue and violent stage business in conjunction with the 'imaginary forces' of the audience.
>
> (1986: 59)

This unusually detailed annotation in the playwright's hand probably only survives because the author, likely an amateur, was unaware that it was superfluous to the company's needs; these instructions therefore point more firmly to what the author hoped might happen than to actual stage business. However, there exists a three-line marginal note written in the bookkeeper's hand that is not cited by Dessen: 'Tritons / m: Bond / Stutf.' (1171–3).[10] This terse cue, far more typical of prompts to action inserted into playbooks by early modern theatre personnel than the playwright's annotations, and probably included only because

---

10 On the author's amateurish preparation of the book and players named in it, see Rebecca G. Rhoads's introduction to her edition of the play, vi–viii.

the bookkeeper had to ensure the entrance of non-speaking actors, seems to confirm both that tritons appeared on stage and that the parts were taken by Thomas Bond and George Stutfield. Without the paratextual evidence provided by the author's and bookkeeper's annotations, there seems little likelihood that modern readers would be able to reconstruct this early staging. Moreover (and more to the purposes of my argument about the difficulties associated with assessing correspondences between textual clues and performance choices), not only is this staging not apparent from close study of the unannotated text, but a theatrical drowning staged by means of tritons and trumpets, if happened on by modern actors, might seem at least to some spectators a distraction or unwarranted departure from the text – an adaptation, rather than performance, of the author's blueprint.

Shaping Shakespeare's plays through performance

Models of theatrical production that take the text as the foundation on which performance is built overlook the feedback loop by which both texts *and* performances are shaped by dominant conceptions of a particular Shakespeare play. This specialized sense of the term 'play' is crucial to an understanding of the reception with which both theatrical and editorial choices are met at any given moment, and over time. One can read and watch *Henry V* in a variety of non-identical editions and stagings, and yet one is able to categorize all of those different editions and stagings as the 'same' play. This is possible only because one already has an idea of *Henry V* that exists apart from its texts and performances (although it may be in part derived from one or more of them), and against which one compares texts and performances that claim to be 'of' *Henry V*. Necessarily, this idea of Shakespeare's history play is radically unstable, varying in its details from one spectator or reader to another. Moreover, far from functioning as an objective yardstick against which to measure performance choices, it continues to take on shape over time in response to new editions and theatrical productions. It is against the play as a subjective and constantly changing concept – not against a supposedly fixed text – that spectators evaluate particular performance choices. Choices seem unexceptionable, not because they are objectively inherent to the text(s), but because they correspond well enough to ideas of the play already held by viewers.

Foakes has recently expressed his frustration with theatrical and editorial studies that draw attention to the instability and indeterminacy of Shakespeare's drama, complaining that such research 'takes no notice of the needs of each new generation of readers and playgoers who come to the plays for the first time, as well as older viewers who wish to hear the text well spoken' (56–7). He characterizes (and perhaps also caricatures) the scholars whose work he addresses as 'wish[ing] to free performance from bondage to the texts' (50). His emphatic 'retort courteous' is that far from 'somehow trapping the director or actor', the text in fact 'may encourage them to choose from a spectrum of possible ways of interpreting language, action, and character so as to enhance their way of presenting the play and the connections they may wish to make with their own time' (56).[11] It may seem that in this chapter I am likewise running foul of Foakes's charges. It is especially worth clarifying, therefore, that the theoretical model I am arguing for here is not inspired by any particular desire to 'liberate' performance from text. As many of the chapters in this volume demonstrate, Shakespeare's texts can be immensely enabling of performance. My rather different point – albeit one undoubtedly shaped by at least some of the intellectual influences Foakes lumps together to dismiss as 'postmodernist theory' – is to attend to the extent to which *both* texts and performances are limited by, and in turn contribute to, the play as a conception that changes over time.[12]

To take an example, a standard convention of performance throughout the nineteenth century was the excision of Fortinbras from *Hamlet*. Far from seeming a mutilation or amputation of Shakespeare's text, this staging was regarded as unremarkable because it fully corresponded to the shape the play at this moment in time had come to assume – critical controversy, tellingly enough, was caused not by productions that cut the part of Fortinbras, but by Johnston Forbes-Robertson's decision in 1897 to *bring on* Fortinbras in the final scene. Another, slightly different, example is offered by the Christopher Sly narrative in *Taming of the Shrew*, which in the First Folio text concludes after Lucentio conceives the plot to change places with his servant, Tranio (using modern scene breaks, at the end of 1.1). Modern production, however, regularly introduces further scenes featuring Sly and the other onstage spectators, including a long exchange with the Tapster at the end of the action. These scenes, not found in the First Folio, are printed in the anonymous *The Taming of A Shrew*, a play whose relation to *The Shrew* remains uncertain – it might have been a source for Shakespeare, or else

---

[11] For a sustained reply to Foakes's position, see Worthen, 2006.
[12] This argument is developed at more length in Kidnie 11–31.

an early draft or later adaptation of the First Folio text. As with the stage convention not to play Fortinbras in the nineteenth century, the convention in the twentieth century of enlarging the part of the drunken tinker into a full-blown framing device by adding scenes from another play seems unremarkable even today. The Sly material may not be part of Shakespeare's *text* (although even here boundaries are blurred by the commonplace editorial practice of including the Sly scenes from *A Shrew* either at the bottom of the page or elsewhere in the book as additional passages), but it has become a familiar component of the *play*. And it is not only performance that is susceptible in this manner to alterations over time. To take an especially celebrated example, the once familiar text of *King Lear*, a conflation of the First Quarto and First Folio versions, was transformed with the publication of the Oxford Shakespeare in 1986 into the now familiar *History* and *Tragedy*, with subsequent generations of readers, teachers and editors grappling with what it means to study a two-text play, and how one might best present it/them, both on the page and in the classroom. The fact that Brian Vickers invokes as a criticism of the second edition of the Oxford *Complete Works* a 'growing consensus' that 'the variations between the two texts are not so great as to constitute two separate plays; that the alterations are theatrical, not authorial; and that the play loses more than it gains' merely reinforces my larger point that (a) text, no less than (a) performance, is constantly measured against something immaterial that stands apart from both text and performance (*Times Literary Supplement* 11 August 2006). Texts and performances are caught up in an ongoing process of alteration, and they are vulnerable in exactly the same manner to charges of adaptation and misrepresentation.

Writing about the preparation of editorial commentary, Barbara Hodgdon recommends approaching a Shakespearean play as something which is 'coming-into-performance', a comment to which she returns in her discussion of Petruccio's final, solitary exit from her edition of *Shrew* (2004: 220; see also Hodgdon, 2010). Her editorial staging is controversial – even 'radical,' to use Hodgdon's word – not because it preserves a First Folio reading, but because it intervenes unusually visibly in the ongoing construction of the play, forcefully demonstrating how a play is not only always 'coming-into-performance' but also, as it were, 'coming-into-text'. The acknowledgement that Shakespeare's plays continue to evolve by means of a dynamic and reciprocal relation between stage and script frees actors from the rhetorical imperative, implicit in theoretical models that present text as the foundation of performance, to justify their creative choices through reference to a supposed original. This is not to suggest that actors and directors will not find texts, both the early quartos and First Folio as well as modern editions, a source of immense inspiration. It is also not to prevent spectators from discriminating among stagings, or to remove from them the authority to value some enactments as being, in their opinion, more 'true' to the play than others. There will always be theatrical interpretations that simply seem more 'Shakespearean' than others. At some historical moments, and with some plays more than others, performance choices such as modern dress or the substitution of guns for swords will provoke a perception that an adaptation is being passed off as theatrical production (so prompting, in turn, appeals to 'the text'). At other times, or with lesser-known plays, whole scenes can be added or cut with little outcry (see Kidnie 32–64). It follows from the model I am proposing that this will *necessarily* happen: it is only through acceptance of some interpretations as corresponding to existing perceptions of the play and the rejection of others as adaptive that a community can arrive at and articulate an idea of the play at any one time. By means of their performance choices, whether innovative or conventional, actors – no less than editors by means of their textual choices – participate in the ongoing formation, and transformation, of Shakespeare's plays.

2
Openings

Peter Holland

> For now sits expectation in the air
>
>   (*Henry V*, Chorus, 2.0.8)

It may have first looked like this: *'Enter Demetrius and Philo'*.

Or this: 'The Prologue'.

Or this: *'Enter Richard Duke of Glocester solus'*.

Or this: *'A tempestuous noise of Thunder and Lightning heard: Enter a Ship-master, and a Boteswaine'*.

Or this: *'Enter a Company of Mutinous Citizens, with Staues, Clubs, and other weapons'*.[1]

Or any of the dozens of other possible examples.

But sooner or later, after whatever preliminaries the printer found appropriate as paratext – title page, half-title, ornaments, sometimes an act and scene indicator, even prefatory poems or a dedicatory epistle – the play, in its first printed guise, began on the page. In a modern edition, that beginning may be after a hundred pages or more of introduction and other editorial material. But still, always, for the reader, eventually the play begins. Whatever preceded it in the printed edition, the opening moment of the play-text, if that is what we can call it, is a simple entrance, occasionally heralded by a sound effect. And, nearly always, it is marked by its bareness, a spare indicator of an actor or two or a larger (sometimes unspecified) number coming onto the stage. The ones for *The Tempest* and *Coriolanus*, the fourth and fifth examples above, appear

---

[1] These are, in sequence, *Antony and Cleopatra* from the First Folio, 1623; *Romeo and Juliet* from the First Quarto, 1597; *Richard III* from the First Quarto, 1597; *The Tempest* and *Coriolanus* both from the First Folio, 1623.

almost opulent in their detail. This chapter starts by looking at these examples primarily in early modern print and performance before turning to ways in which modern productions have begun and how playgoers begin to watch the play, wondering what happens at that moment when the performance begins.

Characters and choruses

Sometimes, even an apparently minimally informative moment of printed text gives more information than a theatre audience will ever learn. Demetrius and Philo, the two characters who open *Antony and Cleopatra*, are never named in the dialogue. No one watching the play at the Globe could have known what their names are; only with the publication of the First Folio in 1623 did the characters gain the names for those reading or watching the play that they had already had for the actors, move from anonymity to specific nominal identity, become individuated rather than generalized.

Their names suggest that both are Romans. Certainly Philo's opening speech points to him as probably having been and perhaps still being a Roman soldier, an officer who in the past has watched Antony in war reviewing his troops and fighting in the thick of battle. Demetrius does not speak until the end of the opening scene, after the appearance and exit of Antony, Cleopatra, her ladies, 'the train' and 'with eunuchs fanning her', after the sight of what Philo, in his opening line, calls 'this dotage of our General's' (1.1.1). But, in the way Philo describes Antony to him, 'you shall see in him / The triple pillar of the world transformed / Into a strumpet's fool' (1.1.11–13), Demetrius seems to have arrived so recently from Rome as not to have seen Antony yet. Actors will, of course, think through these clues, but so too does the reader, trying to make sense of exactly why the play should start with these two unimportant characters. Editions, adding lists of characters to their copy-text, tend to define the two as 'friends and followers of Antony' or something similar, but there is actually nothing in the scene to define whether Demetrius is Antony's friend or follower, simply that he is a visitor from Rome. And neither of these two characters will ever appear on stage again, whoever the actors who played them go on to play later in *Antony and Cleopatra*.

Their presence, almost as minor and barely sketched figures as speaking roles can ever be, functions on the page as a frame to the scene, opening and closing it, giving us a pair of attitudes, a definition of how two Romans view the Antony so passionately and overwhelmingly in love with Cleopatra. They point away from themselves towards the central figures, like supporters on the margins of an image, means by which we see the others, checking whether Cleopatra is the 'gypsy', the 'strumpet' and the 'tawny front' that Philo describes. It is less the speaker than what Philo speaks of that matters, his presence sketched as a character but only as a static mood of barely suppressed fury.

One of the tasks an opening event may be given may well be to frame the action. Quite often Shakespeare begins his plays not with a major event but with something expository, an introduction, a comment on something that will then emerge onto the stage with an attitude towards it already in place. Philo and Demetrius control our view of the title-characters, whether we find when Antony and Cleopatra do appear that we agree with what has been said about them. If the opening of a play in performance is a time of expectation and eager anticipation for the audience, then *Antony and Cleopatra* – and there are many similar examples in Shakespeare – seems to be replicating the audience's emotion as the play itself delays giving us what we want to see, teasing us even as it tells us that the relationship of the central characters has resonances for everyone else in the play's universe. The unimportance of Philo and Demetrius as characters proves precisely to be a sign of their moment in the play's limelight as prelude to that entrance that will somehow get the play 'really' under way. Philo's speech is both a beginning and a hiatus before the start. Openings, in other words, often mark themselves as precisely openings, nowhere more so than when there is a prologue.

Some voices are never characterized, even to the minimal degree of Philo and Demetrius: the Prologue to *Romeo and Juliet* in the First Quarto is not even given an entrance, though in the Second Quarto (1599) the figure has gained a speech heading, 'Corus' [*sic*]. The speaker's 'name' is only a narrow marker of a theatrical function, like 'Prologue', and, however an actor did then or does now tackle the role and make choices about how to represent 'Corus', 'Corus' or 'Prologue' is not, perhaps, a character in any of our usual senses of the word. Reading an opening involves our trying to pick up clues about performance – for instance, questions of identity or tone – with an intensity precisely because we are at the start. But it also needs a wariness about making assumptions. What does a prologue look like, after all?

This prologue lacks even so much as a gendering, for Corus might now as reasonably be female as male. The Prologue to *Henry V* was given an ungendered entrance, 'Enter Prologue', when the speech first appeared in print (F1, 1623, for the speech and indeed all the speeches that make up the chorus's role are lacking in the 1600 Quarto). The twentieth-century performance tradition for *Henry V* has usually made the character male, but in the nineteenth century Chorus was often female: In 1859 Charles Kean cast his wife as Chorus, making her a cross between Clio, the Muse of History, standing in a temple, and Britannia, the iconic essence of the nation (Emma Smith, 2002: 84–5). When Nicholas Hytner directed *Henry V* at the National Theatre in 2003, the Chorus was played by Penny Downie, because, as Hytner explained, 'I felt a female presence in a brutally male play would be a way of theatricalizing the dialectics between rhetoric and reality' (Royal National Theatre, 2010). As directors buck the tradition they draw attention to their reconceptualization of the play's opening, surprising those who know the play in performance and demanding that those experienced spectators pay the moment a different kind of attention.

But the outward appearance of a prologue matters less than what it is saying. Prologues speak *for* the author and the theatre company (they may even speak *of* the author), speak *to* us both authoritatively in their proleptic prefiguring of the action through their knowledge of the plot and humbly in their request for our approval and support. The 'Corus' to *Romeo and Juliet* tells us of the 'star-crossed lovers' and their 'piteous over-throws' (6–7) and promises that 'if you with patient ears attend, / What here shall miss, our toil shall strive to mend' (13–14), completing the formal sonnet of the speech. Outlining plot and seeking approval, the chorus heralds the drama as performance and as narrative fiction.

It is precisely that search for approval that Shakespeare mocks at the end of the prologue to *Troilus and Cressida*: 'Like or find fault; do as your pleasures are / Now good or bad, 'tis but the chance of war' (30–1). But even this 'Prologue armed' (23) is playing with and playing off the functions we expect prologues to discharge and, like others, this unnamed prologue is outside the subsequent action, not a character within it.

Characters as chorus

Inside and outside – the ambivalence of the chorus is a central feature of the activity of entering the play. The drama may take a moment to cross its own threshold, as with the examples I have looked at so far. The opening moments are predicting what will occur or defining an attitude towards the central characters, but they are still a time of arrested development. As the play opens, it has to lure us into its fictive world, define for us the kind of action it will be, enable us to use its framing to approach its events. As the production opens it may make this all the more emphatic by the nature of its choices. Who speaks first can in itself be a strong statement about the meaning of the play. Who speaks first when Shakespeare leaves an option for change can define a production's approach.

Whoever spoke the prologue in an early modern performance of *Troilus and Cressida* (if indeed there were any) would have played another role or other roles in the play. But when a director chooses to have the prologue spoken by a specific character, the meaning of the speech shifts by giving it the character's perspective. Sam Mendes's 1990 production of *Troilus and Cressida* for the RSC had the prologue spoken by a figure in a blazer and flannels, who wryly flicked the medal pinned to his lapel as he identified himself as 'prologue armed' and who spoke with a cultured urbanity that defined a mocking distance from the heroic rhetoric he spoke. As the prologue ended and the first scene began, it became clear that this was Pandarus, though those who had read their programmes and/or knew the actor (Norman Rodway) who played Pandarus would have worked that out already. Since Pandarus speaks a form of epilogue to the play, the choice of speaker made for a neat framing of the whole action of the play, an extension of the way that Philo and Demetrius frame the first scene of *Antony and Cleopatra*, but it also placed Pandarus as the initial point of view of the play's events as fully as if filmed from his perspective. The prologue's language became Pandarus', his identity defining the speech, even if only in retrospect.

With the entrance of Richard, Duke of Gloucester, at the start of *The Tragedy of King Richard the third* (as Q1 calls it), readers and playgoers were and are on different ground. Richard does not name himself. He does not need to. One look at him and we know who he is. The physical presence on stage is always bound to be emphatic: the twisted back, the limp, the arm 'like a blasted sapling withered up' (3.4.69). There is, in effect, a kind of brutal voyeuristic yearning from the audience just before his entrance, a desire to see exactly how that body will appear, how 'deformed', in what ways 'unfinished' (1.1.20). And the reader already knows of Richard Crookback, cannot now read or cannot then have read without that knowledge, and then projects the body onto the speech, not least because the speech starts to make the body's presence a reality in the extraordinary sentence that begins at line 14, 'But I', and does not reach its main verb until line 25: 'Have no delight to pass away the time'. Between the first mention of the subject and the verb come repeated stabbing emphases on that 'I' (16, 18, 24) and on the damaged body, all designed to draw our focus towards that body, towards that self's sense of its bodily self, of the visible self that accompanies the speaking subject (see Plasse). Of course, the turn to the self at line 14 is so strongly made and thereafter so dominant, not only through the speech but effectively through the rest of the play, that it transforms the impact of the preceding passage.

In effect, Richard's speech begins as prologue, the character serving as prologue to his own play as fully as, say, that armed prologue to *Troilus and Cressida*, Rumour 'painted full of tongues' in *2 Henry IV*, Gower in *Pericles* or the choruses to *Romeo and Juliet* and *Henry V* do respectively in theirs. Perhaps the strongest recognition in performance of the switch from generalized prologue, defining the drama's opening moment in the continuum of history, to individualized prologue that defines and keeps defining the nature of the character's opening moment in the continuum of his existence, is apparent in Richard Loncraine's 1995 film. Ian McKellen gives the 'prologue' section (1–13) as a public speech to the court which is partying in style to celebrate the new, hard-won peace, before he moves to give the rest, that bitter analysis of the self and its damaged body, in the ornate lavatories of the 'palace'. The location switch actually comes mid-sentence. Richard says 'He' (12) to the party crowd and then completes the sentence after a sharp edit with a snarling 'capers nimbly in a lady's chamber, / To the lascivious pleasing of a lute' (12–13) as he makes for a toilet cubicle. This Richard may well have said one thing in public and then privately says what he would have liked to say publicly, as a comment both to himself looking in a mirror and, at the same time, to us as spectators, since by looking at the mirror he is also looking straight to camera.

The change of location, from public to private, and the change of addressee, from court to camera (for this is not, here, soliloquy, if by that we mean an address to the self), puts a sharp rule between the segments, turning, as film so often and so easily does, one speech into two scenes, using space, as well as the rare turn out of the frame towards the spectator, to underline emphatically what the speech makes apparent.

McKellen, in his commentary on the screenplay, pointed to the differing effect of the opening speech between stage and screen. In the stage production for the National Theatre in 1990, 'this opening speech was spoken directly to the audience to intensify their identification with the speaker', since 'audiences welcome a character who steps out of the drama to address them, whether in Shakespeare, a pantomime or a musical'. On screen the speech had been prefaced by elaborate action before the opening credits, but 'I never doubted that I should challenge the naturalism of cinema by talking to the camera' (McKellen and Loncraine 62).

Richard's entry is *solus*, 'alone', something Loncraine and McKellen, the joint screenwriters, begin the sequence by brilliantly discarding. But on stage, with Richard Eyre directing, McKellen's Richard made his entry emphatically alone: the black curtain onto which the words 'Edward IV' were projected was whisked away and smoke filled the stage, while the sound system filled the audience's ears with the noise of war – trumpets, horses, cries and crashes. As the smoke cleared and the sound faded, a lone figure in a First World War cap and greatcoat over his uniform moved slowly downstage, no humpback visible, limping only slightly, one hand stiffly in his coat pocket, his face marked by a massive and not totally successful piece of plastic surgery, the very image of a soldier home with a Blighty wound. As he expertly took a cigarette from his silver cigarette-case and lit it, all with only one hand, there was the clear indication of someone whose disability, whose war wounds, if that is what they were, had been conquered by extensive rehabilitation therapy and an effort of will. Talking directly to the audience is now a breach of a naturalistic performance convention that derives from a form of performance centuries later than Shakespeare's theatre. McKellen's Richard was also identified by the detailed realism of costume, the studied movement of the 'deformed' body, the clipped vowel sounds of the voice of the officer class. Such realism works, in effect, against the performance practices of naturalism, creating a tension for us in defining someone who would now and consistently thereafter breach the limitations of practice both as actor and as villain. There was nothing except the syntax, vocabulary and rhythm of the verse lines to tell the audience that this was Shakespeare at all. Whatever history this production of *Richard III* was beginning to chart, it was not a medieval or early modern history, not chronicle so much as alternative history, a counter-history of an inter-war Britain.

The performance choices at this moment of entry may vary, but it is the simple fact of beginning the play with such an entrance that remains startling. An opening solo entry for a play's title-character is unusual anywhere and unique in Shakespeare's work. It functions as a redefinition of a performance trope, so that Richard as his own prologue disrupts the convention of the prologue's not being a character within the play's fictional world. A chorus figure marks the theatre's world, the space of the performance, while Richard, the master-plotter, the author and principal actor in his own drama, begins in a dramatic position even more ambiguously between inside and outside than prologues usually are. Even Gower in *Pericles*, the onstage author of the action, is at the same time always external to Pericles' story, speaking of it as a drama he might be seen as writing even as he presents it. And Richard, Duke of Gloucester, is always writing his own history as he presents it and enacts it.

Waiting for the star(t)

All of Shakespeare's opening scenes operate, it might be fair to claim, within a framework of audience expectation, in part driven by the opening of the play's narrative but also in part through an awareness of a horizon constructed out of the modalities of his theatre. After reading or seeing a few Shakespeare plays, we rapidly learn that there is only a limited taxonomy of recurrent forms, against which exceptions, like *Richard III*, are to be tested. Robert Willson (7–8), giving guidance to a group of scholars gathered to write on openings, suggested that the opening scenes can be distributed into five groups: prologues, ensembles (e.g. formal processions, funerals), informal groupings (like those duologues among minor characters), street scenes and dramatic frames (like the Christopher Sly scenes that open *The Taming of the* Shrew or the Egeon story that opens, and will close, the narrative of *The Comedy of Errors*). We can, of course, try other groupings, but the question is not one that has some implicit right answer. What matters is the audience's awareness of certain, frequent theatrical ways to get things going, to open both the play's world and its narrative, to set up the circumstances in which the action can begin as drama rather than as prose fiction.

There is, for instance, the need to set out what in film would become known as the back story, those events preceding the play's start. At its most elaborate, in Sophocles' *Oedipus Rex*, the entire movement of the action is to uncover and connect together the details of the back story. In *As You Like It*, Shakespeare breaks every rule in later playwrights' rule books by having the play begin with a character, Orlando, telling the back story to another character, Adam, who already knows perfectly well everything that Orlando is telling him.

But there can also be the need to establish something unusual and dominant in the play, as in the way that Richard will dominate *Richard III*. One response to an audience's air of expectation may be to give it something it does not expect, making the entrance to the performance a crashing-out of our reality as we find ourselves terrifyingly in the play's world. One obvious example is the first scene of *Macbeth*, opening with '*Thunder and Lightning. Enter three Witches*', as F1 prints it. The scene anticipates Macbeth's first entrance ('There to meet with Macbeth'), a moment then so intriguingly delayed until after the two messengers, the 'bleeding Captaine' and Ross, have reported to King Duncan on the outcome of the battle and spoken so extensively about Macbeth, again heightening our anticipation for his entry. As Richard Nochimson points out, some Shakespeare plays are striking in their deferral of the moment when the principal character speaks: in *Macbeth* it is 113 lines, in *Othello* 189 lines – and one could compare either with the example of *Richard III* (76). Shakespeare plays on our desire for the title-character in these case, our need to see the star, just as in *Hamlet* the opening scene mentions 'Hamlet' three times but the first two speak of that 'valiant Hamlet' (83) who is already dead and appearing as a ghost. It is not until the scene's end, as Horatio encourages the others to go with him 'Unto young Hamlet', that the play seems to identify a Hamlet who might be 'Prince of Denmark' (as both the First Quarto and the Second Quarto describe him). When the next scene opens with one Hamlet present on stage but the other immediately spoken of ('Though yet of Hamlet our dear brother's death', 1.2.1), the tension between a father and a son, a dead and a living, a ghost and the one who has yet to learn of the ghost becomes clarified and intensified. It takes 156 lines before we see Hamlet, and a further 65 until we hear him speak, his silent presence on stage dressed in black always such a strong marker, even if the playgoers were not bound to be looking at him intently as the play's star.[2]

It is not hard to see 1.1 in *Hamlet* or *Macbeth* as a form of dramatic prologue, clearly far from the kind of conventional expository scene of two unnamed lords as in *Antony and Cleopatra* or the two never-named gentlemen who open *Cymbeline*. Whatever else may be happening, in the definition of the supernatural of *Macbeth*, in the information that there has just been a battle, even in the immediate presentation of inversion (the unholy Trinity of the women), of substitution or equivalence ('Fair is foul, and foul is fair', 1.1.10), and of the miasma and obscurity through which the characters will have to make their way ('the fog and filthy air', 11), the whole scene does not so much begin the action as present a perspective through which that action will be presented.

Plainly the first scene of *Macbeth*, in its reluctance to give anything much by way of narrative detail, operates in this way. Beyond the fact

---

[2] Nochimson notes the long delay, 152 lines, until the central character in *Coriolanus* speaks, but here it is exacerbated further by the fact that Caius Martius has not yet gained the name Coriolanus. We are over 620 lines into the play before Cominius announces that Martius should, 'from this time', be called 'With all th'applause and clamour of the host, / Martius Caius Coriolanus' (1.10.62–4) (76).

that a battle is going on and that there is someone called Macbeth (hardly surprising, given the play's title), the scene is distinctly short on information. Its crucial offering, from its opening sounds of thunder and lightning (for lightning seems to have been a sound-cue more than an instruction for some visual flashes) onwards, is to point to its super-natural world: the phrase was, as Leslie Thomson has established, 'the conventional stage language – or code – for the production of effects ... that would establish or confirm a specifically supernatural context in the minds of the audience' (11).

The sound effects of the opening of *Macbeth* are slightly elaborated in the first printing of the opening moments of *The Tempest*. Ralph Crane, the scribe who wrote the copy that was used by the printers to set the play, was probably responsible for turning a phrase like 'Thunder and lightning' in Shakespeare's manuscript into a more substantial description of the sound, neatly tying it to the play's title: the 'noise' is '*tempest*uous' (my emphasis).[3] Even though it is not until the second scene that Shakespeare makes clear that the tempest is one created for Prospero by Ariel, that it is a magical rather than purely meteorologi-cal event, the sound of thunder and lightning would have indicated its origins. On the one hand, the scene stretches the realism of the early modern stage to its limits; on the other, the sounds act as cues to the audience that the storm is a supernatural signal. In a play in which the sound of thunder will be recurrent (for example, at the opening of 2.2 and when Ariel appears as a harpy in 3.3), the magical sound score is opened by the first sounds of the play. Given that the play will, after this, take place entirely on what F1 describes (incorrectly) as 'an uninhabited island', this opening with the ship in a storm functions as a form of prologue as well, but one that both initiates the action and refers back to the play's title.

Before the beginning

If you have been reading this chapter continuously to this point, you may have been waiting too, expecting my argument to move from the details of individual plays to some more extensive generalizations about how the openings of Shakespeare's plays work. My choice not to do so until now has been the result of my wish to imitate something of the way in which play openings can conform to expectation or not, give

---

[3] See Jowett. On the staging of this scene, see Gurr, 1989.

us what we have been waiting for at once or hold off from satisfying that desire.

All openings involve something of a taking-on of roles, sometimes as a collaboration between audience and performer, sometimes as part of a director's creation of extensive action long before a line is spoken. In Tim Carroll's production of *Richard II* at Shakespeare's Globe in 2003, the doors to the backstage area, the tiring-house, were open so that the audience could watch the actors putting on their tires. Since the company was all male, the audience could watch men becoming women, not only putting on costume and make-up but also putting on gender, taking on their roles, becoming that other they would perform. They performed their transition but also presented it: the actor was not only performing but putting himself into the position of performer, becoming an actor by becoming a character.

Beginnings involve a shared tension in the theatre, the actors' anxieties and the audience's expectations meshing in those moments before, in most modern theatres, the house lights go down. In most theatres, few of which have a curtain any more, the set may already be visible, its definition of the nature of the production asking to be read, to be used as a group of parameters for its way of seeing the play or of enabling us to see the play. For many of us, that time before the lighting states alter is always thrilling, always a moment of anticipation as we move firmly from our world of light into our world of darkness and then to be watching the newly lit world of the stage, from settling in our seats, reading the programme, looking around, standing up for new arrivals in our row, sitting again, checking our watches, always waiting for that awareness of the lighting cue which will move our bodies into an alertness of attention, from relaxation to the diminution of the sense of our bodies into becoming little more than eyes and ears. It is a pure experience of liminality and transition, of the threshold of the performance being formulated.

Going to theatre involves its own transitions, from the audience's individual journeying to assembling as an audience, as the community for the performance. What draws the audience is always an awareness of the object, the production to be seen. But familiarity or lack can transform the nature of attention, of what is being watched and what is being watched for: seeing *Hamlet* for the 85th time is radically different from seeing, say, *Cymbeline* for the first time (see Trewin). The crucial decision – to attend and hence to buy a ticket to attend – may be driven by widely differing motives: a school party to see a set play, a romantic evening for two, a wish to see a particular play or, just as often, to see a particular company or performer. Tickets for a production of *Hamlet* will sell out far more quickly if it stars Jude Law or David Tennant, and the audience will watch the opening waiting not for Hamlet, but for the presence of celebrity. The motives drive differing patterns of attention, differing ways of watching the play's opening.

From the moment of the production's announcement, the buzz may begin in ways that, from poster design to website materials, will start to control how the audience will start to watch. If you were wondering whether to buy tickets for the Shakespeare Theatre Company's *Henry V* in Washington, DC, in 2010, you could not only watch three excerpts from it on the company's YouTube channel but also see vox-pop audience members giving their responses to the show, accompanied by some stills from the production. If they liked it, so might you. Their responses would have defined something of your expectation as you entered the theatre.[4] The location of the theatre, the structure of the front-of-house, the price of tickets, the nature of seating – or, at Shakespeare's Globe, standing – and all the other physical factors of the space and its operation as commercial enterprise have their particular effects on the way in which the play's opening will be perceived as the show starts.

And when exactly does the play start? The performance may already have started as the audience enters the auditorium, the space of performance. Gregory Doran's 2006 RSC production of *Antony and Cleopatra* began not, as usual, with Philo and Demetrius bursting onto the stage as if in mid-conversation (as if, that is, Philo's 'Nay' is a response to something Demetrius has said just before they enter), but with three Romans standing on the stage, waiting, long before the house lights dimmed, replicating, as it were, the audience's state of expectation and of waiting. It is the same trick that productions of *Hamlet* often adopt, having the audience enter to find Francisco already on stage pacing on guard-duty, a time of sustained expectation that is doubly disrupted, both by the arrival of Barnardo and by the wrong-footing when it is the arriving sentry, not the one already on guard, who issues the challenge, a moment that teeters almost on the edge of performance mistake, as if the wrong actor, not the wrong guard, has spoken: 'Who's there?' 'Nay, answer me' (1.1.1–2; see Nuttall 84.)

---

[4] See, for instance, www.youtube.com/watch?v=J4NVTZIUicM&feature=channel for a play excerpt and 'Audience Testimonials' at www.youtube.com/watch?v=NxWmyi3nb6s&feature=related or at www.shakespearetheatre.org/plays/details.aspx?id=183&source=l (i.e. it is also available on the company's website), both accessed on 9 May 2010.

Two of the Romans bore all the signs of having had a long journey. All three, as they paced to and fro, were clearly annoyed to be kept waiting. The lights went down and the wait continued, for them and for the audience. Nothing was happening and the audience began to experience that slight restlessness, a tinge of anxiety as to whether all was well backstage. Perhaps someone was late or ill. What if it were Patrick Stewart (now back with the RSC after 25 years' absence)? The opening, in other words, was not yet felt by the audience as part of the performance but as a potential sign of accident, an intervention in the act of attentiveness and in the beginning of the play. A slight, bare-chested figure appeared running through the stalls and onto the stage, showed the three soldiers the whip he was carrying, then, after putting his finger to his lips to demand their secrecy, ran off. The audience probably barely realized that it was Patrick Stewart before he ran back across the stage, laughing loudly, pursued by a woman who was now holding the whip and was also laughing. Michael Dobson describes it as a 'little powerless brush with self-indulgent celebrity'; only now can one of the soldiers 'burst out with the indignant comment that has been building up in him since before we even arrived at the theatre': 'Nay ...' (Dobson, 2007: 294.)

The performer's celebrity and the character's play off each other. The audience has come to see Stewart and been kept waiting. Philo and Demetrius have come to see Antony and been kept waiting. The wait is over for each at the same moment but in a way that is hardly satisfying for any. All want to share in the space of celebrity, not just to glimpse it. Reordering Shakespeare's sequence allows the audience to share the frustrations of the soldiers.

Doran's was a new take on a recurrent device to open the play: showing the audience Antony and Cleopatra behaving in ways that may or may not justify Philo's anger. Robert Helpmann at the Old Vic in 1957 began with 'an Alexandrian revel, with Antony's dotage "o'erflowing the measure"'; Trevor Nunn's 1972 RSC production opened with a 'parade of Cleopatra's court', with the two dressed as 'Egyptian god monarchs'; Caird (RSC, 1992) created a silhouetted upstage image of the two 'wantoning with each other while ... the Egyptian servants smile' (quoted in Madelaine 144–5). Barrie Rutter's production for Northern Broadsides in 1995 mocked the audience as well as Antony and Cleopatra by beginning not in Alexandria, but with Philo as a comic MC who spoke his lines as a trolley was wheeled out with two actors, both male, on it. They spoke some of Antony and Cleopatra's lines from 1.1, creating a savage mockery of a performance of the heroic lovers, presented to a sole onstage audience member, Caesar, offering us what Cleopatra at the play's end will fear: 'I shall see / Some squeaking Cleopatra boy my greatness / I'th' posture of a whore' (5.2.215–17). Then the 'real' Antony and Cleopatra walked rapidly onto the stage, speaking the same lines, offering us in their presence a sense of just how much of a fictional lie the performance of them for Caesar had been. Their power denied the possibility of finding their love ridiculous.

These varying choices reflect that anxiety of beginning. Most wanted to make the opening easier on the audience by glossing Philo's words. Doran, equally deliberately, wanted to play with the audience's tension, our awareness of exactly what we had come to see: Patrick Stewart as much as Antony, the performer as much as the play. We were a crowd of expectant eyes, 'Straining upon the start' (*Henry V* 3.1.32).

The roar of the crowd

I have touched on plays that start slowly and ones that start explosively. Only one Shakespeare play begins with a crowd arriving on stage as they head towards an event, as if what we are seeing happening on the stage is ourselves rushing collectively towards the performance. Their sense of an opening, a salvo in the battle with the patrician authority, is matched by our sense of the play's beginning. With the arrival on stage of a 'company of mutinous citizens', *Coriolanus* lands us in the middle of the action as explosively as the crash of thunder in *Macbeth* or *The Tempest*. Some productions have begun with offstage sounds of the crowd. In 1838, for instance, Macready's crowd were first heard offstage 'like the surging murmurs of the sea ... till the multitude burst on the stage, rivalling in numbers and violence the actual Roman mob that thronged to the Capitol', as a contemporary reviewer described it (quoted in Ripley 165).

It is often easy to see how spoken language in the opening scene of a play might set up questions and problems that the play will explore, but *Coriolanus* begins with a stage direction whose terms will prove to be complexly crucial to the play's debates: in what sense are the protesting people 'mutinous', an explicitly condemnatory word? Are they fully 'citizens', 'possessing civic rights and privileges', as the *Oxford English Dictionary* defines the word (*n*.1), or only half-accepted members of this city-state subordinate to the rights of the patrician class? Are they a 'company', like, say, the City Companies of early modern London, or are they, as Caius Martius and later stage directions will describe them (e.g. 1.1.207, 3.1.182 SD), a 'rabble'?

What all editions of the play leave open but what all performances quickly define is how many people there are in this crowd. Very few productions since the nineteenth century have matched the size of Macready's group of citizens, no fewer than 300 of them. Tim Supple's production at the Chichester Festival Theatre in 1992 had a crowd of over 50 who filled the stage powerfully and threateningly. Early modern performances, probably using no more than six or eight actors, could not have produced anything like the same effect of a crowd that could overwhelm any group of patricians. As well as the numbers, the physical appearance of the crowd will impact the audience's response, defining the frameworks for understanding the protest. The citizens complain of shortages of corn and some may therefore be visibly weak and starving, as in David Thacker's production for the RSC in 1994. Most productions have made their crowd all-male, as the early modern theatre presumably did. Now such a gender choice would be read as if only men can be a violent mob, but there may be women among them, either equally determined in carrying weapons or more passively showing the effects of famine. Some productions, short of numbers of men, will draft in women actors but dress them as men. In a play of such violent political confrontation the gender of the Citizens says much about a production's view of the nature of the city. So too will the nature of their costume: well-dressed or ragged, showing signs of their trades or not, entirely workers or also including some middle-class (what Shakespeare's audience would have thought of as 'the middling sort'). Their choice of weapons, too, is now less likely to be staves and clubs than 'other weapons': a design note in the prompt book for Thacker's production opted for 'a mixture of scythes machetes etc. In David Thacker's words "If you wouldn't feel safe taking on an opponent with a sword, it's not frightening enough".'

If the production sets *Coriolanus* in a period other than Rome or Elizabethan London, the crowd can take on other resonances, quickly and potently conjuring up different protests. In Michael Bogdanov's production for the English Shakespeare Company in 1989, at the time of the rapid collapse of the Soviet bloc, the crowd were workers protesting as trade unionists, carrying banners proclaiming 'Solidarity' and threatened with being crushed by military opposition. It immediately suggested the Solidarity union (Solidarność) that Lech Wałęsa was then leading in Poland against Soviet control, with the closing of the Gdansk shipyards by strikes and, eventually, shortly after the date of this production, the establishment of a new non-communist government in Poland, the first in the Soviet bloc. While Shakespeare's playgoers probably saw these citizens as strikingly like themselves, Bogdanov found a mode of representing this crowd that foregrounded the play's immediacy as contemporary political debate.

The crowd in *Coriolanus* productions is read quickly and effectively by the audience; we read the resonances and meanings, the ways the production wants us to find relevancies and disjunctions, to find a connection with or distance from ourselves. The audience notes, too, how the director's choices are balanced by economic exigencies that limit how many actors can be employed to fill out the crowd. That balance led Peter Hall at the National Theatre in 1984 to sell tickets for seats on stage to playgoers who then became the crowd, manoeuvred by a small group of actors-as-crowd. Inevitably inept, the audience-as-crowd was watched by the rest of the audience as they tried to follow the actors-as-crowd's instructions, to shout as directed, to improvise their performances, always awkward beside the professional performers. They could be seen to be trying to become a crowd, to change their role in the performance from audience to actor, just as we change into audience as we move towards and into the theatre, taking on our role.

All's well

I have finally worked through the sequence of five plays with which I opened this chapter, so that my opening is now complete. What follows the opening? If one of the recurrent questions I have been exploring is 'when does the performance begin?', it seems as if I ought to be ending with the reverse question: 'when is the opening over?' But instead I want to close by turning to a different play, a play whose title promises ending rather than beginning, as a way of seeing how many of the concerns of this chapter play out across a different text in performance.

It is always the case that the play's world and the theatre world intertwine in the choices of performance. I want to end with another example of the restructuring of a play's beginning to take specific account of the star performer, as a way for me to pinpoint how opening sets up everything that will follow on. The opening of *All's Well That Ends Well* in F1 brings onto the stage four figures 'all in black': the young Count, his mother, Helena and Lord Lafeu. In a very few lines it is clear that the Countess's husband has recently died, that 'yong Bertram Count of Rossillion', as the first stage direction in the First Folio defines him, has succeeded his father and is leaving to become the King's ward (effectively, until Bertram comes of age), that the King is seriously ill and that Helena's late father was a skilled physician. As Bertram is being consigned to the king's patronage, so Helena was 'bequeathed' to the Countess's 'overlooking' (34–5).[5]

The entering quartet says much about the ensemble of the play. But, just as Peggy Ashcroft played the Countess as her last Shakespeare role (in Trevor Nunn's production for the RSC in 1981), so Judi Dench played the Countess in what was widely expected to have been (but proved not to be) her last Shakespeare role, directed by Gregory Doran in 2003. And her presence skewed the possibility of groupings that Shakespeare's opening defines. Instead of entering with others, she was given a sudden and disturbing solo entrance, 'half-running toward us, breaking the decorous codes implied by her clothes, clearly under the pressure of some strong emotion'. Indeed, as Michael Dobson notes, her entrance induces in the audience an emotion 'of intense familiarity: it feels suddenly that we are in the presence not just of a grief-stricken woman but of a grief-stricken member of our own families'. Celebrity creates connection of actor beyond character and 'the stature of this particular performer, her presence over time in the minds and lives of that audience, both mandated and vindicated this small initial piece of adaptation' (Dobson, 2005: 162–3). Where Shakespeare wanted us to see four actors, Doran knew that his audiences had come only to see one and that, by giving them what they wanted, the play would subsequently be able to proceed without diverting the audience's attention, for, as Dobson noted, 'Dench threatened to dwarf the Countess' (167).

But openings are much more than a chance for the audience to get what they have paid for: here the sight of the celebrity whose presence in the cast had kept the box office busy. For, as well as watching out for Dench, the audience was also working hard at absorbing, at speed, the vast quantity of information that a play's opening pushes at them. There was the set, where, without detailed stage realism, the gauze scrims were dappled with the suggestion of leaves; the lighting, which used yellow and green to begin to suggest autumn; the music, pastiching Purcell (a little out of period but sufficient to suggest early modern), played live by a small consort with a cello dominant; and the costumes, which were reassuringly Jacobean and aristocratic so that the audience could relax into the play's period and the conventions of costume drama.

Openings may produce an adrenalin rush of excitement – what the audience has travelled and paid to see is finally beginning – but they also produce a kind of information overload that needs controlling by

---

[5] On the opening of the play see Styan; Levin, 1997–98.

the theatre company and processing by the audience's collective and individual brains. For some, the frequent theatregoers, it is a familiar demand; for some, less versed in the arts of decoding performance, it may be strange and even confusing. In seconds the mapping of the conventions of the performance onto the conventions of the play is accomplished. The virtuosity of the production is matched only by the skill of the audience in grasping, intuitively if not necessarily articulately, what it is expected to understand from this opening, learning how to respond to the specifics of the choices, from the unending possibilities for creative transformation of text into performance, that have been made by this production by this company in this theatre on this day. The arts of theatre write over the printed text – and the play begins.[6]

---

[6] For a remarkable exploration of how the opening of a very different kind of drama is understood by an audience well versed in its meanings, see Riley.

3
Entrances and Exits

Rob Conkie

Entrances and exits both signify and effect change. When someone comes onto the stage they change it: they populate an empty stage; they bring new information; they cause an emotional reaction in the onstage characters; they interrupt, advance, reverse, slow down, hasten, stop what is already happening. When someone leaves the stage they change it: they cause an absence; they suggest what will happen off stage; they give the remaining characters a chance to reflect and to focus on their subsequent actions. Entrances and exits, therefore, are one way by which the dramatic trajectory and impetus of a play might be charted (indeed, a common rehearsal technique in the Stanislavskian tradition is to divide the play into smaller units than scenes, often marked by entrances and exits). Furthermore, this notion also points to the way that carefully scheduled stage traffic can shape an audience's affective response to a play in performance, something understood most clearly, and metonymically prefigured, by those of Shakespeare's characters who plan, plot, devise and scheme. Shakespeare's schemers know, perhaps better than most, this potential of well-orchestrated entrances and exits to effect change. They know – somehow intuitively, or via an unholy dramaturgical alliance with their author – that timely comings or goings can alter what other characters see and know, or what they think they see and know, and thus, what they feel and how intensely. In the majority of these cases the schemer attempts (usually successfully) to frame an innocent character, the entrances and exits carefully calculated to exploit yet-unsurfaced suspicions and insecurities in the onstage watcher/s. Consider, for example, Aaron's 'stratagem, cunningly effected' to implicate Martius and Quintus in the murder of their new brother-in-law Bassianus (*Titus Andronicus* 2.3.5, 6, 192–306) or Edmund's betrayal of his credulous father and half-brother (*King*

Lear 2.1.17–89) or, indeed, Don John and Borachio's offstage staging of Hero's supposed infidelity (*Much Ado About Nothing* 3.2.51–91). Here are plots within plots, actions which propel the momentum of each of these plays, and which signal one of their author's chief means of schematizing dramatic effect and affect: entrances and exits.

Schemer-in-chief, Iago, is the stage-manager of entrances and exits, *par malevolence*. Having plotted Cassio's drunken and violent disgrace, he makes his very first poisonous insinuation to Othello (that his marriage to Desdemona might be under threat) – 'Ha? I like not that' (*Othello* 3.3.37) – by capitalizing on the overlap of the entering General (30) and the exiting Lieutenant (36). This is an example of Iago responding to a fortuitous entrance/exit. Later in the play, when Othello, much further ensnared in the plot, lies incapacitated by the psychosomatic epilepsy, a 'lethargy' (4.1.58) Iago himself has provoked, the schemer sets in motion a series of further comings and goings designed to exacerbate the torment: here, Iago demonstrates the potentially devastating effects of carefully judged (and manoeuvred) entrances and exits. As Cassio enters during Othello's seizure, an entrance perhaps prompted by Desdemona's encouragement in the previous scene to 'walk hereabout' (3.4.172), and which might have proved a considerable hindrance to his malicious plans, Iago begins to organize the ensuing action to his advantage via a manipulation of who comes and goes when and where. He instructs Cassio to 'withdraw yourself a little while' (61), which is both a spatial and temporal orchestration of the stripped Lieutenant's movements, a pattern which he repeats to the newly conscious General. Given that Othello is emotionally distraught and disoriented, Iago has thrice to instruct him: he suggests that Othello should 'Stand you awhile apart' (82), repeats 'Do but encave yourself' (89) and, perhaps slightly desperately, but continuing to control the temporal and spatial, 'But yet keep time in all. Will you withdraw?' (102). Having left the stage for a 'little while', Cassio returns seven lines after Othello's withdrawal, during which Iago gleefully reveals his plan to the audience: the First Folio text confirms Iago's mastery of the dramaturgy (and thus, of the other characters); first he announces 'Here he comes' (109) and then the stage direction complies, '*Enter Cassio*'. In the following action Othello, withdrawn (or partially exited), but then beckoned forward (or partially re-entered), hears Iago question Cassio about the 'bauble' (142) Bianca but supposes that the (most unflattering) answers that he gives refer to his wife. Iago is then able to use the unlooked-for entrance of Bianca, complete with Desdemona's handkerchief in hand, as further confirmation of the cuckolding of which Othello assumes he is the victim. Iago directs Cassio to exit 'After her, after her' (162) in order that he can intensify Othello's misery once they are alone: only a few lines later, having succumbed totally to the combined effects of these carefully crafted entrances and exits, some planned and others improvised, Othello declares, 'I will chop her into messes' (193).

My scheme for the remainder of this chapter is to further consider the significance of entrances and exits in the making of Shakespearean theatre via a kind of variorum explication of the first scene of *Titus Andronicus*,[1] mainly focused on entrances, and the last two scenes of *The Comedy of Errors*, more focused on exits. Variorum editions of Shakespeare typically collate observations by editors and commentators. Here, my exposition of *Titus Andronicus* 1.1 and *The Comedy of Errors* 4.4–5.1 will concentrate on: stage directions, especially as they are interpreted by modern editors; staging possibilities, on both early modern and contemporary stages; and stage histories, particularly the 1987 RSC and 2006 Globe Theatre productions of *Titus Andronicus* and of *The Comedy of Errors* from 2002 by the Bell Shakespeare Company (BSC). The variorum will illustrate the two foundational points introduced thus far. First, that entrances and exits always implicate some kind of change: Bernard Beckerman observes on this point that 'entrances plunge the audience into the midst of a new situation or a more highly developed stage of an earlier situation' (178). And secondly, that entrances and exits chart the organizational schematic of a play, especially in terms of its capacity to involve and affect its audience: Tim Fitzpatrick thus defines dramaturgy as 'the playwright's capacity to structure the

---

[1] The authorship of this scene is contested. None of the single editions of the play that I have used – Waith, 1984; Hughes (updated edition 2006, but original edition 1994); Bate, 1995 – support the notion that George Peele wrote as many as four scenes of *Titus*, but they each pre-date Brian Vickers's comprehensive 2002 study, which makes just this argument based on 'verse style, vocabulary, syntax and other linguistic habits' (215). Bate's introduction to the RSC *Complete Works* concedes that the play is 'Mostly by Shakespeare, but the first act and possibly the beginning of the second and fourth acts have the stylistic marks of George Peele. It is not known whether this was an active collaboration or whether Shakespeare took over an older play by Peele and revised the later acts much more thoroughly than the first one. Francis Meres in 1598 and the 1623 Folio editors had no hesitation in attributing the play to Shakespeare' (1619). Therefore, I am using *Titus* 1.1 as generally Shakespearean: if it is not, indeed, by Shakespeare himself, it provides a template for much of Shakespeare's dramaturgy for the remainder both of the play and his subsequent career, but also a means of comparison in terms of how this dramaturgy developed.

performance by orchestrating its rhythms and flow by the manipulation of entrance and exit patterns' (1999: 6).

Killer entrances

Eugene Waith, editor of the Oxford Shakespeare edition of *Titus Andronicus*, observes that the First Folio text 'has stage directions presumably derived from the prompt-book and hence reflecting stage practice, though not necessarily the author's intention' (83). This state-ment perhaps implies a hierarchy between Shakespeare as a writer of dramatic literature and as a theatre practitioner; indeed, this latter category is to some extent elided. The emphasis here, by contrast, is on Shakespeare as a maker of theatre, especially via the crafting of entrances and exits. In any case, the first such First Folio stage direction for *Titus Andronicus* reads:

> *Flourish. Enter the Tribunes and Senators aloft, And then enter Saturninus and his Followers at one doore and Bassianus and his followers at the other, with Drums & Colours.*[2]

Alan Hughes, editor of the New Cambridge edition, writes of this open-ing that 'The play starts with a bang'; it is a figurative bang, given that Alan C. Dessen and Leslie Thompson note that a 'flourish' most often represents 'a fanfare usually played *within* on a *trumpet* or *cornet*, pri-marily when important figures *enter* and *exit*' (original emphases, 94). The productions to which I will refer below were certainly aggressively percussive, Deborah Warner's actors rattling the metal ladder on which the victorious Titus sat, and the mobile towers on which the brothers entered through the crowd in the new Globe production were similarly struck fiercely and repeatedly. Hughes continues, prologue-like, with 'Two factions enter through opposite tiring-house doors' (67). The Arden (Third Series) editor, Jonathan Bate, similarly glosses this action: 'The doors were at either end of the tiring-house; the rival brothers thus take up confrontational positions on opposite sides of the stage, with the powers of arbitration between and above them in the gallery' (127). This notion of opposition and symmetry is further underlined later in the scene when the fractious brothers re-enter, each having secured a

---

[2] Unless otherwise noted, all stage directions are taken from the First Folio (1623).

bride, but also having slighted one another. All of the three editions already mentioned set this stage direction as it appears in the Quarto edition of the play, in two parallel columns reflective of the division it describes. Waith writes that 'The layout of the First Quarto stage direction is reproduced since its unusual form emphasizes the symmetry of another spectacular entrance, comparable to the one which opens the play' (102), and Hughes concurs, offering, via a statement which closes the gap between author and theatre-maker, that 'The symmetrical form of the Quarto stage direction, in double columns, may reflect Shakespeare's intended staging, and has therefore been retained' (83).

These types of symmetrical and standoff entrances (and exits) are common and well known in Shakespeare. As Andrew Gurr and Mariko Ichikawa point out of the characters staring antagonistically at each other across the stage, 'Their difference and division are symbolically shown by their split entrance' (99). Gurr and Ichikawa list several examples, including: the Montagues and Capulets in *Romeo and Juliet* 1.1; Oberon and Titania and their respective retinues in *A Midsummer Night's Dream* 2.1; and, more wistful than hostile, the departing paramours of *Love's Labour's Lost* 5.2. Gurr and Ichikawa themselves, who argue for three entry/exit points on the Shakespearean stage – those at either side and one in the middle – stand to one side squaring up against proponents of a two-door stage, most defiantly and comprehensively championed by Tim Fitzpatrick. The Quarto of *Titus Andronicus* might represent the argument thus:

It is generally agreed that Shakespeare's playhouses had three entry-ways in the *frons*, i.e. two flanking doors and a central doorway or aperture. (Gurr and Ichikawa 14)	It is my contention that Shakespeare intended his plays to be performed using only two doors for entrances and exits. (Fitzpatrick, 1995: 27)

Indeed, the two parties appealed for 'patrons' and 'favourers' of their 'right' in an extended debate in the pages of *Theatre Notebook* between 1999 and 2002. I confess to being somewhat Leontes-like – 'a feather for each wind that blows' (*The Winter's Tale* 2.3.183) – in my capacity to evaluate this debate, partly because I favour Gurr and Ichikawa's three doors, and yet Fitzpatrick argues more rigorously and ingeniously. What I find difficult to believe, though, is that a central space, even if it did not provide access to the tiring-house in the 1580s, did not do so by the time the Lord Chamberlain's Men became the King's (in 1603). Theatre people are practical, problem-solving people (Ichikawa, 2006: 20), and if a central discovery space represents a site of dramatic potency, including for the use of entrances and exits, then only exploiting such a resource at the opening of a play seems to me derelict of practical and artistic duty. On the other hand, Fitzpatrick offers many highly nuanced dramaturgical interpretations, which suggests that practical (and pedagogical) work on the plays, especially within the context of 'original practices' Shakespeare, might be similarly derelict in not sometimes experimenting with the restrictions/opportunities of two-door staging.[3]

My tentative preference for the staging of the opening entrances of *Titus Andronicus* would require three doors, such as at the reconstructed Globe, with the central opening accommodating Titus' spectacular entry between those made by the opposed brothers.[4] This First Folio stage direction, one of the most expansive in the canon, reads:

> *Sound Drummes and Trumpets. And then enter two of Titus sonnes; After them, two men bearing a Coffin covered with blacke, then two other Sonnes.*

---

[3] Irrespective of the side of this debate, both parties work out a series of elaborate schemes or rules to explain how the rehearsal-challenged actors (Stern, 2000: 52–79) knew where to make their entrances. Indeed, the advocates of the three-door stage still make rules for two, given that a major platform of their argument is that the central door is reserved for special and symbolic entries and that the majority of the stage traffic passes through the flanking doors. These rules include:

Beckerman: the O rule – a character enters from one door and exits through the other (Gurr and Ichikawa 97; Beckerman 72–3, 176–82).

Gurr and Ichikawa: the S rule – a character enters and exits through the same door (122).

Fitzpatrick: the basic arrangement is of triangulation, where one door provides access to a place more inside than the stage space and the other door to a place more outside (1995; see also 1999; with Millyard, 2000; 2002; with Johnston, 2009).

Mahood provides a fascinating refinement of the two-door arrangement according to gender and status: she suggests that hired men playing the bit parts would have used the 'outside' door, the boy actors playing the women would have used the 'inside' door, and that the experienced actors could use either door, used as they were to the conventions (42). Mahood goes on to offer a stunning analysis of the staging of Ophelia's madness according to this stage logic and the expectations it would have created for the audience well-versed in these patterns (48–9).

[4] Though Ichikawa champions the use of the central door for spectacular entries, her list of early Shakespeare plays requiring 'a discovery space or a third entrance' (18) does not include *Titus*.

> *After them, Titus Andronicus, and then Tamora the Queene of Gothes, &*
> *her two Sonnes Chiron and Demetrius, with Aaron the Moore, and others,*
> *as many as can bee: They set down the Coffin, and Titus speakes.*
>
> (1.1.69 SD)

Here, I am persuaded by Gurr and Ichikawa's suggestions that 'where the entrance or exit itself is meant to be spectacular, the case for the use of the central opening is a strong one' and that 'kings are likely to make their ceremonial entrances through the central opening' (109, 110). As soon as the temporarily appeased brothers (and their followers) begin their ascent to the balcony, back through the opposite doors by which they entered, the Captain announces Titus' entry, the beginning of which perhaps overlaps with the last of the brothers' followers disappearing into either of those flanking doors. At the conclusion of this lengthy central entrance the coffin[5] is placed 'upstage' (by which I mean closer to the tiring-house) of the trap, with Titus centre-stage facing downstage (or at the majority of the audience), the prisoners and sons assembled on either side. After acknowledging the rulers on the balcony, Titus begins the ritual burial of his sons, which includes Lucius' entreaty and his agreement that Tamora's eldest son be sacrificed. Throughout this action, and as the coffin is lowered into the trap, Titus stands with his back to those above and instead faces the audience, whom he has ascribed as Roman citizens. When he is called by Marcus into political affairs he reverses this and turns his back on the majority of the audience in order to face the high-status dignitaries, both on the stage, in royal and political persons, and perhaps also off it, if the Lords' Rooms are populated with high-paying audience members. These series of entrances, and the subsequent stagings they encourage, communicate several important aspects of the play: they are revelatory of character, story and theme, in particular of warring and intractable leaders, of sublimated desires, of deafness to pleas for mercy and of slight regard for human life. The entrances are also demonstrative of a play delighting in its own theatricality; here, a society which revels in bloodshed is mirrored by a theatre which revels in spectacle.

The productions of *Titus Andronicus* by Deborah Warner at the Swan and Lucy Bailey at the Globe fully exploited this sense of the spectacular, partly via an expansion of the entrance/exit possibilities

---

[5] The stage direction at line 69 stipulates one coffin; at line 149 the stage direction reads '*and lay the coffins in the tomb*'.

in their respective theatres. Isabella Bywater's design for the Swan *Titus Andronicus* included a bridge at the level of the first gallery with entrance/exit points at either end, which added to the standard openings at upstage left (USL) and right (USR) and the often deployed access through the audience at downstage left and right (DSL and DSR).[6] Two coffins were illuminated centre-stage, either side of the trap; a sheet was hung USC from the bridge obscuring the back wall of the theatre; then, the Hughes-like bang starting the play was a sudden burst of light. Saturninus ran through the audience from DSL, past the coffins, and then turned to the audience to present his case. Bassianus was already delivering his attempt to recruit the audience as he walked through them to the DSR entrance, stopping downstage of the coffins and turning about-face to reinforce his message. Marcus entered the balcony bridge from SL and began his intervention from its centre; his words convinced the brothers to retreat, which they did, upstage but on different sides. Warner's next move was a much-celebrated *coup de théâtre*:

> With a crescendo of drumming and male voices yelling, the curtain that has hitherto hidden the Swan's backstage (brick) wall falls to reveal the stage picture of the victorious Titus, along with his sons and prisoners.[7] Titus is sitting aloft on a ladder, which is held horizontally by four prisoners, chained to the ladder with their heads poking out through the rungs. Titus sits in the middle, with two prisoners either side. Tamora is on a leash ... . When revealed, they all step forward (with Titus' sons beating on the ladder as though it were a horse, making the prisoners move) to the spot just upstage of the trap door and the coffins, where they stop and Titus begins his speech.
>
> (Rogers 2)

---

[6] Of the number of entrance/exit points one might ask with Regan, 'What need one?' (*King Lear* 2.2.437). Two notable productions that did without them were Trevor Nunn's RSC *Macbeth* (1974–76), where the actors sat on crates in a circle and stood to enter when the action required them, and the 2001 Globe *Cymbeline*, played by six actors doubling and trebling, who sometimes, for the sake of narrative clarity, spoke their entry stage directions aloud.

[7] In that there was no access point for it to be brought in, this entrance – Titus at the top of the ladder with his prisoners and sons – was set behind the makeshift curtain before the play began, and thus perfectly instances Fitzpatrick's notion of the pre-established discovery (see Fitzpatrick and Millyard 2–23).

Now, that's an entrance: expository and symbolic, in its encapsulation of sexualized brutality; spectacular and theatrical, via its Artaudian assault on the audience's senses (and many more [and more] shattering assaults were to follow); and iconic, as if the suddenly revealed opening entrance instantly etched itself on future incarnations of the play in performance, the Julie Taymor film (1999) and the new Globe production alike.

Though somewhat indebted to the earlier RSC production, William Dudley's design for the Globe production of the play was even more daring. Perhaps inspired by early modern references to inky-cloaked theatres in lines such as 'The stage is hung with blacke, and I perceive / The auditors prepared for tragedy' (*A Warning for Fair Women*, Induction 74, quoted in Gurr, 1999: 18), Dudley transformed the reconstructed Globe stage into what several reviewers called a temple of death. Of this aesthetic Nicholas de Jongh wrote: 'Black cloth swathes the stage, covers pillars, turns exits into strange, cavernous tunnels and obliterates the gallery' (*Evening Standard* 26 November 2006). Thus, some entrance points were eliminated, but then others, primarily through the audience, were created. Saturninus and Bassianus arrived this way on mobile scaffolding towers, pushed raucously by their ardent followers; their appeals for adherents were thus somewhat compromised by almost running many of them over in the dodgem-cars competitiveness that ensued. The towers elevated the brothers about six feet above the ground; that is, with their feet near the groundlings' eye-line but able to communicate very directly with other audience members in the lower and middle galleries. Marcus appeared from the centre-stage cave opening, spewed out into the ugliness of the play, but took them both back with him into the belly of the dark beast once they had been placated. The followers took their trolleys off and then a very drunk Captain entered on foot through the yard and staggered up the ramp placed at the 'downstage' edge of the stage. Then Titus entered, standing on a barge (with Tamora sitting in front of him) carried by eight actors, and therefore recalling the Swan ladder entrance, as black confetti, ash-like, fell from the obscured heavens. This was a bold, physical entrance, the entrance of a warrior and a conqueror.

I have sampled these first few entrances from *Titus Andronicus* for a number of reasons. First, they seem to me to offer excellent possibilities for the, to use Gurr's phrase (2001: 65), 'optimal' use of Elizabethan theatre architecture.[8] Second, the production examples above reveal

---

[8] I do not have space here to explore the vertical entrances and exits required of going aloft or of lowering into the trap (but see discussion of *The Tempest* below);

how modern directors and designers have created spectacular, and probably undreamt-of, interpretations of the stage directions provided in the First Folio text. Third, in terms of my opening argument about the significance of entrances and exits as markers of change within a play and of its affective force, these comings and goings (and others within this scene) chart an escalation from political aggression into extreme barbarity and, perhaps because of this, an audience response of bewildered numbness which culminates in Marcus' later reaction to his brutalized niece. I want to turn now, from these horrors, to the much more palatable delights – at least for the audience, if not for the bemused characters – of comic entrances and exits towards the end of *The Comedy of Errors*.

It's all in the timing

My favourite essay in all six volumes of the *Players of Shakespeare* series is Donald Sinden's analysis of playing Malvolio in John Barton's lauded RSC production of *Twelfth Night* from 1969, whereby he rates his success in garnering laughs with scores out of ten. Of the moment in the play when he dismisses those who have duped him into yellow-stockinged smiling (3.4.95), Sinden writes: 'I will admit to a dissatisfaction on this exit – I never really succeeded in bringing it off theatrically, even if I did it truthfully' (62). Here, the actor has to discover a balance between internals – characterized by Sinden as truth and, in the words of Otto Brahm, being 'sensitive to the inner spirit of a work' (quoted in Chinoy 30) – such as character, narrative, situation and mood, and externals such as theatricality, presence and craft; the best theatre practitioners, actors like Sinden or perhaps Mark Rylance at the Globe and directors like Warner and Bailey, are able to transcend this dichotomy in order that their stagecraft, including entrances and exits, whether spectacular or simple, illuminates the ontology of the play, at least as they have interpreted it. In this next section I would like to focus on the craft of performing entrances and exits, particularly with skills such as comic pace and timing. In the earlier section on *Titus Andronicus* I began with historical and theoretical considerations of entrances and exits before providing contemporary examples; here I will reverse that procedure to structure the

---

each of the three single editions of the play I have drawn on interpret both the going aloft and the placement of the tomb in uniquely different ways.

following discussion via the last two scenes of the BSC production of *The Comedy of Errors*.

The BSC's *Comedy of Errors* provides a comparison to the earlier *Titus Andronicus* productions in ways other than generic: both of those productions, though neither of them adhered to Ralph Alan Cohen's injunction to 'employ the stagecraft of the author' (214), were produced on thrust stages, one on the reconstructed stage of the Globe and the other on the approximately Elizabethan stage of the Swan. The BSC's main house productions tour nationally throughout (the eastern states of) Australia, playing in proscenium spaces, and are thus blocked presentationally towards the audience, almost always in a darkened auditorium (though there were exceptions for this production). Stage architecture, of course, determines much of the potential (or limitation) for entrances and exits, a point borne out by Warner and Bailey's decisions to alter their respective playing spaces. Jennie Tate's design for the BSC created several entrance/exit points; stage right was, as described by one reviewer, 'an oriental bazaar where characters appear and disappear amid the clutter and coffee-making steam' (*Sydney Morning Herald* 16 September 2002). Moving across the stage from the bazaar was another door, still right of centre, a centre door not used until the last scene (more of that below), and a further door at stage left. Added to this was a curved recess on the stage-left wall housing a concertina screen which was used for the central scene of the play (3.1) when Antipholus of Ephesus is locked out of his house and both the inside and outside action is represented at the same time.[9] With two entrances from the bazaar this makes a total of five entrance/exit points, a neat historical synchronicity, given T.S. Dorsch's description of the Elizabethan screen in the Great Hall of Gray's Inn, the location of the first recorded production of the play on 28 December 1594, with its 'five handsome arched doorways with finely carved doors' (23).[10]

---

[9] Dorsch's edition of the play uses a C. Walter Hodges illustration of this scene – 'a conjectural reconstruction of the Gray's Inn performance' (27) – with a portable door held perpendicular to the forestage so that both parties, inside and outside, can be witnessed by the audience. This device was also used in the 1999 Globe production of the play, although here the twins were each played by one actor, which necessitated considerable physical shenanigans to make the scene work.

[10] Dorsch's suggestion that the screen would have been 'very suitable', even 'ideal', for the staging of *Errors* is, somewhat lamentably, squashed by Ros King's

Tate's five doors, the maze-like bazaar and the moveable screen provided the actors, as the review above attests, with the means to appear and disappear. This is, to some extent, anachronistic Shakespearean staging, given Peter Thomson's observation that entrances and exits in Shakespeare's theatre are unlikely to surprise: first, because they are almost always announced in dialogue; and secondly, because a surprising entrance to or 'an unobtrusive exit from an open stage is almost a contradiction' (43).[11] In this contemporary proscenium production, however, and especially one which featured a magician (playing Dr Pinch), the *mise en scène* was deliberately used to misdirect the audience so that entrances and exits could surprise both them and, it seemed, the characters. The other constant in the reviews of the production was of its breakneck and interval-less pace, what Colin Rose called its 'lickety-split tempo'. Such pace is important to the execution of comic entrances and exits, a point reinforced by Cohen's cautionary observation that 'Shakespeare's plays average roughly 100 entrances and exits. If each entrance or exit is accompanied by just three seconds, the pauses to enter and exit will add 300 seconds or five minutes to a show' (217). For most of this production such three-second gaps were nonexistent, because the majority of entrances and exits overlapped, a practice with a definite historical precedent. Ichikawa writes of the 'many instances where no sooner has a character begun to exit than another character enters', and that 'there are some cases in which the overlapping of exits and entrances can be meaningful' (2002: 57). In *The Comedy of Errors* the main pleasure for the audience with overlapping is whether or when the twins will finally run into one another. Shakespeare keeps them relatively discrete until the end of 2.2 which requires the '*Exeunt*' of Adriana, Luciana and Antipholus of Syracuse, with Dromio of Syracuse instructed to remain as porter and the immediate entrance of the Ephesian Antipholus and Dromio with Angelo and Balthasar; this overlap establishes the to and fro of the next scene, where one

---

revised introduction to his edition of the play. Not only does she clarify that only two of the 'fine carved arches' actually 'conceal doors', but she also argues that the performance would have occurred at the opposite end of the Hall (34).

[11] This refers to the audience not being surprised; characters can, of course, depending on the staging, be surprised by entrances they have failed to notice; see, for potential examples, *Much Ado About Nothing* 2.1.182 or *1 Henry 4* 3.3.62.

master dines within and the other is locked out, and the Dromios banter rhythmically, if not exactly poetically.[12]

Here is a brief recap of the errors-driven dramatic momentum leading up to the penultimate scene of the play, mostly caused, of course, by the two sets of twins being mistakenly supposed, even by themselves, for each other: the visiting Syracusian Antipholus leaves his money at his lodging, is mistakenly accosted by his twin's wife, dines with her, falls in love with her sister, is given a gold chain, but decides, not unreasonably, that 'sorcerers inhabit' (4.3.11) the city and that he will therefore take flight; the Ephesian Antipholus dallies too long at the market, is locked out of his own house and dinner, takes solace with the Courtesan and is arrested for failing to pay for his chain; 4.4 begins with Antipholus of Ephesus being escorted by the Officer. In the BSC production these two entered by the door right of centre, but not through the bazaar (which was mostly used for slapstick entrances and exits). Six lines later Dromio of Ephesus also entered stage right, full of pride that he had procured the rope, though Antipholus was hoping for 500 ducats. The First Folio text lists the next two entrances as *'Enter Adriana, Luciana, the Courtizan, and a Schoole-master, call'd Pinch'* at line 31 and *'Enter three or foure, and offer to binde him: Hee strives'* some 65 lines later. In this production all the characters entered on the former instruction, the four called for, and two others for subsequent binding duties, all stage left. Apprehended DSR, the two presumed madmen were bound back-to-back and thus made their exit, hopping like a kangaroo and joey – a particularly Australian exit – all the way to stage left. From here there were a number of deftly judged comic entrances and exits.

---

[12] A more poignant overlapping of twins occurs in *Twelfth Night*. Sebastian's first entrance is 24 lines after Viola/Cesario's exit (1.5.222–2.1.1); then he exits and Viola enters five lines later (2.1.29–2.2.1); after she has survived what appears a deadly duel with Sir Andrew and is then accosted by Antonio, she leaves and Sebastian enters nine lines later, another near miss (3.4.305–4.1). They do not share the same physical space, although some directors contrive such moments, until the very last scene. Overlapping entrances and exits are not, of course, the sole preserve of twins; the plays offer resonance-filled juxtapositions, comings and goings that comment one upon the other. In *The Two Gentlemen of Verona*, for instance, Proteus ends the first scene, having just given a love letter to Speed to deliver to Julia, worrying about how she will receive it. He exits, she enters: with her is Lucetta, who already has the letter. If Speed exits holding the letter aloft and then six lines later Proteus exits as Julia and Lucetta enter (at the other door), perhaps with Lucetta also holding the letter momentarily aloft but unseen by Julia, the connection and the comedy are made explicit.

Shakespeare allows 13 lines between the exit of the bound Ephesian pair – time just enough for the shocked witnesses to collect themselves and draw breath – before their Syracusian twins re-enter unbound. Adriana drew the Officer DSL in order to settle her errant husband's debts and was accompanied by her concerned sister and the implicated Courtesan. The specific skill of the dramaturgy here is to lure Adriana into high-status pronouncements, which Blazey Best did most haughtily, just before the next entrance completely knocks the wind out of her sails. She reproved the Courtesan to her left, turned back to the Officer on her right and then, like a dutiful youngster crossing the road, looked scornfully again to the Courtesan at her left. This meant that she did not see the frenzied stage-right entrance of her (unbeknownst) brother-in-law and his servant. As Luciana hollered, 'God for thy mercy, they are loose again' (137) everyone froze for a moment, though the women's surprise was greater, given that they thought the two who had just entered right had only just exited, all tied up, left. Antipholus thrust out his fly-swat rapier – another Australianism – and then four lines later, with the Officer leading, the women fled stage left, hands in the air, shrieking loudly, carefully obeying the stage direction of '*Run all out. Exeunt omnes, as fast as may be, frighted*' (140).

The energy of the play is maintained here by the constant entering and exiting, where neither the characters nor the audience can predict when and where someone will next emerge or disappear. Antipholus is required to exit with Dromio at the end of 4.4, another ten lines after the 'frighted' exit. In this production he did not, but loitered DSR as Angelo and the Second Merchant entered USL lamenting his seeming misconduct. Then Dromio re-entered, for once the right servant meeting the right master with the right instruction carried out. The argument that followed between the two parties leads up to the stage direction of '*They draw. Enter Adriana, Luciana, Courtezan, & others*' (32). Here, after the Second Merchant challenged, 'I dare, and do defy thee for a villain' (32), Antipholus confidently drew his fly-swat and he and Dromio proclaimed, 'hah'! The Merchant replied by drawing a gun from his pocket and he and Angelo countered, louder, 'hah'! On the resultant pause, set up by the comic one-two punch, the remainder of the stage direction was enacted, Adriana bursting in breathlessly and shouting, 'Hold, hurt him not, for God's sake, he is mad' (33). The Courtesan snatched the fly-swat and there began a Keystone Kops chase in and out of the bazaar, with each of the hunters and hunted off stage long enough for an unscripted entrance and exit of the still-bound Antipholus and Dromio (of Ephesus) hopping from stage left to right. Their Syracusian brothers re-entered from the bazaar, were surrounded by those aiming to subdue them and were backed to the upstage centre door, the entrance to the Priory, by which they made their exiting escape. The final cascading exits of the production, made shortly after these errors were explained and put right, exemplified Gurr and Ichikawa's notion that 'At the ends of the romantic comedies and some other plays, the central opening is fit for the joint departure of the two groups of characters who have achieved a harmonious relationship' (112): first, *'Exeunt omnes. Manet the two Dromio's and two Brothers'* (5.1.410), where the BSC cast gleefully accepted the invitation 'to a gossips' feast' and 'such festivity' (5.1.408, 409) in the central Priory; then, *'Exit'* the brothers Antipholus (5.1.416), patting one another on the back; finally, *'Exeunt'* the Dromios (5.1.429), and having played paper, rock, scissors to determine who would go first and, not being able to decide, they exited Jake the peg-like – very Australian – each with his arm around the other.[13]

The big exeunt

Shakespeare's works have often been accorded near-sacred status. Like the Bible, the first words of which are 'In the beginning' and the last of which is 'Amen', Shakespeare's *Works*, as collected within the First Folio, begin with *'A tempestuous noise of Thunder and Lightning heard: Enter a Ship-master, and a Boteswaine'* (*The Tempest* 1.1.1) and finish with '… such a peace. *Exeunt'* (*Cymbeline* 5.4.569). According to this scriptural (and fanciful) conceit, Shakespeare's canon (and canonization) begins with a tempestuous big-bang entrance and then he presides, Prospero-like, over, according to Ralph Alan Cohen's mathematics (217), approximately 3,600 entrances and exits until the resolution of a peaceful exeunt. Prospero, of course, is a different, if not altogether antithetical, schemer of entrances and exits to Iago (with whom I began). Iago directs traffic, for the most part, from behind a stage pillar, a position of strength he perhaps discovers in the very first scene whilst taunting Brabantio. By marked vertical contrast, the stage space from which Prospero controls entrances and exits would appear to be the theatre's uppermost point:

> *Solemne and strange Musicke, and Prosper on the top (invisible). Enter several strange shapes, bringing in a banke; and dance about it*

---

[13] One last exit, and appropriately not centre, was the Duke chasing the Courtesan off left for some 'good cheer' after the curtain call.

with gentle actions of salutations, and inviting the King etc. to eate,
they depart.

(3.3.17 SD)

This reference to 'on the top', one of Ralph Crane's scribal flourishes
(see Vaughan and Vaughan 126–30), has intrigued theatre historians.
C. Walter Hodges writes of this moment that 'I have assumed he
must have been on the upper stage, and "on the top" of that small
central porch projecting from it' (135–6). This observation (and the
conjectural illustration on the facing page) puts Prospero in the same
sort of place as Juliet in her balcony. Dessen and Thompson offer a
further (and more elevated) possibility: that it was 'used seldom for
a location where one figure appears *above* the main platform and
possibly above the upper playing level' (233; original emphasis).
Even more appealing, perhaps, is the suggestion Andrew Gurr makes
to Christine Dymkowski that Prospero may have 'appeared looking
down out of the roof-trap' (Dymkowski 257). Irrespective of exactly
where Prospero may have stood (or perched, suspended even) whilst
'on the top' – and the place would obviously have altered depending
upon which space the play was performed in – what the top position
affords, in terms of entrances and exits (and one not available to
Iago), is an overview.

The overview of entrances and exits reveals interesting (quantitative
as well as qualitative) details. The shipwreck of the first scene, minutely
orchestrated by Prospero – 'Hast thou, spirit, / Performed to point the
tempest that I bade thee?' – and executed by Ariel – 'To every article'
(*The Tempest* 1.2.193–5) – contains 12 entrances or exits within just
54 lines; this is a coming or going every 4.5 lines (and the need for
an alert stage manager). The second scene, wherein Prospero length-
ily exposits his enforced deposition to Miranda, contains 9 entrances
or exits within 591 lines, or a coming or going almost every 66 lines.
Thus, quite obviously, the frequency, or lack thereof, of the stage traffic
helps to create an entirely opposite dynamic and tempo – desperate to
perambulatory – in the opening two scenes. Up until the time Prospero
appears on the 'top' his surveying, as well as directing, of entrances and
exits has allowed his plan, and the subjects within it, to meander: from
this point he manoeuvres them more purposefully, via Ariel, towards
his desired conclusion. And here, in the character perhaps most often
associated with the author, do the scheming of onstage entrances and
exits most compellingly and spectacularly evidence the dramaturgical
function of direction change and manipulation of affect.

The travellers enter this scene (3.3) exhausted. Gonzalo complains, 'My old bones ache' (2), the King himself is 'attached with weariness' (5), and though Antonio and Sebastian keep themselves alert in the hope of assassinating Alonso (and the others), all have been readied by Ariel's Puck-like leadings for the 'banquet' which is about to appear before them. The entrances of the shapes with their 'gentle actions of salutations' change the mood of the men: Alonso asks, 'What harmony is this?' (18), Gonzalo praises the 'Marvellous sweet music!' (19), and the rest remain somewhat stupefied until Sebastian prompts, 'Will't please you taste of what is here?' (42). Lulled into a notion that the island is beneficent, the men prepare to eat just as the next spectacular entrance shatters this recent calm: '*Thunder and lightning. Enter Ariell (like a Harpey) claps his wings upon the Table, and with a quaint device the banquet vanishes*' (52 SD). Dymkowski lists many of the various ways by which this entrance has been staged, most of which fall within descending from the flies, ascending through the trap or simply running on (261). Now are the men, particularly the three former plotters of Prospero's usurpation, battered by Ariel's apocalyptic condemnation, after which '*He vanishes in Thunder: then (to soft Musicke.) Enter the shapes againe and daunce (with mockes and mowes) and carrying out the Table*' (82 SD). Such is the impact of these closely co-ordinated and emotionally charged entrances and exits that the three men soon exit in near-suicidal calamity.

I have concluded with Prospero because he offers, in contrast to Iago, such an alternative approach to, and perspective of, entrances and exits. And yet, both characters metonymically represent their author via their manipulation of the onstage action: as Prospero calmly observes of his three panic-stricken enemies, 'They now are in my power' (3.3.90), so Iago maliciously declares that his plans 'shall enmesh them all' (2.3.326). Prospero and Iago exert and model an author-like power in that those they enmesh include not just Alonso, Antonio and Sebastian or Othello, Desdemona and Cassio, but also the willingly credulous audience: to put this in a slightly different way, their machinations become one of Shakespeare's chief means of organizing his story. Further, in light of the theme of this volume, Prospero and Iago can themselves be seen as *makers* of theatre: the former creates a storm and shipwreck; gives and takes away a magical banquet; organizes a wedding masque; arranges a stunned reunion: the latter causes a late night ruckus; stages a drunken brawl; cashes in on a distraught courtesan; plays murder in the dark (almost all of these staged events are designed to be viewed by other characters). Here, perhaps, is a secret to Shakespeare's mastery of entrances and exits: with Prospero, he sees them from the top – and in Robert Weimann's term, composes them with his 'author's pen' – where each coming and going can be minutely plotted for maximum effect, but also arranges them with Iago from behind the pillars – drawing on his 'actor's voice' (2000) – from whence he can observe the beads of sweat on the actors' brows and the anguished, perplexed or delighted faces of those in the yard; his manipulation of persons both on and off the stage via entrances and exits – to register change, both subtle and extreme; to affect an audience; provide spectacle, symbol, symmetry, opposition, juxtaposition, a comic punchline, a tragic conclusion – are therefore, to extend my bardolatrous fantasy above, equal parts heaven and hell.

4
Endings

Paul Prescott

Prologue: Hamlet gets jiggy

Let us begin with an ending from the middle of *Hamlet*. King Claudius rises and calls for lights. The play, *The Murder of Gonzago* (aka *The Mousetrap*), is aborted and court and actors scatter off stage. Hamlet and Horatio are left alone among the detritus of the hastily abandoned performance. The King's conscience has been caught, perhaps sooner and more effectively than Hamlet could have hoped for, and the play has ended. What happens next is odd. Hamlet starts to sing:

> Why, let the stricken deer go weep,
> The hart ungallèd play,
> For some must watch, while some must sleep,
> So runs the world away.
>
> (3.2.249–52)

Has Hamlet finally lost it? What does song – and this song in particular – have to do with the fact that his uncle has seconds earlier revealed his guilt? Is this an appropriate reaction to such a profound moment? 'Some must watch' – yes, we have just watched Hamlet and Horatio watching Claudius watch the actors. 'So runs the world away' – agreed, the world has just run away. But why is Hamlet singing? The next lines clarify what is happening, as Hamlet steps out of the clownish character he has temporarily adopted and comments on his own performance: 'Would not this, sir, and a forest of feathers, if the rest of my fortunes turn Turk with me, with two Provençal roses on my razed shoes, get me a fellowship in a cry of players, sir?' (3.2.253–5). Horatio agrees that it would, and Hamlet returns to the song. Like Feste at the end of *Twelfth Night*, he provides a musical

50

conclusion that bears a tantalizingly enigmatic relationship to the action that has preceded it. His choice of a balladic closing device is unsurprising, for Hamlet has a borderline obsession with jigging: he accuses Polonius of being for 'a jig or a tale of bawdry or he sleeps' (2.2.480–1) and slanders Ophelia as a jigging, ambling lisper (3.1.143–4). When he makes obscene jokes to her about 'country matters' before *The Mousetrap*, Ophelia points out that he is merry and he responds, 'Oh God, your only jig-maker' (3.2.113); moments later, he will indeed make a jig about a 'stricken deer'. What this short post-*Mousetrap* sequence dramatizes, then, is the curious ways in which human beings seek to draw lines in the sands of experience. The play is over, but Hamlet is still playing, trying to find a suitable way to conclude, searching for the appropriate ending. *The Mousetrap* has had a dumbshow and a brief prologue, both introductory, inductive devices; so where's the epilogue? Hamlet supplies it. The sequence could easily be cut with no harm to the plot of the play. Hamlet's first line after the court has exited could well have been, 'Oh good Horatio, I'll take the Ghost's word for a thousand pounds' (3.2.263–4). But as so often in this play, Shakespeare thickens the texture of the action, choosing to dramatize the end of the performance-within-the-performance, the transition between the 'stage world' of *The Murder of Gonzago* and the return to the 'real world' of Elsinore. This transition is complex and many-layered: Hamlet clowns, draws attention to his clowning, and metatheatrically compares himself to an actor and a shareholder in a theatre company (like his author, like the actor, Richard Burbage, playing him). Like every ending, however, this marks the beginning of something new: Hamlet now has proof of his uncle's guilt. The clownish epilogue is also the prologue to the second half of the revenge tragedy.

'They say he made a good end'

The construction of an ending is a central component of Shakespeare's stagecraft. After another bout of spontaneous song in *Hamlet*, mad Ophelia tells the startled onlookers: 'I would give you some violets, but they withered all when my father died. They say he made a good end' (4.5.180–1). Making a good end is vital to playwrights of all times, but perhaps the significance was even richer in the early modern period. Ophelia's sense of making a good end is eschatological; that is, it is concerned with theories of what actions – prayer, repentance – one should undergo in the last moments of life in order to secure the best possible afterlife. In her madness, she mistakenly believes her father has died a good because well-prepared-for death. In Shakespeare's time there was a keener imaginative association between the end of the play and the end of one's life. The notion that all the world is a stage, all the men and women merely players, is not original to Shakespeare and his contemporaries. We find it in the Ancients, most succinctly in the saying attributed to Democritus (d. *c.*370 BCE): 'The world is a stage, life is the play: we come on, look about us, and go off again.' Four centuries later, Seneca expanded the metaphor: 'It fareth with our life as with a stage-play: it skilleth not how long, but how well it hath been acted. It importeth nothing in what place thou makest an end of life – die where thou wilt, think only to make a good conclusion' (323). Shakespeare adopts the trope with relish, but it was part of the furniture of the early modern mind. In the Preface to his 1614 *History of the World*, Sir Walter Raleigh described God as the 'Author of all our Tragedies', a divine playwright who 'hath written out for us, and appointed us what every Man must play'. It therefore follows that 'Death, in the end of the Play, takes from all, whatsoever Fortune or Force takes from any one' (D1–2). The end of a play, then, is a microcosm of our journey's end, a dress rehearsal for a greater departure. When Doll Tearsheet enjoins Falstaff to 'leave fighting o'days, and foining o'nights, and begin to patch up [his] old body for heaven', the fat knight responds, 'Peace, good Doll, do not speak like a death's-head, do not bid me remember mine end' (*2 Henry IV* 2.4.207–10). If all the world is a stage, the end of the play speaks like Doll's death's-head and bids us remember the ultimate closure of death. In *Richard II*, dying Gaunt calls for an audience to watch his final performance: 'More are men's ends marked than their lives before' (2.1.11). So it is with the play: the closing moments are a time of intense marking and heightened interpretation. While the theological dimension may no longer so strongly apply, we in the present still feel the existential intensity. In *Sweeney Agonistes*, T.S. Eliot offered the mantra: 'Birth, copulation and death, / That's all the facts when you come to brass tacks, / Birth, copulation and death.' Having got the birth bit out of the way, the only facts we can look forward to are copulation and death, and of these two the only certainty, alas, is death. In short, as creatures acutely bound by and uniquely conscious of time and mortality, we are hard-wired to take endings very seriously.

What did it mean to 'make a good end' in the early modern theatre? There is surprisingly little explicit theorizing in the period. Perhaps the nearest thing to a concise statement of practice comes from Ben Jonson who, reflecting on the arts of writing in general, maintained that endings require special attention: 'Our composition must be more accurate in the beginning and end, than in the midst; and in the end more, than in the beginning; for through the midst the stream bears us' (119). By 'accurate',

Jonson meant 'executed with care; careful' (*Oxford English Dictionary* 1). If we develop the image of the stream, Jonson seems to be saying that the artist needs to take care launching the audience downstream – the exposition of the play. Once launched, the spectator can be borne along relatively freely through the rapids and vast central expanses of the play's action. The greatest care must then be applied at the end of the journey.

How to make an end

What kinds of endings did Shakespeare make? We should not be afraid of the obvious: 19 of Shakespeare's plays feature the death of a major character within the last seven minutes or so of stage action. These 19 plays are mostly what Heminges and Condell described as 'Histories' or 'Tragedies' in their arrangement of the First Folio, although we should note that the anomalous *Troilus and Cressida* and the late romance *The Two Noble Kinsmen* (not included in the First Folio) also qualify. We might also want to add to this list *Love's Labour's Lost*, where the offstage death of the King of France changes everything in the closing minutes of the action. If roughly half of Shakespeare's plays end in death, most of the other half end in the prospect of marriage and/or some form of reunion or reconciliation. We generally call these plays 'comedies', although here we would have to include *Henry V* as well as some very dark offerings such as *Measure for Measure*. Put simply: the major events of Shakespeare's endings are death and marriage, separation or reunion, integration or disintegration. (In probably his last play, *The Two Noble Kinsmen*, we extraordinarily have both.) Beyond this binary – death or reunion – is there something like a deep structure or grammar to Shakespeare's endings, a DNA of stagecraft running through the plays? What does a statistical reading of 38 plays reveal about how this particular playwright wrought his endings?[1]

---

[1] This survey includes the 38 plays printed in the Norton edition of the *Complete Works*. Plays have been generically classified following that edition's 'Table of Contents by Genre', except that the four Romances have been subsumed under the larger heading of 'Comedies'. A number of caveats must be attached to this enterprise. Generic categories are hardly as rigid as presented here. For many reasons, too, the number of lines (especially of prose) in any final scene (or even speech act) will vary from edition to edition. These figures should therefore be taken as broadly indicative rather than forensically accurate. However rough-hewn these figures might be, it would be fascinating – but sadly beyond the scope of this piece – to compare them with those generated from the complete works of other early modern dramatists.

How long does an ending last?

The theatrical experience is time-bound. One of the major differences between reading and seeing a play is that as readers we can control our durational experience of the text, but in the theatre we are at the mercy of the playwright and the production's tempo. As Shakespeare wrote in Sonnet 60:

> Like as the waves make towards the pebbled shore,
> So do our minutes hasten to their end,
> Each changing place with that which goes before;
> In sequent toil all forwards do contend
>
> (ll. 1–4)

Shakespeare's stagecraft is about controlling the ebbs and flows of this sequent toil. It is very hard to say exactly when a play begins to end. We know from the very beginning of *Romeo and Juliet* that the piteous end of the script has already been written, as it were, and that the following two hours will propel us towards inevitable tragedy. But if (following Emrys Jones) we take the scene to be the basic unit of construction in Shakespeare's dramaturgy, the first thing we notice is the astonishing range and variety of Shakespeare's final scenes. The average length is 228 lines. What does this mean in terms of duration? If the lines are spoken 'trippingly on the tongue' as Hamlet recommended, it takes about an hour to speak 900 lines. The average final scene in Shakespeare therefore lasts about 15 minutes. But only four plays closely conform to this normative average: *The Taming of the Shrew*, *Titus Andronicus*, *The Merry Wives of Windsor* and *As You Like It*. The finales of most plays are either significantly longer or shorter. At one end of the range we have *Macbeth* and *Richard III*: these final scenes are the shortest in the canon and are near-identical: the tyrant has been slain and his successor defines the terms of the regime change. Malcolm promises, 'We shall not spend a large expense of time' (5.11.26), and neither he nor Richmond do – both scenes dispatch their business in a mere 41 lines. At the other end of the spectrum, the final scene (5.2) of *Love's Labour's Lost* is gargantuan, roughly an hour long in an uncut performance. Quite brilliantly, it shows a sequence of mass disguises and disrupted plays-within-the-play, before the entrance of Marcade and the announcement of death pulls the rug from under our feet, and the play itself is cheated of its expected ending. Lest we miss the thrill of this formal experiment, Shakespeare has Berowne spell it out: 'Our wooing doth not end like an old play' (5.2.851). It is unsurprising that (as a rule of thumb) the more elaborate the plot, the longer the final scene – the final movements of *The Comedy of Errors, Measure for Measure* and *Cymbeline* are all at least twice the average length. (It was the latter's prolixity that compelled George Bernard Shaw to offer his streamlined *Cymbeline Refinished*.) In general, comedies have the most long-winded closing scenes (an average of 301 lines; or 266 if one excludes the freak-ish length of *Love's Labour's Lost*). In comparison, the ten Tragedies average 227 (with a wide range between *Macbeth* [41] and *Othello* [381]). Most striking is the relative punchiness of the closing scenes of the ten History plays. The average here is only 97 lines, but if we remove the anomalously long last scene of *Henry V* (which features the inset roman-tic comedy playlet of Henry and Katherine's bilingual wooing), then the average History play needs only 70 lines or just under five minutes to conclude its weighty business.

What is the average length of the closing speech act?

The average length of the closing speech act is 9.25 lines. There is a slight generic difference here. The last speakers in Tragedies and History plays speak for just over ten lines, while the last speaker of a Shakespearean comedy speaks eight. We might also distinguish between the two halves of Shakespeare's comedic output: in the first decade of plays (from *Two Gents* to *Twelfth Night*), Shakespeare's marked prefer-ence was for short (an average of 3.5 lines) closing speech acts; perhaps unsurprisingly, the problem Comedies and Romances from *Troilus and Cressida* onwards require an average of 14 lines. It is typical of the sheer variety of Shakespeare's dramaturgy (and of the shortcomings of a statis-tical reading of drama) that none of the closing speech acts is either 3.5 or 14 lines long. But these rough figures do alert us to some instructive anomalies. For example: the only play in the canon to end on a one-liner is *The Taming of the Shrew*:

> HORTENSIO. Now go thy ways, thou hast tamed a curst shrew.
>
> LUCENTIO. 'Tis a wonder, by your leave, she will be tamed so.
> (5.2.192–3)

The ending of this play has been seen as problematic for 400 years, and the problem is generally perceived to be Kate's speech of capitula-tion to her new lord and master. John Fletcher, Shakespeare's younger contemporary and collaborator, thought this ending so unsatisfactory that he wrote a sequel, *The Tamer Tamed* (*c*.1611), a revenge comedy in which Petruccio's second wife settles the score. But regardless of what we might think morally or politically of Kate's apparent capitulation, we might note that this is a weird ending *dramaturgically*. Just before the last two lines are spoken, Kate and Petruccio leave the stage; this may not sound remarkable but in no other Shakespeare play do such important protagonists quit the stage so close to the end of the play. The general principle across all genres is for a mass simultaneous exit (with or without corpses). What Kate and Petruccio leave behind are the somewhat stunned banquet party and the curiously lame split couplet between Hortensio and Lucentio. In later comedies, as we will see, Shakespeare is keen to provide some kind of motivation (often food-based) for the final exeunt, but here there is none: having already eaten and with no compelling reason to go anywhere, the onstage characters seem stuck in a postprandial limbo. It is the experience of this stunted finale – as much as the palatability or otherwise of Kate's speech – that creates the phantom limb feeling, the sense that the play is missing something. (This sense is the opposite to that which we feel at the end of *A Midsummer Night's Dream*, a play which doesn't quite know how to stop, and which offers a superabundance of closural devices – the Mechanicals' bergamask followed by Theseus' apparently concluding 'off to bed' speech, then the dance of the fairies with Oberon and Titania, and finally, *finally*! Puck's epilogue.) The anonymously authored *The Taming of A Shrew* (pub. 1594) may be based on Shakespeare's play or it may have inspired it, but one of the most radical differences between the two surviving texts concerns the plays' treatments of the framing device. Shakespeare's play begins with two long induction scenes in which Christopher Sly is duped into believing himself a Lord and a play is put on for his benefit. After the Induction, we see Sly once more, at the end of 1.1, when he is clearly having trouble staying awake (or possibly wants to carry off to bed the cross-dressed boy he believes to be his wife). Following this brief moment of metatheatre, however, we never see Sly again, and the play-within-the-play becomes *the* play. In Shakespeare's text, metatheatre silently falls away; in *A Shrew*, Sly is a consistent and noisy presence throughout the action and the play concludes with his being returned to 'reality'. Woken up at dawn by a tapster on his way to work, Sly believes he has dreamt it all – the lordship, the free wine, the play about the shrew – but the dream will prove useful:

> I know now how to tame a shrew,
> I dreamt upon it all this night till now ...

> ... I'll to my
> Wife presently and tame her too.
>
> > (19.16–20)

The closing lines in *A Shrew* are the tapster's: 'Nay, tarry, Sly, for I'll go home with thee / And hear the rest that thou hast dreamt tonight.' Read beside Shakespeare's text, this seems like a much more persuasive conclusion. It reminds us that the whole of the play-within-the-play called *The Taming of A Shrew* was a piece of theatre put on by an all-male cast to pander to an all-male audience. Sly is repeatedly shown to be an incompetent reader of drama, and his final resolution to apply the play's 'message' to his own domestic life is surely meant to be laughable. It is not inconceivable that this is how Shakespeare's play originally ended when it was first performed in the early 1590s, but that an equivalent epilogue did not find its way into print. Perhaps, then, the anomalously stunted end of the published version of *The Shrew* provides compelling evidence that Shakespeare wrote a different and fuller ending than the one we have inherited from the First Folio text.

Who speaks the last words of the play proper?

Shakespeare's plays always end with masculine speech. The nearest Shakespeare comes to a feminine ending is when Rosalind delivers the Epilogue to *As You Like It*, an epilogue during which 'she' turns back into a boy player. But the closing words of the play proper are always spoken by a male character. Beyond noting the obvious patriarchal implications of these masculine endings, we might also speculate some typecasting here, with the responsibility for resonant closure perhaps often falling to the same actor. In the mature Tragedies, it is not impossible that the same actor played a sequence of play-ending characters: Fortinbras, Edgar (in the First Folio *Lear*), Malcolm and Octavius Caesar – the last of whom closes both *Julius Caesar* and *Antony and Cleopatra*. The situation changes with the Romances, largely because the established authority figure and the lead actor has, tragicomically, survived the plot: it was presumably Richard Burbage – as Pericles, Leontes and Prospero – who enjoyed the privilege of vocally closing the main action of those late plays.

What time elapses between the death of a major character and the end of the play?

On average, 64 lines are spoken between the key death and the end of the play. That is roughly four minutes of stage time. If death is what happens to those left behind, this buffer zone, as it were, allows the survivors both on stage and in the audience to acclimatize to the catastrophe and negotiate its meaning. The protagonist's death or deaths are mediated, their life evaluated, by the onlookers. The buffer zone is generally wider in the History plays by a minute or so; the median length in the Tragedies is 44 lines or three minutes – somewhere between *Macbeth* and *Hamlet*. Again, it is fruitful to dwell on the anomalous. In Shakespeare's two earliest tragedies – *Titus Andronicus* and *Romeo and Juliet* – more than twice the average length expires. In *Romeo and Juliet*, Friar Lawrence notoriously spends 31 lines telling the audience what it already knows: 'I will be brief' (5.3.228)! These drawn-out endings have been widely seen as problematic by theatrical practitioners across the centuries and have generally been heavily cut. Purists have responded by accusing the players of squandering important material and of distrusting Shakespeare's stagecraft. But one might equally argue that practitioners have improved the work of the young playwright by making it more closely resemble the work of the mature Shakespeare. The two most painful endings in the canon are, arguably, those of *Othello* and *King Lear*. The pain is multi-faceted and certainly has much to do with the spectacle of female suffering and death. But it is also noticeable that in both plays, only 16 lines (in *Othello* and the First Folio *Lear;* 17 in the Quarto *Lear*), roughly one minute, elapses between the death of the titular hero and the death of the play. Shakespeare's final tragedy *Coriolanus* is comparably terse, even clinical. The craftsman's decision to minimize the buffer zone is a masterstroke: because less is said, 'the weight of this sad time' (*Lear* First Folio 5.3.298) appears less supportable, less amenable to discursive anaesthetic. In heavily cutting the final speeches in *Titus* and *Romeo and Juliet*, theatre practitioners have sought to maximize the emotional intensity, the unmediated pain of these earliest tragedies by exploiting the stagecraft of their illustrious successors. Woody Allen once observed: 'I'm not afraid of death. I just don't want to be there when it happens.' Shakespeare's tragic endings force us to be there when death happens, and the craftsman, whether early modern playwright or postmodern practitioner, must choose the duration of that happening.

How many plays end in rhyming couplets?

Approximately three out of four plays end with the form of aural closure that is the rhyming couplet. Tragedies and histories more often end in couplets than comedies. Only two plays in the whole canon end in prose (*Love's Labour's Lost* and *Much Ado*). A couplet is a recapitulation and summation of all the preceding couplets and exits in the play. Though a small-scale effect and by no means reserved for the ends of plays, the final rhyming couplet's aptness and efficiency can best be judged by our sense of unease when it fails to arrive. A shift in pronunciation makes it very hard for the poor actor playing Malcolm at the end of *Macbeth*: 'So thanks to all at once, and to each one, / Whom we invite to see us crowned at Scone' (5.11.40–1). Human error can also intervene: I once took part in a production of *Romeo and Juliet* in which the Prince of Verona (somewhat the worse for wear) stumbled on and solemnly slurred over the dead couple: 'For never was there a story of more woe / Than this of Romeo and her ... er, Juliet' (cf. 5.3.308–9). There is no doubt that this frustrated rhyme had the lamentable effect of spreading the actor's confusion across the audience and retarding (and perhaps diminishing) the eventual round of applause.

How many plays end with the promise of an offstage discussion?

Fourteen plays end with the fascinating convention of an offstage discussion. At the end of *Romeo and Juliet*, the Prince (if he is sober) orders his onstage subjects to 'Go hence, to have more talk of these sad things' (5.3.306); Portia closes *The Merchant of Venice* by initiating a similar withdrawal:

> Let us go in,
> And charge us there upon inter'gatories,
> And we will answer all things faithfully.
> (5.1.296)

Mistress Page's final words conjure up a cosier, less legalistic scenario in which all will retire to her Windsor home and merrily 'laugh this sport o'er by a country fire' (*Merry Wives of Windsor*, 5.5.219). It is tempting to see this 'let's go off and chat' device as perfunctory, a convenient excuse to shift bodies off stage now that the real business of the play is done. But the frequency with which Shakespeare employs the motif hints that something more meaningful is at stake. What these lines underscore is the essentially Janus-faced nature of endings – while these closing moments will inevitably look back over the action at all the events that have brought this group of characters to this particular position, they will also look forward to the continuation of relationships and of conversation. The rest will not be silence. This I take as an inbuilt invitation to the audience to go forth and multiply meaning. In their Preface to the First Folio, Heminges and Condell instructed the 'Great Variety of readers': 'Read him, therefore, and again, and again, and if then you do not like him, surely you are in some manifest danger not to understand him.' Something like this injunction is embedded in the end of Shakespeare's plays: discuss him, therefore, and again, and again. Some of the plays (most notably *The Comedy of Errors* and *The Merry Wives of Windsor*) close with the anticipation of gossiping and feasting. Hamlet talks of a play being 'well digested in the scenes' (2.2.420–1), but a play in early modern London must also have been well digested in the tavern over a post-show meal. Everyone had to eat something after what was, in effect, a matinee: by concluding their action with the prospect of gossiping and feasting, a retelling o'er of the play's events, these endings mimic and predict the post-performance activities of their audiences (see Weimann, 1996; Meek).

How many performances ended with an epilogue or a jig?

It is impossible to say how many performances ended with an epilogue or a jig. The earliest published editions of Shakespeare's plays feature ten epilogues. But it is highly likely that some epilogues may have been spoken at original performances but did not find their way into the printed texts. It is also probable that most, if not all, epilogues were designed to be performed at the conclusion of the play's premiere, but might be discarded should the play be fortunate enough to be revived again. The epilogue is a liminal convention that takes place in a twilight zone between fiction and reality; it both prolongs the play and the actor–audience relationship whilst simultaneously announcing that all the playing is over, at least temporarily. It is generally ingratiating, offering an apology for the quality of the performance and soliciting the audience's applause – we should remember that no performance is complete without the consent of the audience. None of these ten plays whose epilogues survive in print are, according to the First Folio definition, tragedies. Nearly all – with the exception of *2 Henry IV* – are comedies. Perhaps Shakespeare thought that his tragic apocalypses required no postscripts and no apology; perhaps the epilogue to *Hamlet* simply did not survive the passage from playhouse to printing house.

As with epilogues, so with jigs: it is impossible to know the full extent to which this type of afterpiece was a regular addition to Shakespeare's endings on the early modern stage. We probably have one eyewitness account of a Shakespearean jig. When a Swiss tourist, Thomas Platter, visited London in September 1599 he went to 'the house with the thatched roof' and watched 'the tragedy of the first emperor Julius Caesar': 'At the end of the comedy, according to their custom, they danced with exceeding elegance, two each in men's and two in women's clothes, wonderfully together' (Greenblatt *et al.* 3301). But it is impossible to say how many performances at the Globe or elsewhere ended in this quite civilized fashion or, indeed with the more bawdy, rambunctious song-and-dance farce that was more typical of the genre (see Baskervill; Clegg and Thomson). And we can only guess at the effect such afterpieces had on an early modern audience. However limited the archive, the existence of at least some traces of these conventions alerts us to the range of sub-literary and sometimes nonverbal devices that conspired to create the sense of an ending for Shakespeare's first audiences.

Remaking Shakespeare's endings

Ben Jonson cautioned the need for accuracy in the construction of an ending, so it is striking that one of the most notorious attacks on Shakespeare's craftsmanship accused the playwright of carelessness, of *in*accuracy. Samuel Johnson complained in 1765:

> In many of his plays the latter part is evidently neglected. When he found himself near the end of his work, and in view of his reward, he shortened the labour to snatch the profit. He therefore remits his efforts where he *should most vigorously exert them*, and his catastrophe is improbably produced or imperfectly represented.
>
> (Johnson VII: 71–2; emphasis added)

Of all aspects of his stagecraft, the ways in which Shakespeare ended his plays has endured the most widespread and sustained disapproval. If his characterization is almost universally admired, his dialogue clearly unparalleled, praise has been far from unanimous for Shakespeare's ability to make a good end.

The theatre's habit of remaking Shakespeare's endings began in the early modern theatre. Fletcher provided a sequel to *The Taming of the Shrew*; Shakespeare himself seems to have had second thoughts about exactly how *King Lear* should end, though he knew he wanted it to end differently than his source texts. The late Romances, with their reunions between husbands and wives, parents and children, revisit, rewrite and redeem the apocalyptic severances of the Tragedies. In the same optimistic spirit of revision, the Restoration theatre provided its audiences with radical refashionings in which the perceived roughness and injustices of Shakespeare's finales were polished and corrected to suit the taste of the age. Nahum Tate allowed his Cordelia and King Lear to live and for good to triumph in his adaptation (1681), a conclusion so popular it held the stage until the nineteenth century. John Dryden, understandably baffled by the way in which Shakespeare ended *Troilus and Cressida*, contrived to tie up the loose ends in the neat apocalypse of tragic misunderstandings and multiple suicides that concludes his own adaptation of 1679. Elsewhere, actor-managers inserted or elaborated dying speeches to milk every ounce of pathos from their onstage demises. For Restoration theatre-makers, Shakespeare's scripts were considered more like fair game than Holy Scripture. Whatever care (or lack of it) Shakespeare had devoted to creating his great variety of endings, from the Restoration onwards these endings would be treated as the raw materials from which each subsequent generation of practitioners would seek to create the most striking possible finale.

A strong tendency, as in Tate's *Lear*, has been to sugar over the pain of Shakespeare's endings. As Shaw wryly noted: 'The practice of improving Shakespear's [*sic*] plays, more especially in the matter of supplying them with what are called happy endings, is an old established one which has always been accepted without protest by British audiences' (133). But things were about to change. By 1977, Richard Levin could observe that 'over the past decade the number of ironic endings in Shakespeare has been increasing at a remarkable rate' (337). By 'ironic', Levin meant readings or productions in which the upbeat and harmonious ending apparently suggested by the text is discarded in favour of an atmosphere of discord or uncertainty. Frequently these endings emphasized the impossibility of progress and the circularity of history – a common Modernist trope (T.S. Eliot: 'In my beginning is my end') – and one reanimated in Shakespeare studies by Jan Kott's influential theory of 'The Grand Mechanism'. Kott argued that in Shakespeare 'history stands still. Every chapter opens and closes at the same point' (6). There are no grounds for optimism as the new king (Malcolm, Fortinbras, Richmond) will be just as hated as the last, his regime just as corrupt. Thus Roman Polanski's film of *Macbeth* ends with Donalbain visiting the Witches, an action replay that takes us back to the play's opening and which casts severe doubt upon the ongoing security of Malcolm's kingship and kingdom. Many stage productions of *Macbeth* and other history plays have closed with some variation of this *da capo* coda. Indeed, so common is this directorial flourish that these ironic or pessimistic endings have become almost as reassuringly cosy and clichéd as the harmonious, optimistic endings they originally sought to subvert.

Cyclical or ironic endings are less common in productions of the Comedies, the nonverbal conclusions of which are more likely to follow *Much Ado about Nothing* and stage a celebratory dance than they are to cast doubt on the future happiness of the couples. Here, nevertheless, directors have frequently mined the closing moments of Shakespeare's plays for signs of unhappiness and future discord. Cheek by Jowl's *Twelfth Night* (2003) ended with a single spotlight picking out Malvolio, his features rigid with determination as he pronounced 'I'll be revenged on the whole pack of you' before a snap blackout. Ian Judge's RSC *Love's Labour's Lost* (1993–94) was set on the threshold of the First World War and ended with the young men silhouetted against a cloudy cyclorama, the distant rumble and boom of heavy artillery chillingly ruling out a happy sequel. Somewhat more subtly, the close of Declan Donnellan's Maly Theatre production of *The Winter's Tale* (1997) shaded the joy of reconciliation with an unforgettable image of the irrecoverable. Immediately after Hermione had implored the gods to look down and pour their graces upon her daughter's head (5.3.122–4), the scene of reunion froze. No further words were spoken. Mamillius entered, guided by the young woman who personified Time. They wove their way around the statuesque bodies like after-hours trespassers at Madame Tussaud's. Finally, inevitably, they stopped next to the kneeling Leontes, the father whose mania had destroyed this son. The boy briefly placed a hand upon his father's head before leaving the stage as silently as he entered it. The lights faded and (on the occasion I saw it at least) the effect of the interpolation was so moving that it was some time before the audience could bring itself to applaud. As with many endings in contemporary Shakespearean theatre, Mamillius' spectral re-entry was unscripted, nonverbal and its effect overwhelmingly emotional.

Making a good end for theatre practitioners is always intimately bound up with the observation or subversion of decorum, the appropriate tone and style for the specific circumstance of the performance. The fundamental aim – to manipulate collective feeling in a certain direction – is common to theatre artists of all eras. The timbre of that feeling and the means used to trigger it, on the other hand, will vary greatly depending on the historical moment, the audience's horizon of expectations, and the technological means available to the production team. As Peter Brook wrote of style in Shakespearean production: 'A production is only correct at the moment of its correctness, and only good at the moment of its success. In its beginning is its beginning, and in its end is its end' (1967: 256). We might illustrate this dictum with a whistle-stop tour of *Hamlet*'s stage history. On Shakespeare's stage, the play would presumably have ended with Fortinbras' closing speech, a Death March and a sound effect (*'a peal of ordnance are shot off'*). Throughout the eighteenth and nineteenth centuries, however, Fortinbras was customarily omitted from the play completely, partly so that *Hamlet* might terminate more or less precisely and pathetically with the Prince's last breath. Thus in the Cumberland acting edition of 1829, the play's last words are 'the rest is silence'. Later in the nineteenth century, Henry Irving allowed for a little eulogizing when he ended his *Hamlet* with Horatio's lines:

> Good night, sweet prince,
> And flights of angels sing thee to thy rest.
> Whilst I behind remain to tell a tale
> Which shall hereafter make the hearers pale
> (based on 5.2.302–3)

The closing couplet is painful (in a bad way), but the truncation combined a romanticizing instinct with the atmospheric and adjustable effects of gaslight and must have worked some emotional magic on a great part of the Lyceum's audience. One of the greatest differences between endings on Shakespeare's stages and on Irving's or our own is technological: lighting. Once the stage has retreated behind a proscenium arch and its curtain, any moment can be petrified into an indelible image as the curtain descends or the lights fade. This moment of mnemonic intensity is beautifully captured in Ronald Bryden's description of the closing seconds of David Warner's *Hamlet*:

> The four captains kneel on either side of the body. Awkwardly they hoist it on their shoulders, its arms outflung as if in horizontal crucifixion. As they pick their way upstage through heaped bodies, pale courtiers and dumbfounded soldiery, its head lolls behind them, staring back sightlessly at the audience. The lights dim, the stage darkens, a faint spotlight clings with a halo of luminosity to the receding arched throat and hanging head ... [It] deliberately ends with the image which has closed every *Hamlet* you remember, formally conventional as a Byzantine icon. Hamlet has become Hamlet, statue, legend, the starry Prince.
>
> (*New Statesman* 27 August 1965)

If Hall's knowing deployment of that familiar closing image was, in Brook's term, 'correct', so too was Charles Marowitz's conscious iconoclasm when, also in 1965, he concluded his sceptical, anti-heroic *Hamlet Collage* with Hamlet intoning the lines 'From this time forth, my thoughts be bloody or be nothing worth' to hoots of derision and catcalls from the suddenly reanimated corpses that littered the stage. More recently, we might wonder what it says about our own historical moment that Gregory Doran's 2009 RSC production starring David Tennant returned to the star-centred conventions of the nineteenth century, and verbally ended the play with Horatio requesting that flights of angels sing Hamlet to his rest. Fortinbras *did* then enter, ominous yet strangely mute, but more or less the full focus remained on Tennant/Hamlet as the lights faded and a sound-cue poignantly provided 'a swan-like end, / Fading in music' (*Merchant of Venice* 3.2.44–5).

As the foregoing examples show, performance always exceeds the text. A Shakespeare script can only tell us certain things about how a performance might end, whether on Shakespeare's stage or our own. The script tells us what the characters are supposed to say and offers occasional implicit or explicit stage directions. But major dramaturgical components are unscripted and implicit at best: how should those lines be delivered? What gestures should accompany the words? What is everyone wearing? How are the bodies on stage spatially arranged? How do those bodies leave the stage? *Exeunt*, like *They fight*, is an exceptionally flexible stage direction. The openness of Shakespeare's texts invites even demands that subsequent collaborators refashion and reimagine those endings, just as Shakespeare rewrote the endings he found in his sources.

Epilogue: when does the fat lady stop singing?

It is very hard to say when a performance ends. Even after the curtain (figuratively or literally) comes down, the communal event continues to signify. Almost invariably, actors will invite and receive an audience's applause, but these curtain calls have their own semiotics and usually serve to prolong, rather than curtail, the production's play of meaning. Curtain calls seek to tell us what kind of production we have just seen. Peter Brook's production of *A Midsummer Night's Dream* (1970) famously concluded with the cast jumping down from the stage and into the auditorium to shake hands with the audience, the giving of hands (Epilogue, 15) made literal and reciprocal. When the RSC mounted productions of eight history plays in 2006–08, the curtain call varied

depending on whether one was attending a single stand-alone performance or whether one was in for the long haul of a four- or eight-play
cycle. When performed alone, many of these productions ended with a
solo, 'star' curtain call for the lead actor, the exalted 'he who plays the
king' (*Hamlet* 2.2.308). Yet during the 'Glorious Moment', an eight-play
marathon performed over four days, these were avoided: hierarchical
star bows would have run counter to the story the event wanted to
tell, a story of a democratic and egalitarian ensemble who were all in it
together. In most curtain calls, actors are still acting, still demonstrating something. It is common, for example, to see hearty backslapping
as they retreat to the wings – ostensibly this demonstrates camaraderie,
but as aficionados of peace talks or coalition governments will recognize, the gesture can also perform power. If the actors are still performing, so is the audience, performing (or failing to perform) those actions
expected of us, clapping too early, or too late, with gusto or with reser-
vation. The warmth or otherwise of this moment can alter the actor's
and company's perception of the performance they have just given, a
perception that has more or less subtle consequences not only for the
post-show mood in the pub, but also for the attitude that the performers will bring to their job on the next day's work. When the audience
leaves the theatre, too, the performance experience is not quite over.
(After the RSC's 2009 *As You Like It*, this was true of the world we exited
into as the trees and buildings outside the Courtyard Theatre had, during the second half, been magically papered with love letters resembling
those Orlando had earlier posted around the Forest of Arden.) We might
also choose to read reviews on posters outside the theatre, or write our
own, or follow the injunction of many of the plays and go forth and
have more talk of these sad or happy things – all of these activities help
stay the moment of performance while also retrospectively recalibrating
our thoughts and feelings about what we have just experienced.

Many decisions – not all of them conscious – conspire to create a live
ending. What happens when this intricate choreography malfunctions?
Theatre programmes routinely publish the approximate running time
of a show (the consultation of which is always a moment of truth for
the reluctant theatregoer). Visitors to the 2010 Stratford, Ontario festival website could learn that that season's productions of *The Tempest*
would last for 2 hours and 32 minutes and *The Winter's Tale* for 2 hours
and 59 minutes. This precision mimics those of movie listings, but in
the theatre (unlike the cinema) any number of things could happen to
shorten or lengthen the running time. The audience is a key constituent
of Shakespeare's endings. Not only are we required to liberate Prospero

or pardon Puck, but we are also capable of intervening in the performance in ways limited only by the extent of our imaginations. We might
through the quality of our silence serve to magnify the intensity of the
closing moments. When Henry Jackson watched the King's Men perform *Othello* in Oxford in 1610 he recorded the profound impression
made on him by the spectacle of the dead Desdemona: 'she moved
[us] more after she had been murdered, when, lying upon her bed, her
face itself implored pity from the onlookers'. This account reminds us
of the power of the nonverbal in our sense of an ending (the players
'aroused tears not only through their words, but even their gestures'),
but Jackson's response also hints at the quality of attention he and his
fellow spectators contributed to the performance event. Conversely,
bathetically, any single audience member is capable of wrecking these
moments. There are many accounts of the intense pathos of David
Garrick's performances as King Lear. On one such evening, the house
was entirely hushed and spellbound by the great actor's genius, when
an Italian violin player, Cervetto, seated in the orchestra pit in front of
the stage, gave a loud, unmistakable and tension-sapping yawn. The
thread of attention thus crudely snapped, the audience dissolved in
laughter.

> The enraged [Garrick] sent for Cervetto and demanded why he
> behaved so? In broken English poor Nosey apologised: 'Sare, I begs
> ten tausend pardons, sare; but *ven mooch* interested I always open *ma
> mouths* and yawn very louds.' This excuse did not satisfy [Garrick]; he
> was forbidden to be so 'mooch' interested again.
>
> (Stirling 2:293)

Given that the theatre is the most volatile of art forms, endings can
sometimes come unexpectedly. Shakespeare knew this to his own cost.
At a performance of *Henry VIII* at the Globe in 1613, a small cannon was
shot off as a sound effect, but managed to set fire to the thatched roof.
Within an hour, the Globe had burnt to the ground. No one died, but
one man, finding his breeches on fire, was forced to douse the flames
with his beer. Shakespearean theatre history is littered with such abrupt
endings. When touring America in 1849, William Macready suffered
a barrage of abuse during his Shakespearean performances. Evenings
ended early as performances were disrupted by missiles hurled from
the auditorium: eggs of doubtful purity might be endured, but when
the carcass of a dead sheep was lobbed on stage some pause must have
been necessary. Macready's ill-fated tour ended when a performance of

Macbeth in New York was terminally disrupted by an outbreak of rioting that spilled out of the theatre and into the adjacent streets around Astor Place; the militia was called, opened fire and killed 31 civilians. But for a spontaneously unexpected ending, nothing quite beats the story (perhaps apocryphal) of a nineteenth-century performance of *Othello* during which a man in the audience, infuriated by Iago's dastardly behaviour and hopelessly confusing actor with character, rose to his feet, informed Iago, 'You, sir, are a scoundrel' and shot the actor dead. That is one way of making *Othello* end happily. It is also a stern reminder that when we go to watch Shakespeare in the theatre, we can never be entirely sure how we will react or quite how the evening will end.

5
Visual Scores

Christie Carson

This chapter explores the extent to which Shakespeare's plays *play* with our vision, our expectations and our understanding of the way the theatre can make us 'See better' (*King Lear* 1.1.152) by seeing differently. It looks at the increasing complexity of visual imagery throughout Shakespeare's writing career by highlighting the relationship between textual and visual rhetoric and the foregrounding of the audience's interpretation of the visual score. In order to illustrate this argument I have chosen to highlight three pairs of contrasting visually significant moments on stage. By combining a close reading of the text in these moments with examples from performance it is possible to demonstrate that Shakespeare's work shows a developing sense of the importance of collective understanding of the visual on stage. The performance of the plays through 'original practices' experiments, particularly in the reconstructed theatres of Shakespeare's Globe and the Blackfriars in Virginia, has helped to reanimate the collective visualization process that is embedded in the dramatic structure of Shakespeare's work. The plays have not changed, but our understanding of their dramatic effect has, owing to the participatory nature of the audiences in these new old spaces.

This argument combines a close analysis of references to seeing and looking in the texts with examples taken from experiments in original practices (productions that aim to reanimate the 'original' theatrical aesthetic of Shakespeare's texts in various ways), particularly experiments with all-male companies, to illustrate the gap between what is seen and what is described on stage. I will begin by examining the use of stage twins in *The Comedy of Errors* and *Twelfth Night* to create cases of mistaken identity. But I will also indicate how *The Comedy of Errors'* simple employment of farcical conventions of confusion develops into a complex discussion of perception and gender identity in *Twelfth*

Night. The gender debate is one that I will carry through to examples taken from *Othello* and *Antony and Cleopatra* – in which the bodies of boy actors are highlighted through undressing in one case, and dressing in the other – to mark a clear gap between what the audience sees on stage realistically and what it is asked to imagine. The relationship between reality and illusion, as well as between physical attributes and gender assignment, are opened to debate when the audience is dared to see something other than what is physically presented before it on stage. The third pair of visual moments moves a step further, examining the very nature of existence as well as the purpose of art. The death of Cordelia in *King Lear* and the rebirth of Hermione in *The Winter's Tale* help to articulate visually where the line between life and death, illusion and reality might be. The large philosophical questions, which it may be argued sit behind the theatrical illusions of the earlier plays, are made the subject of the action in these final two examples.

Thoughts about the importance of the visual in Shakespearean performance have been circulating for some time. Dennis Kennedy writes: 'the visual history of performance, which has been mostly excluded from Shakespeare Studies, rewards extended investigation because of its intriguing relationship to the status and uses of Shakespeare, both in the theatre and in the culture at large' (1993: 4). Theatre practice for many years has been influenced, even dominated, by a dependence on pictorial and then later filmic visual codes of realism and beauty that devalued the input of the audience's imagination. I do not believe that original practices experiments reconnect with Shakespeare's own audiences, but rather operate to reinvigorate the dialogue within the plays between an audience, the actors on stage and the playwright through the idea of collectively agreeing to see, as Mark Rylance says, 'the actor and the audience [as] one group of imaginers' (109). In all Shakespearean production the world of the play is communicated to the audience through visual cues. As Kennedy says: 'There is a clear relationship between what a production looks like and what its spectators accept as its statement and value. This seems obvious: the visual signs the performance generates are not only the guide to its social and cultural meaning but often constitute the meaning itself' (1993: 5). Kennedy's exploration of the visual is embedded in the design tradition of his own period of writing. Directors' theatre, with its conceptual understanding of the plays, has often been accompanied by complex visual instructions for the audience through detailed set and costume designs. Original practices performances, while often elaborately costumed, strip away the realistic settings and return to the audience the power to 'see better' (1.1.152) by looking collectively. Perception, perspective and identity become the subject of the gap between what is and what is not seen on stage.

Twins: realizing the limitations of realism

The first theatrical moment I will focus on to illustrate the way these conventions operate is the coming together of the two sets of twins in *The Comedy of Errors* which takes place for the first time in 3.1 when Antipholes of Ephesus is locked out of his own home. The central image of the scene is the door trick which pits the two sets of twins against each other both physically and verbally, particularly in terms of the Dromios' ability to reason through their positions and identities.

> Antipholus E. Who talks within there? Ho, open the door.
>
> Dromio S. *[Within]* Right, sir. I'll tell you when, and you'll tell me wherefore.
>
> Antipholus E. Wherefore? For my dinner. I have not dined to-day.
>
> Dromio S. *[Within]* Nor today here you must not. Come again when you may.
>
> Antipholus E. What art thou that keepest me out from the house I owe?
>
> Dromio S. *[Within]* The porter for this time, sir, and my name is Dromio.
>
> Dromio of Ephesus. O villain, thou hast stolen both mine office and my name.
> The one ne'er got me credit, the other mickle blame.
> If thou hadst been Dromio to-day in my place,
> Thou wouldst have changed thy face for a name or thy name for an ass.
>
> (3.1.38–47)

The initial exchange in this passage between Antipholus of Ephesus and Dromio of Syracuse articulates the confusion felt by the local servant and master but also differentiates the two servants, since Dromio S. is initially more polite and rhetorically sophisticated than Dromio E.

However, as the two Dromios are differentiated they also become one, through the fact that they have not been accurately recognized by their masters when they met previously in the market. They appear to be entirely interchangeable given that their identity is attached to their position, therefore the 'office' and the 'name' become one. These servants are seemingly simply the beast of burden they are compared to, the ass.

But this exchange is not as simple as it might first appear. The rhetoric that each of the Dromios uses both mimics and parodies the rhetoric employed by their masters. This helps to separate the two pairs but also sets up quite different relationships between each master and servant.

ANTIPHOLUS E. There is something in the wind, that we cannot get in.

DROMIO E. You would say so, master, if your garments were thin.
Your cake there is warm within. You stand here in the cold.
It would make a man mad as a buck, to be so bought and sold.

ANTIPHOLUS E. Go fetch me something. I'll break ope the gate.

DROMIO S. *[Within]* Break any breaking here, and I'll break your knave's pate.

DROMIO E. A man may break a word with you, sir, and words are but wind,
Ay, and break it in your face, so he break it not behind.

DROMIO S. *[Within]* It seems thou want'st breaking. Out upon thee, hind!

(3.1. 69–77)

Antipholus' philosophical musing about what is keeping him in the street is quickly turned by the literal interpretation of the Dromios into the fear of madness by Dromio E., a physical threat by Dromio S., a joke about flatulence (Dromio E.) and a further play on the idea of breaking in bucks by whipping their behinds (Dromio S.). Dromio S.'s threatening behaviour is countered by Dromio E.'s fears and jokes creating a sense of two very different servants. The Ephesus pair of servant and master have a clearly defined domestically enshrined relationship of service, while the visiting Syracuse master and servant appear to have the closer bond of travelling companions.

On stage the constant realigning of power between these two pairs can become quite complicated visually. It is necessary to have both actors on stage at the same time, pointing out that their similarities may or may not be a mistakable likeness. This struggle for individuality alongside indivisibility is tricky to create visually. Different solutions to this problem have been found in performance. In two 2009 touring productions, one from the RSC and one from the Globe Theatre, quite differing visual strategies were applied. In the RSC schools production, directed by Paul Hunter of the Told by an Idiot company, the twins, while played by two actors who were dressed identically, were physically paired with their masters rather than with each other (one set were taller and thinner than the other). In the Globe touring production, the same actor played both parts using a cut-out image of himself to stand in for the character that was not speaking. While this second solution avoids the difficulty of making the characters' identicalness believable, it shifts the audience's attention from the progress of the story to the appreciation of the actor's virtuoso performance. This, I would argue, illustrates that any attempt at visual realism in fact takes away from the audience's pleasure of collectively suspending disbelief. The presentation of the scene at the Globe became clever rather than involving.

The twins come face to face in 4.4, but it is not until the reconciliation of the brothers in the final act when the characters talk each other into and out of their own identities. Intriguingly, at the end of the play the two Dromios look to each other to sort out their new-found state, but with an assumption of audience involvement in and acceptance of their assessment:

> DROMIO E. Methinks you are my glass, and not my brother:
> I see by you I am a sweet-faced youth.
> Will you walk in to see their gossiping?
>
> DROMIO S. Not I, sir. You are my elder.
>
> DROMIO E. That's a question. How shall we try it?
>
> DROMIO S. We'll draw cuts for the senior. Till then lead thou first.
>
> DROMIO E. Nay, then, thus:
> We came into the world like brother and brother,
> And now let's go hand in hand, not one before another.
> *Exeunt*

(5.1.417–25)

This ending to the play focuses on the power of the pair to realign their own identities and the hierarchy which might separate them. This small attack on the logic of the laws of primogenitor is a theme which returns in the character of Edmund in *King Lear*. The fact that the play ends with the servant characters and their questioning of the social order places the vision of the servant characters at the centre of the audience's experience. When played by two actors who are similarly dressed the audience sees *through* the Dromios, both physically in that it understands that they are not really twins, but also metaphorically in that it takes on their perspective. The audience members can leave the theatre 'hand in hand, not one before the other' imaginatively despite their varying social and cultural positions. This effect was lost somewhat in the Globe production, where the audience was asked to enjoy the union of an actor with an image of himself.

Twins: confronting gender expectations

The gentle encouragement in *The Comedy of Errors* to join in the fun of co-creation is further developed but also debated in *Twelfth Night*. A lesson that Shakespeare seems to have learned from *The Comedy of Errors* is the wisdom of keeping the two actors playing the twins apart for as long as possible. The confusion that occurs in *Twelfth Night* is very similar to the scenes in *The Comedy of Errors*, but it is made more convincing by the fact that the two characters are not seen on stage together until the final reconciliation. The confusion between the two twins is also augmented by the fact that the audience know that Cesario is a woman. Rather than the characters questioning, defining and redefining their own identities as they do at the end of *The Comedy of Errors*, Viola is faced with the consequences of her false identity being taken as true. She is the 'poor monster' (2.2.31) that must see what time has in store for her. The idea of identity in this play becomes an interesting combination of physical appearance, reputation and recognition by others. The relationship between outward appearance, actions and expectation is the subject particularly of the scene when Sir Andrew Aguecheek challenges Cesario to a duel. The humour in this scene comes from the fact that Sir Andrew, although a man, is no more brave than Viola in disguise. But it is Sir Toby, with his claims that Cesario is 'a very devil' (3.4.232) who 'will not be pacified' (3.4.238), that present a new identity for this character. Viola's aside, 'Pray God defend me! A little thing would make me tell them how much I lack of a man' (3.4.223–4), puts her in the position of confiding in the audience, setting up a new contract of conspiracy with it. However, this allegiance is quickly challenged when the fight is interrupted by Antonio. What begins as a performance of false masculinity on both sides quickly becomes a dangerous and deadly duel with real consequences. When Antonio claims his love and devotion to Cesario and begs for him/her to prevent his arrest, the audience is placed in an awkward position not knowing whether it is better to see Viola exposed or to let the true-hearted Antonio be jailed. This is a much more complicated use of the confusion of the conventions of mistaken identity than is seen in *The Comedy of Errors*, since the audience is engaged in thinking through the consequences of the confusion. What the audience sees is the outcome of putting forward a false identity or self-image, but it is also given a potential opportunity to rectify the problems that result from mistaken identity.

This first confrontation of the audience's expectations of a playful game of confusion is then augmented by a further test of what it sees when Sebastian appears on stage in the next scene. As in *The Comedy of Errors*, the issue here in performance must be whether the actor playing Sebastian is sufficiently like the actor playing Viola/Cesario to be mistaken for her/him from his first entrance. It is only once the difference in Sebastian's actions, and possibly his voice, are made clear that the audience becomes sure a new character has entered the scene. Sebastian's entrance is, however, supported by the descriptions of Sir Toby in the preceding scene since *this* young man now fits the image of the hot-headed adversary that Toby describes. When Sir Andrew strikes him Sebastian replies without hesitation.

> SIR ANDREW AGUECHEEK. Now, sir, have I met you again? There's for you.

> SEBASTIAN. Why, there's for thee, and there, and there. Are all the people mad?

> (4.1.16–17)

Sir Andrew's challenge is met by Sebastian's quick and ready response, but what is perhaps more interesting is the exchange of two seemingly inconsequential rhetorical questions. While in *The Comedy of Errors* the questions posed on stage are for the other characters to answer, in this play these questions raise interesting issues for the audience as well. Sir Andrew's 'Now, sir, have I met you again?' puts the audience in the position of having to either agree or disagree. Sebastian's actions help to confirm that he is not in fact Cesario but he follows up his action with another question: 'Are all the people mad?' Again, the audience is implicated. Sebastian, as an outsider to the world of the play up to this point, provides a new perspective on the action. The assumption of madness is a conventional response to mistaken identity (Antipholus E. greets Dromio S. with 'How now? A mad man?' at 4.1.95) when he is told a ship is waiting for his passage home), but here the audience is included in 'all the people' that might be mad, clearly pointing out the form of conspiracy that exists. The audience's acceptance of the vision of a boy playing a girl playing a boy is challenged by the appearance on stage of a boy playing a similar-looking boy asking if the characters and spectators are all mad.

This challenging behaviour, however, quickly disappears in *Twelfth Night* since Sebastian allows himself to be led to wed Olivia without questioning his own identity or self-image to any great extent:

> OLIVIA. Do not deny. Beshrew his soul for me,
> He started one poor heart of mine in thee.
>
> SEBASTIAN. What relish is in this? how runs the stream?
> Or I am mad, or else this is a dream:
> Let fancy still my sense in Lethe steep.
> If it be thus to dream, still let me sleep.
>
> OLIVIA. Nay, come, I prithee; would thou'ldst be ruled by me!
>
> SEBASTIAN. Madam, I will.
>
> OLIVIA. O, say so, and so be.
>
> (4.1.54–61)

Olivia's hope that to 'say so' is to 'be so' provides a clear sense of one way of looking at the audience contract. The audience should simply accept as real everything it is told to see. This is essentially the assumption that underlies the character's actions in *The Comedy of Errors*. Antipholus S., like Sebastian, accepts a wife he does not know with very little resistance: 'Until I know this sure uncertainty, / I'll entertain the offer'd fallacy' (2.2.185–6). This speech makes clear that the audience know the play is a 'sure uncertainty' but are asked to 'entertain the offer'd fallacy'. The play will work only if the audience is willing to 'play' along.

However, *Twelfth Night* ends with a more complex relationship between identity, perception and belief in the scene when the two actors playing the twins come together. Orsino says: 'One face, one voice, one habit, and two persons – / A natural perspective, that is and is not!' (5.1.200–1). Orsino's lines provide direction regarding what the audience is expected to see: both 'One face, one voice, one habit' but also what 'is and is not' on stage visually. Orsino acts as the director on stage of the audience's imagination and, like Olivia, assumes that to 'say so' is to 'be so', highlighting the theatrical convention rather than relying on the audience to 'accept the offer'd fallacy'. The audience is given the opportunity to struggle to sort through its own preconceptions and expectations, weighing up what it sees against what it is told to see. This acceptance of the reality of the twins, and in particular their gender identity, is further complicated in performance by all-male casts.

Seeing Viola/Cesario and Sebastian on stage in all-male productions

Looking at the twins in two productions that have used all-male casts, it is possible to illustrate the issue of identity and its relationship to onstage illusion. Discussing the Globe's 2002 production of *Twelfth Night*, Farah Karim-Cooper identifies the way that costumes and make-up helped to give the appearance of identicalness for the twins: 'The effects of their identicality were created not just by wearing identical costumes, but also by the application of a white facial makeup base; it was dizzying, particularly when one twin was exiting just as another was entering the stage' (2008: 71). I would argue that this dizzying effect was created not only by the make-up and costumes, but that it is an element of the onstage illusion which is embedded in the dramatic structure of this play. The audience is meant to be disoriented by the actors' quick entrances and exits, set up as they are by the descriptions of these characters by others on stage. The original practices experiments at Shakespeare's Globe clearly endeavoured to address the gap between Elizabethan expectations and audiences today, but also tackled the current assumptions that audiences bring into the theatre of men dressed as women coming primarily, although not exclusively, from the pantomime tradition. Karim-Cooper writes:

> The *Twelfth Night* company in 2002 asked its audience to believe that thick white face paint on grown men was a clear sign of femininity. A modern audience would not have access to the meanings that

painted faces had in Elizabethan and Jacobean England or on the Renaissance stage, but clearly through such experiments, the new Globe was shifting the established associations that white face paint has with sophisticated forms of theatre, Kabuki and opera, as well as with clowns and pantomime, but curiously, the Globe was also drawing upon these associations to intensify the comic and symbolic effect of white makeup in the play.

(2008: 69)

The question of whether the audience accepts a boy dressed as a girl dressed as a boy cannot be separated from the other elements of stage illusion. Yet expectations of sexuality in the twenty-first century are necessarily different from those of a Renaissance audience, and this point is worthy of some investigation, particularly in the context of all-male productions.

Abigail Rokison, looking at two different productions of *Twelfth Night,* the Globe production in 2002 and Edward Hall's production for the Propeller Company in 1999 (which was remounted in 2006/7), articulates the implications of all-male casts when presented to a twenty-first century audience in contemporary rather than Renaissance costume:

> According to Hall, with an all-male company 'the audience stops being interested in the sexual chemistry between the actors and starts listening to the words' ... [quoted by Alek] Sierz, *Independent on Sunday* 14 August 2003]. However, when Mark Ravenhill asked the rather flippant question 'Surely this is a bit poofy?' in his *Guardian* article on Propeller [24 January 2005], he raised a serious point about the homoerotic undertones of cross-gendered casting in Shakespeare.
>
> (77)

The physical practices of costuming and make-up and the architecture of the space at the Globe contribute to a sense of getting closer to the theatrical practices, but also the sensibilities of the period. However, contemporary all-male productions cannot rely on an understanding of Renaissance erotic practices; there is an undeniable gulf between what an audience now might feel and how an audience then might have responded. Rokison points out that, 'For James C. Bulman, all-male casting, far from distancing the audience from such issues, highlights the themes of sexuality and gender identity' (77; Bulman, 2004). She also makes clear that a similar series of conflicting anxieties about sexuality

still confront an audience watching an all-male production of the play
at the Globe:

> members of a modern audience, unaccustomed to seeing men taking
> on Shakespeare's female roles, may indeed find themselves aroused
> or indeed amused by the relationships enacted on stage. Paul Taylor,
> writing on the performance of *Twelfth Night* at Middle Temple
> Hall [*Independent* 2 February 2002], asserted that Eddie Redmayne's
> 'scandalously persuasive' performance as Viola 'would bring out the
> bisexual in any man'.
>
> (78)

Therefore whether presented in Renaissance costume or in contemporary clothing, the visual presence on stage of a man dressed as a woman
provides conflicting visual signals that make it difficult for an audience
to uniformly 'accept the offer'd fallacy'. What is said, what is seen and
what is felt by the audience intersect in very interesting ways in these
two productions. Contemporary experiments with all-male casts have
helped to reintroduce the sexual ambiguity of the role of Viola/Cesario
providing the opportunity for audience engagement that is very personal and individual, since it relies on both assumptions about masculinity and femininity and the unpredictable laws of sexual attraction.

Of course it is not just the twins that provide a debate about the
nature and substance of gender performativity in *Twelfth Night*, as
Karim-Cooper points out:

> Olivia in *Twelfth Night* provides a crucial example, because her beauty
> is a subject for consideration in the play: she protests that her beauty
> is natural (as would any self-respecting aristocratic lady who paints
> her face), although Viola (as Cesario), being female and acquainted
> with the secrets of a lady's chamber, boldly insinuates that the oppo-
> site may be true. Whether or not Olivia is a painted lady, this scene
> clearly marks a self-reflexive moment in the theatre, as the boy actor
> playing her emphatically denies his character is painted, even as he
> is painted up to signify his female role.
>
> (2010: 103)

Drawing attention to the visual construction of gender in this scene opens
up a debate about acceptable forms of desire in the plays, and at the same
time highlights the artificiality of the performance currently in front of
the audience. As Karim-Cooper observes: 'The scene also interrogates

contemporary definitions of female beauty, by demonstrating that the impersonation of it is so viable' (103). What it is to be beautiful as well as what it is to be female are debated with the audience through the physical form of the male actor on stage. The male actor's femininity becomes the substance of the scene, but the action also highlights the gap between the ideal vision of beauty described and the actor's face that is presented.

Boy actors exposed on stage

Looking further at the idea that Shakespeare increasingly used the contradiction of a female body being portrayed by a boy actor on stage to his advantage, I turn to two other theatrical moments that draw attention to the body and its physical attributes which stand in obvious contrast to the discussion of gender by the characters. The slow undressing of Desdemona before she is murdered in her bed points out her frailty but also potentially the masculinity of the actor. Emilia asks a pragmatic question of her mistress: 'Shall I go fetch your nightgown?' (4.3.35). Desdemona's reply, 'No, unpin me here' (4.3.36), is followed by a rather strange change of subject: 'This Lodovico is a proper man' (4.3.37). This statement leads to a discussion of what constitutes a proper man. Emilia says, 'A very handsome man' and Desdemona replies, 'He speaks well' (4.3.38–9). Emilia's concentration on a man's physical attributes and Desdemona's attention to his education may be partly a difference of class, or it could simply be the division in experience of men between these two women that is increasingly evident as their conversation progresses. In the privacy of Desdemona's bedchamber these two women have a sensitive and frank debate about the difference between the sexes in terms of their attitudes towards marriage. This debate then moves quickly to an assessment of the biological similarities between men and women:

> EMILIA. Why we have galls, and though we have some grace,
> Yet have we some revenge. Let husbands know
> Their wives have sense like them: they see and smell
> And have their palates for both sweet and sour,
> As husbands do.
>
> (4.3.95–9)

Emilia's description of the similarities between men and women in terms of their physical appetites is accompanied by the increasing exposure of the boy actor's body. On stage the similarities but also the differences between the clothed boy actor performing as Emilia and the undressed actor playing Desdemona make a striking visual counterpoint to the argument made by the characters in conversation.

Like Cleopatra's self-conscious declaration of the inadequacy of her portrayal on stage ('I shall see / Some squeaking Cleopatra boy my greatness'; 5.2.218–19) the recognition of the limitations of the illusion presented on stage is followed by the careful creation of the tragic death of each of these women. I would argue that in both of these cases the theatrical intensity of the moment is heightened, rather than under-mined, by the recognition of the gap between what is seen and what the story requires the audience to believe. The symbolic and visually striking nature of both these deaths requires a separation of the actor and the role. The actor must himself be aware of the impossibility of attaining the artistic aim of symbolism while at the same time striving for it. However, in practice, when the struggle to maintain the illusion is shared with the audience it becomes a collaborative act rather than an attempt to fool the audience. Mark Rylance, in discussing acting on the Globe stage, says: 'I had to become a storyteller as well as a part inside the story' (105). But he acknowledges the extent to which this element of the performance style is demanded by the plays themselves:

> I do not know how it works, but I find I can be in the story and in the audience making fun of myself in the story at the same time, in certain places in Shakespeare. Now this may sound like a contradiction of what I was saying earlier about not commenting on the story, but if we are all in the story, audiences and actors alike, then I found I could flip between these two seemingly contrary realities as if they were one. The actor and the audience are one group of imaginers somehow.
>
> (109)

The recognition of the boy actor within the role helps to illustrate the increasingly complex process of combining the audience's imagination with the presentation by the actors in particular visual moments on stage.

Death on stage bringing the audience together

The last two moments I would like to consider demonstrate the way that in the plays written in Shakespeare's mature period the actor on stage becomes the catalyst for a profound and philosophical understanding of the nature and purpose of the theatre. In *King Lear*, Cordelia's death, and in *The Winter's Tale*, Hermione's rebirth, both represent the relationship between the physical and the spiritual, between life and art, between reality and illusion. It is in these moments that Shakespeare exploits the full capacity of the theatre to develop a complex audience engagement that allows it to see what 'is and is not' (*Twelfth Night*, 5.1.201) simultaneously. By looking in some detail at these two scenes, it is possible to argue that, as Shakespeare developed as a theatrical writer, he used his understanding of the limitations of theatrical illusion to develop a dialogue with the audience that relies entirely on the presence of live actors at the centre of an increasingly complex argument about the relationship between the material body and identity, but also between the body and perception.

In *King Lear*, Gloucester falls forward on a flat stage. While Edgar's description of the steep cliff and the view of the beach below prepares the audience for the scene, it is impossible to tell whether the fall on stage itself could ever be seen to be in any way convincing. Edgar, too, is confused about the implications of the onstage action: 'And yet I know not how conceit may rob / The treasury of life, when life itself / Yields to the theft' (4.5.41–3). He has to ask his father (and the audience) 'alive or dead?' (4.5.45). It is up to Gloucester to move and Edgar to act as the audience's cue on stage to tell it what to see: 'Thus might he pass indeed. Yet he revives' (4.5.47). This exchange with the audience is crucial for setting up the final scene of the play. Even as Gloucester revives he must ask his son, 'But have I fall'n or no?' (4.5.56). Again, this is a question that Edgar and the audience must answer together. Edgar repositions his character, in performance often both vocally and physically enacting another person, at the bottom of the cliff, providing himself with a new identity both visually and through his description of the events on stage which the audience has both seen and not seen. Visually this scene is interesting in that it presents the central characters as unhelpful witnesses of their own actions, deceivers of each other as well as of the audience. But this scene also places rather large demands on the audience to keep up with the imagery presented verbally, while very little is offered visually to support these images. Edgar becomes the stage magician who orchestrates the audience's visual *and* imaginative experience. He becomes the audience's imaginative guide on stage in this moment.

In the final scene of the play the intermingling of practical and philosophical questions again depends on the audience's response to piecing together the description of what is seen with the theatrical presentation of the actors on stage.

> *Enter Lear, with Cordelia [dead] in his arms, [Edgar, Captain, and others following].*

LEAR. Howl, howl, howl, howl! O, you are men of stone.
Had I your tongues and eyes, I'ld use them so
That heaven's vault should crack. She's gone for ever!
I know when one is dead, and when one lives.
She's dead as earth. Lend me a looking glass.
If that her breath will mist or stain the stone,
Why, then she lives.

(5.3.231–7)

The audience is told categorically that Cordelia is dead – 'She's dead as earth' – only to be told one line later that perhaps there is still a sign of life. The idea of checking her breath on a looking-glass is pragmatic and verifiable on stage, but this test also clearly has two outcomes, the real and the symbolic. This testing of the audience's engagement with the symbolic nature of the presentation of the tale on the stage is then taken a step further with the two rhetorical questions that follow on in the text:

EARL OF KENT.   Is this the promis'd end?

EDGAR. Or image of that horror?

(5.3.237–8)

The bleakness of the vision presented is called into question by the realization that it can never be anything but an 'image of that horror' rather than the real thing. The audience is told by Edgar that what it sees is not real and yet is asked to believe in it at the same time.

Lear's continued attempts to prove that Cordelia is alive involve the audience imaginatively but also empathetically in the central tragedy of his fall. The King says, 'This feather stirs, she lives' (5.3.239), and this is followed by the announcement of the death of Lear's other two daughters and then Edmund's death. The piling up of these unseen bodies is given very little consideration in comparison with Cordelia's central visible corpse, because it is only her life that can save Lear: 'if it be so, / It is a chance which does redeem all sorrows / that ever I felt!' (5.3.239–41). The idea that a single breath might save the play puts a great deal of pressure on the actor playing Cordelia in that moment not to breathe in an obvious way. When Lear finally gives up on his own life he focuses the full attention of the audience on the one thing it cannot see properly but it knows to be there: the breathing Cordelia; 'do you see this? Look on her? Look her lips / Look there, Look there' [*He dies*] (5.3.283–5). This line is an addition to the First Folio and one which I have argued elsewhere (see

Carson, 'Quarto of *King Lear*') might well indicate a rewriting of the play to accommodate the public playhouse audience. Performances on the Globe stage suggest that the groundlings might perceive some breath in Cordelia. Drawing attention to the collective act of seeing at the same time as requiring a silence that encourages a collective act of not breathing too loudly brings the audience together in a way that acknowledges that everyone in the theatre has 'sense in them' (*Othello* 4.3.97), as Emilia says. The silence of the audience in this moment helps to create a unified interpretation which elevates what it agrees to believe above what it can see. Therefore the audience allows Lear's direction to draw it towards a consensual acceptance of the symbolic vision of the dead Cordelia in his arms. This challenge to the audience, but also this acceptance of the audience's power to decide what it sees, demonstrate Shakespeare's sophisticated use of theatrical craft as well as his increasing acceptance of the power of the audience to determine meaning. This final moment seamlessly orchestrates physical, emotional and imaginative solidarity in the audience.

Rebirth on stage: setting the audience free

The final example, of the statue in *The Winter's Tale*, points to a complex understanding of the role of the theatre in making its own illusions transparent in order to make them more, rather than less, convincing. Paulina's attempts to keep Leontes and Perdita away from the statue draw attention to the physical body of the actor playing Hermione: 'The statue is but newly fix'd, the colour's / Not dry' (5.3.47–8). The debate about whether or not the 'stone' is convincing again draws attention to the fallacy of the illusion. What I would suggest is added to this scene is a debate about the relationship between the theatrical illusion and the potentially conflicting emotions and beliefs of the onlookers.

> PAULINA. No longer shall you gaze on't, lest your fancy
> May think anon it moves.
>
> LEONTES. Let be, let be.
> Would I were dead, but that, methinks, already—
> What was he that did make it? See, my lord,
> Would you not deem it breathed? and that those veins
> Did verily bear blood?
>
> POLIXENES. Masterly done:
> The very life seems warm upon her lip.

LEONTES. The fixture of her eye has motion in't,
As we are mock'd with art.

(5.3.60–8)

The notion of being 'mock'd with art' is crucial here as it points to the heart of the problem in the audience contract – that solidarity of response requires the inclusion of any potential sceptics. In *The Comedy of Errors* and *Twelfth Night* there is a developing dialogue with conventions assuming the audience will play along; with *Othello* and *Antony and Cleopatra* the playwright points out the limitations of art and requests the audience's participation in the illusion. Cordelia's death demands attention and respect. However, this scene leaves the choice of whether to believe or not fully with the audience, but with one additional argument:

PAULINA. It is required
You do awake your faith. Then all stand still;

On: those that think it is unlawful business
I am about, let them depart.

(5.3.94–7)

The addition of the idea of faith is coupled with the removal of any accommodation made to the audience members that might think the scene damnable, blasphemous or simply unbelievable. The sceptic is banished. The audience is given the choice to stay and participate in the illusion or to depart; staying means believing and joining in the illusion, 'accepting the offer'd fallacy' rather than feeling that one is 'mock'd with art'.

Ralph Cohen describes the way that this moment worked in the reconstructed Blackfriars Theatre in Staunton, Virginia:

At first, when Paulina says, 'Behold and say 'tis well' (5.3.20) they craned their necks, but when Leontes began to speak three lines later – 'her natural posture!' (5.3.23) – and then began to comment so specifically on the age represented in the 'statue,' as many as twenty of them ... would finally get up and move down the aisle behind the gallery seats to see. Their curiosity simply overwhelmed their conventional theatre behaviour.

(223)

As Cohen points out, staging these plays in reconstructed spaces has helped to develop a greater understanding of the careful attention paid by Shakespeare to audience response and interaction freed of 'conventional' or traditional twentieth-century theatre behaviour. It has also helped to reinvigorate this responsive process for modern audiences. Cohen goes on to say:

> Then came the best part: they stood watching to see if Leontes or Perdita would touch the statue, while Paulina threatens all the while to close the curtain. Every evening, about fifty lines later, a few of those who had stood would start to return to their seats, but Paulina's line 'if you can behold it, / I'll make the statue move indeed' (5.3.87–88) would stop them, and Paulina would take the next lines, 'It is required / That you do wake your faith. Then all stand still' (5.3.94–95) first to the seated audience and then to the standees. Leontes would second her, 'Proceed' (5.3.97) and direct his next order to the standing audience members above and below: 'No foot shall stir' (5.3.98) It was as though the playwright had anticipated the way an audience would respond to the architecture of the Blackfriars.
>
> (223–4)

While it is impossible to argue decisively that this reaction proves Shakespeare intends what Cohen seems to suggest, I would like to point out what this reconstructed theatre allowed. 'See[ing] better' in this case has three interconnected meanings. The first is that real involvement in the theatrical moment requires a physical response as well as an imaginative one, in this case getting into a place where one can see the onstage illusion properly. Second, it is essential to see with an eye to sympathetically imaging the symbolic implications of a woman turned to stone for 16 years while simultaneously accepting the further pragmatic imaginative possibility that Hermione was hiding at Paulina's house until the oracle was fulfilled and Leontes had repented. The third aspect of this moment that must be highlighted is that any inclination towards realism and rationality inevitably gets in the way of real engagement. Leontes' line makes this point clear: 'No settled senses of the world can match / The pleasure of that madness. Let 't alone' (5.3.72–3). Why bother to come to the theatre if one fears or does not value the 'pleasure of that madness'; in other words, the ability to see what is not there with a group of other imaginers?

Seeing Shakespeare 'feelingly' (*King Lear* 4.5.152)

The articulation of identity as it relates to perception and the purpose of art is dealt with in the plays most acutely when the stage picture does not fully satisfy the audience and when the rhetorical questions in the text confront the logical and pragmatic assumptions of the audience but also its prejudices. The fear from the period that the illusion of the theatre was a form of dreaming, madness or even damnation is dealt with directly in these plays. While initially it is the subject of debate on stage, later in Shakespeare's writing the issue of believability is overlooked in order to reach towards bigger questions. By increasingly relying on the audience to participate in creating symbolic meaning on stage Shakespeare's visual illusions become increasingly engaging. In the final example from *The Winter's Tale* magic and realism are created at the same time. Hermione both 'is and is not' real, the magic that brings her to life 'is and is not' Leontes' love and the audience's willing participation in the 'pleasure of that madness'. Convincing visual spectacle ceases to be the goal of the plays once authority to determine if the audience is being 'mock'd by art' is handed over to the audience members themselves. The pure pleasure of being tricked by the illusion is celebrated in this final image which both 'is and is not' entirely magical. Shakespeare takes on Olivia's imperious notion that to 'say so' is to 'be so' but also Dromio E.'s egalitarian plea to the audience and actors to 'go hand in hand, not one before the other'.

Reconstructed spaces have helped to demonstrate how this process can continue to engage audiences in the larger philosophical ideas addressed in the plays. But these experiments have also made it clear that the plays are designed to be re-created with each performance. Mark Rylance states: 'It became paramount to say to the actors, "Don't speak *to* them, don't speak *for* them, speak *with* them, play *with* them." Eventually, in my last years, I really came to feel it was not just about speaking, it was about thinking of the audience as other actors' (107). The visual rhetoric of Shakespeare's plays, therefore, is a union of textual imagery, visual spectacle and audience imagination. The playwright engages *with* the audience but *through* the actors on stage, combining visual cues with poetic imagery to instigate a playful and complex imaginative conversation about the nature of identity, perception, beauty and art. When Lear says to the blind Gloucester, 'yet you see how this world goes' (4.5.150–1), Gloucester replies, 'I see it feelingly' (4.5.152). Ideas about reality and fiction, life and death, spring out of the imagination of the present audience. It is the audience's interaction with the visual world of these plays both on stage and in the mind's eye that creates a new discussion of these topics every time these plays are performed.

6
Props

Farah Karim-Cooper

> When props are regarded as properties, they may no
> longer seem to be so trifling: as objects owned by act-
> ing companies, impresarios and players, as objects
> belonging to – proper to – the institution of the
> theatre, stage properties encode networks of material
> relations that are the stuff of drama and society alike.
> (Harris and Korda, 2002: 1)

During the previews of the 2009 Globe production of *Troilus and Cressida*, Achilles' Myrmidons murdered the unsuspecting Hector with a machine-gun. The rest of the production was set reasonably firmly in the ancient world, achieved through the lavish set, pseudo-Greek costumes, tattoos and hairstyles and the props themselves, which were deliberately designed to be temporal signifiers. However, the introduction of the machine-gun seemed to rupture the audience's sense of place and time, and the gun's lack of transhistoricity was a cogent reminder of the intrusion of the materials of the present when performing the past; but the rupture may have been too great, according to the director (Matthew Dunster), who felt he had lost 'control' of the theatrical event. He thus removed the offending prop from the rest of the run. What this example illustrates is the role that objects play in constructing an audience's sense of history. As Andrew Sofer writes, 'in addition to locale, props silently convey time period' (21). Equally, one object can change the entire temporal meaning of a production and remove a director's 'control'. By the very nature of its materials and its reconstructed design, the Globe Theatre imposes history on to its performers, actors and audience alike. When directors are invited to create a production there, they are forced to consider the historical implications of the space.

At times the historicity is an artistic deterrent and designers and directors respond by concealing the evocative signifiers of the past, either by hammering wooden panelling on to the elaborately painted tiring-house façade or building large-scale sets that force the stage to thrust out deeper into the Yard, rationalized by spatial instinct, or by a sense that the space does not 'work' based on essentialist notions of what 'feels' accurate or inaccurate about the reconstruction.[1] However, there are many directors who embrace the space's historical identity and who creatively attempt (now without recourse to 'original practices' conventions, discontinued at the Globe in 2006) to reconstruct a sixteenth- or seventeenth-century aesthetic or 'feel'.

Turning to the subject of props, as Jonathan Gil Harris and Natasha Korda have pointed out in their remarkable introduction to *Staged Properties in Early Modern English Drama*, 'early modern scholarship has become obsessed with materiality ... . In the process, theatrical objects have increasingly joined subjects as privileged sites of materialist critical inquiry' (15). Although in theatre studies, the analysis of props as constituting a fundamental part of the sign-system of theatre has long been a part of semiotic studies from the era of the Prague School until now, early modern literary scholars have begun, as Harris and Korda note, to examine the importance of objects, their cultural biographies and how they transmit meaning within a particular social, political and cultural moment. Within these studies of clothing, food, cosmetics, drugs and a wide range of other objects on the early modern stage, critics have mapped out approaches to analysing the sexual and cultural politics of early modern culture in an attempt to consider what might have been at stake when these plays were first performed. In particular, Sofer's study

---

[1] In interviews with actors and directors, the word 'instinct' often emerges in discussions about the architectural features and the playing conditions they create at the Globe. However, what is often overlooked is the anthropological fact that spatial instincts are not transhistorical or universal and that this type of 'theatrical essentialism' (as Alan Dessen has termed it) does not necessarily constitute evidence about how early modern actors responded to the architectural features of their theatres. Part of the project of reconstruction was to reorientate a performance community (actors and audience) towards a theatrical tradition that was absent so long as to seem alien and therefore unlock hidden potentials for interpretation of the plays performed at the new Globe. This is not to suggest that generally, the instinct of a theatre artist is not valuable; however, if it is trying to recover how early modern actors might have responded to a theatrical space, the Globe should not rely on the spatial instincts of current actors/directors alone.

is concerned with the 'mobile, material life [of props] on the stage' (vii), namely, how

> on the one hand, props are *unidirectional*: they are propelled through stage space and real time before historically specific audiences at a given performance event. At the same time, props are *retrospective*: in Marvin Carlson's apt expression, they are 'ghosted' by their previous stage incarnations, and hence by a theatrical past they both embody and critique.
>
> (viii)

Nowhere is this 'unidirectional'/'retrospective' dialectic more true than in the Globe theatre space, where the past and the present are both simultaneous contributory units in the making of theatre. This chapter will address the ways in which props construct history at the Globe and will explore this issue in part by examining the point of view of modern directors. Here we are concerned with the processes of making meaning and making theatre, in Keir Elam's sense of the word: 'the complex of phenomena associated with the performer–audience transaction' (2), through single objects, specifically, historically evocative ones. The case study for this chapter will be the Globe's 2007 production of *Othello* directed by Wilson Milam. I want to examine what happens when a director deliberately sets out to construct a historical moment through the visible constituents of theatre, such as costume, set and props, and how props, specifically, can participate in but simultaneously contradict such an aim.

'Original practices' and the reproduction of history

Although quite a bit of ink (including my own) has recently been spilled over the Globe's deployment of 'original practices' production in its first ten years, it is worthwhile examining some of the historical residue left behind that Dominic Dromgoole, the Globe's artistic director, is attempting to scrape off. The term 'original practices' has different meanings within varying contexts and theatre companies: the American Shakespeare Center's reconstructed Blackfriars Theatre in Staunton, Virginia, for example, use the term to refer to the practices of the theatre companies working in early modern commercial theatres. Thus in their annual Actor's Renaissance Season, based on Tiffany Stern's research (2000), the resident theatre company performs several early modern plays, using actor's parts, with no director and very little rehearsal time, such as three days. At the Globe, however, it means something entirely different.[2] In 'original practices' productions, costumes, props and music, as well as manners, deportment and socially appropriate codes of conduct would be researched to the finest detail, using only methods and materials available in the sixteenth and seventeenth centuries, replicated and put into performance. The result was often startlingly beautiful productions that enlivened Renaissance materiality and reorientated audiences to the aesthetic of the period in tangible and constructive ways. Mark Rylance characterizes the original practices experiment in terms of the guiding principles that informed the reconstruction: 'research, materials and craft' (Karim-Cooper, 2010: 103). He emphasizes the importance of these principles in creating performances at the Globe. The historical research that went into the productions was 'radical', as Rylance remarks, because 'being faithful to a period … is pretty unfamiliar in the theatre' (104). However, whether or not we now know more about the way Shakespeare's plays were originally staged because of these productions remains uncertain. There is, of course, much value in making costumes and props out of 'authentic' materials, as a great deal has been learned about clothing and dressing practices, particularly among early modern actors. Christie Carson discusses the 'confusion of myth and historical fact' when she describes the tension between the attempt to mock up history televisually when an episode of *Doctor Who* was filmed at the Globe, and the 'original practices' project: 'ironically, the careful "original practices" project of Shakespeare's Globe was in the popular imagination overridden by this filmic attempt to recreate a former reality. The "reductive or the simplified" televisual realism of the programme helped to undermine the carefully researched experiments of the real theatre' (Carson, 2010: 283). A similar tension exists when directors at the Globe post-Rylance attempt to diligently reconstruct a historical period without deploying the principles that underpinned 'original practices' productions. For example, in Chris Luscombe's production of *The Merry Wives of Windsor* at the Globe in 2008, the Elizabethan period became something of a motif; through the use of costume, music, props and design, the Tudor aesthetic was alluded to throughout the production and seemed to mock any serious attempt at reconstructing a historical period theatrically. For example, in that year, while the Architecture Research Group were conducting carefully researched experiments in decoration and

---

[2] See Carson and Karim-Cooper for scholars' and practitioners' attempts to define this movement at the Globe in its first ten years.

painting in the Gentleman's Rooms in order to begin the process of carrying out the decorative scheme exemplified in the tiring-house façade throughout the rest of the auditorium, in Luscombe's production, designer Janet Bird hung faux plaster and timber panels upon the heavily decorated walls on the *frons scenae* to evoke a sense of the past through pastiche. Institutional incoherence is not always a feature of Globe performance practice, as we shall see.

The power of original practices productions is such that directors working at the Globe during the Dromgoole era with the mandate to do a production in 'Renaissance style' nevertheless feel the need to break out of this prescription. Many directors at the Globe are often radically opposed to the constraints of history, while ironically, some Globe directors feel challenged by the historical imposition of the space and go to great lengths to engage with the past, but without the excessive budgets original practices productions once boasted. For example, Mark Rosenblatt prepared for his production of *Henry VIII* (2010) by researching the visual details as well as the historical 'facts' surrounding the Reformation and the court of Henry VIII. Trips to Hampton Court Palace inspired much of the visual feast that the production provided, and the props department sent representatives to the Palace to take pictures and then re-create as much as possible each of the relevant objects for the production, which perhaps had one of the most extensive props list of any at the Globe. Although Rosenblatt's methodology seems similar to that of the Rylance-era original practices method, it only *seems* similar; a 'Renaissance-style' production at the Globe is not the same as an 'original practices' production is, and this is not to say that it should be.

Wilson Milam's production of *Othello* began with the 'Renaissance-style' mandate, and early rehearsals consisted of intensive textual analysis, lectures and historical research. In an interview with the research team, Milam admitted that he 'really needed to dig into that period into what were his [i.e. Shakespeare's] historical references, what was his own particular London historical reality, because most people think he had never been to Italy' (Milam, October 2007). As it turned out, Milam became somewhat obsessed with Renaissance history and his self-imposed mandate became to reconstruct Venice and Cyprus *circa* 1570 rather than have the actors perform as Jacobeans playing Venetians, which is the kind of temporal styling that Dromgoole has tended to deploy in his productions, for example *Coriolanus* (2006) and *Antony and Cleopatra* (2006).

The company of actors performing *Othello* were told in the first week of rehearsals that they would be the first group of actors to perform this tragedy at the Globe in 400 years,[3] and that Eamonn Walker would be the first-ever black man to play Othello on the Globe stage. Thus the production and the performers were laden with the unquantifiable burden of historical weight just by virtue of the theatrical venue. The historicity, in this particular example, carried with it a distinct responsibility not only on the part of the actors, but on the director as well, an American who had never directed Shakespeare at the Globe – or anywhere else, for that matter. Milam referred to his sense of historical duty in the space: 'this was the Shakespeare god smiling and saying "learn about the source"' (October 2007). Milam's artistic and intellectual journey began with the stage, and it was clear to him from the start that it should be mostly bare – to establish 'primacy of the actor' (October 2007) – that there would be no masking of the tiring-house structure or extensions of the playing space into the Yard. However, what would need to happen was an intensive exploration into the period around 1570, and the reconstruction of this would rely primarily on the visual details of performance, such as costumes and props. The only adherence to supposed Elizabethan conventions of playing was the desire for a mostly bare stage, but as Harris and Korda point out, 'the objects of the early modern stage were often intended not merely to catch, but to overwhelm the eye by means of their real or apparent costliness, motion, and capacity to surprise' (4), and that, as evidence suggests, it is more than likely a myth that the early modern stages were not replete with 'dazzling properties' (4). Thus, in the early weeks of rehearsal, historical details about early modern staging practices did not figure in the reconstruction of a historical moment on the Globe stage. However, the irony of a bare stage in a production of a play that is set in Venice, a city which, historically, was 'crammed with both people and things' (Allerston 12), did not go unnoticed. What remained unexplored, however, was the relationship between the ubiquity of 'things' and female sexuality, links made in early modern England and in the play.

In Lena Cowen Orlin's collection, *Material London ca. 1600*, Ian W. Archer explores the growth of London's urban population and the corresponding increase in the availability and consumption of goods. He finds a tension between morality and the growing acquisitiveness of Londoners in the early 1600s: 'consumption was a moral problem because the desire for goods was linked with sexual desire' (187). The

---

[3] It was not entirely true; as this chapter will show, Globe Education produced an 'Our Theatre' production of *Othello* in 2004.

alignment of material consumption and sexual consumption is an important one in this play. The Globe production's use of large suitcases to accompany Desdemona when she arrives in Cyprus was meant to gesture towards her status as a Venetian lady, a lady who would have had 'things' and would have carried many of them with her when she travelled; the fact that, in the willow scene, she is not surrounded by the contents of those suitcases adheres to Milam's minimalist approach, as well as perhaps a symbolic reading of her character's virtue. The idea to present Desdemona minimally was an interpretative choice, not only to highlight the handkerchief in her hands during the crucial scenes, but also to indicate to the audience that she is in fact innocent of sexual infidelity; however, to suggest to a modern audience the relationship between objects and sexuality presents a danger of replicating the early modern practice of polarizing and overdetermining female sexuality. Milam's intended portrayal would not have been consistent necessarily with what we know about Patrician ladies in sixteenth-century Venice, but the production was not entirely free of the ideological baggage that historical replication can bring with it.

By staging a Venetian *Othello*, Milam felt he was honouring Shakespeare's knowledge of Italian history and in this way was 'being faithful' to Shakespeare as such; the obvious tension that would emerge, however, was that between the director's vision of the play, the accurate details, or minutiae, of the history of the period around 1570 and the history of Shakespeare's theatrical practices in 1604 when the play was first performed. Nonetheless, there was an apparent need to get the props right, to give them a historical focus. This chapter explores the deliberate staging of history by examining closely two important props in the production: the handkerchief and the portrait of the Moorish Ambassador *circa* 1600; moreover, it will question whether or not physical objects on stage can be determined in such specific and historically centred ways. 'The theatrical sign inevitably acquires secondary meanings for the audience, relating it to the social, moral and ideological values operative in the community of which performers and spectators are part', argues Elam (8), which inevitably interrupts their historical continuities; however, it would be useful to identify exactly what communities are converging within a theatre like the Globe.

The performers in a production like Milam's *Othello* are operating within a dialectic of invoked historical communities. There are layers of significations at the Globe from a performer's point of view through which such a production makes meaning. The *Othello* company were made aware of the historical significance of the Elizabethan theatre space in which they would be working. For example, they learned the history of Elizabethan playhouses, their unique vertical structure and the world in which they were constructed. Yet the actors were being asked to represent to a modern audience a period earlier than the play's original composition, and a far-distant setting. The three communities represented here would therefore be consistently present through the production's run. The props were designed to signify history, but paradoxically, partly because of these multiple communities, worked simultaneously to undermine this historicity.

Textile witness: the handkerchief and the erasure of historical weight

From the painted hangings draping the auditorium, decorating the stage and perhaps the Lord's Rooms, to the actor's costumes and gloves, cloth properties would have been familiar sights in the Elizabethan and Jacobean playhouses and handkerchiefs were another expression in this vocabulary of textile. Originating as a property in the civilization of social selves, the handkerchief, through the centuries, has since acquired a multiplicity of meanings. Andrew Sofer traces the use of handkerchiefs back to the 'sacred cloth' used in 'devotional drama' and shows that 'in the course of launching revenge tragedy as a popular genre, [Thomas] Kyd appropriated and sensationalized' the tradition (62). The handkerchief in *Othello* is a much discussed prop; so rather than provide a survey of its critical and social history, I will highlight one or two studies that shed particularly useful light upon its role as a theatrical sign that transmits identifying codes about gender, race, commerce and psychology. Examining early modern portraits in his chapter on handkerchiefs in *Materializing Gender in Early Modern English Literature and Culture*, Will Fisher argues that the handkerchief is a kind of 'prosthesis', 'since it was to some extent "incorporated" into the (female) body' (41). In *Othello* the handkerchief actually becomes an emblem for the female body and Desdemona's presumed transgressions are written there. Fisher argues that 'if Othello sees the handkerchief as an integral part of Desdemona's hand and a necessary means of controlling her "watery" nature, the play as a whole nevertheless insists upon the accessory's detachability and transferability' (56). It is the transferability of the handkerchief that problematizes its meaning for spectators today. The early modern notions of how objects absorb identities would carry little weight among the current Globe audience. The network of early associations with handkerchiefs, such as its memorializing of 'sacred cloth', its contribution to the Anglo-European civilizing process and the regulation of the body, its importance to courtship rituals and the plurality of meanings it acquired in the social contracts between men and women in the sixteenth and seventeenth centuries would somehow have to be concentrated into the prop handkerchief in impossibly obvious ways. The new Globe, with its multi-faceted, postmodern audience, refuses to enable one culture or cultural moment to be represented singularly. Sofer refers to the work of Marvin Carlson, who 'reminds us that spectators bring associations from previous productions with them to the theater, and that these "ghosts" color their experience of the current performance' (6). The play does do the work, however, of inscribing its own meaning on to the prop, and for *Othello*, it emblematizes female deception, when Othello 'thinks' it is 'ocular proof' of Desdemona's infidelity, when Emilia actually steals it from her Lady and when Cassio asks Bianca, his 'whore', to make a copy of it. The play makes us aware of the handkerchief's 'ability to circulate between different hands' (56), and Othello misreads this circulation as a register of his wife's transportability, her presumed movement between different beds. But for a modern audience seeing the handkerchief in play at the Globe, the object itself must shake loose current signifying attachments and assume the early modern connotations as well as those prescribed by Shakespeare's play. To enable this assumption, it was decided that in the Globe production, the prop would need to be visually exceptional and distinctive; thus the handkerchief had motifs of large strawberries concentrated into the centre of the panel. Because the production had very few props in it other than scenic devices, such as benches, stools, tankards, and so on, the idea was to place due emphasis on the handkerchief: 'We had beer tankards, swords, a handkerchief' (Milam, October 2007). The actors attempted to demonstrate the transferability of the prop throughout the production. Zoe Tapper's Desdemona clutches it adoringly, but nervously; Walker's Othello tosses it to the floor when Desdemona attempts to wipe his forehead; Lorraine Burroughs's Emilia displays it, holding it up high for the audience to take note, demonstrating that, in her hands, it becomes a register for the pivotal moment of the play when she passes it to her husband, effectively trading it for his affections. Tim McInnerny's Iago kisses it and places it inside his jerkin (jacket), while Zawe Ashton's Bianca waves it about jealously when Cassio asks her to 'take out the work'. Thomas Rymer's famously excoriating rant about the play condemns 'our poet' for making 'so much ado, so much stress, so much passion and repetition about an Handkerchief' (quoted in Vickers, 1974: 51). The handkerchief is indeed central to the play, but why shouldn't it be? As Sofer reminds us, it had a complex religious significance for early moderns, but in the play it also has a history that is exotic, 'foreign'; this orientalizing discourse of the handkerchief enables the cloth to extend beyond the local to incorporate other worlds.

For years, critical discussions of the handkerchief have denied it its crucial role ascribed to it in the play as an alien artefact, an object that derives from a 'foreign' country and whose biographical history calls to mind the increasingly mysterious backgrounds of objects in circulation in sixteenth- and seventeenth-century England due to the increase in trade:

> That handkerchief
> Did an Egyptian to my mother give;
> She was a charmer, and could almost read
> The thoughts of people. She told her, while she kept it,
> 'Twould make her amiable, and subdue my father
> Entirely to her love; but if she lost it,
> Or made a gift of it, my father's eye
> Should hold her loathed, and his spirits should hunt
> After new fancies. She, dying, gave it me,
> And bid me, when my fate would have me wiv'd,
> To give it her.
>
> (3.4.55–65)

Its history is woven into the drama through Othello's narrative, the back story that gives the handkerchief its magical powers and its historical identity as a measure of fidelity; as Harry Berger, Jr remarks: 'he [Othello] makes the handkerchief symbolize first the wife's sexual power over her husband and then the chastity that the husband demands as an always-inadequate place-holder for the virginity she lost when she subdued him to her love' (239). For Milam's production, the research team at Shakespeare's Globe were asked to provide images of Renaissance continental handkerchiefs with the idea that if the prop was accurately sourced, then the production would be able to do the work of reproducing some of the original meanings or associations of handkerchiefs. But such an endeavour is never entirely possible; Catherine Silverstone has observed that those working at the Globe have acknowledged 'that they cannot produce a fully authentic early modern theatre' (quoted in Carson and Karim-Cooper 67), and neither can they produce a 'fully authentic' early modern prop or audience to rightly interpret that prop. The prop was ultimately sourced from a combination of descriptive references in the play-text itself and an earlier incarnation of the play staged by Globe Education, demonstrating its transferability as not only an object in the play, but as a prop on the stage.

In 2004, Globe Education launched its Shakespeare and Islam initiative as way of creating a dialogue between Shakespeare's Globe and the British Muslim community. Part of the project's aim was to educate people about the ways in which Shakespeare and his contemporaries were engaged with the East primarily through the exchange of goods, and that Shakespeare's London was establishing itself already as a proto-multicultural metropolis. One strand of the initiative was the 'tent for peace' project, in which 'students from around the world created [panels], inspired by Islamic designs, for the handkerchief from Egypt "spotted with strawberries" which Othello gives to Desdemona. Ninety were hand-embroidered and sewn together to create the lining of a Tent for peace – now used for storytelling' (Carson and Karim-Cooper 137). In addition to the Tent, as Spottiswoode relates, there was a presentation of *Othello* on the Globe stage by over four hundred Southwark schoolchildren. He states: 'to demonstrate the power and presence of the handkerchief as a character unto itself, this production deliberately had a hand-embroidered love token clearly visible at Desdemona's first entrance in 1.5, unlike many productions in which a small modern hankie is not seen until 3.3, thus marginalising its role in the play' (138). The handkerchief used in the 2007 Globe production of the play copied the design of one of the panels created for the Shakespeare and Islam project, thus unconsciously inheriting Globe Education's reformulation of the handkerchief, constructed through a deliberate semiotization of the prop as a symbol of peace, community and positive religious multiculturalism, which worked towards but was fundamentally unsuccessful at undermining the misogynistic and racist discourses articulated by the play. Although the audience's access to this reformulation might have been as limited as their access to the handkerchief's early modern resonances,[4] taking what Carson calls an 'institutional approach', I am arguing that this particular articulation of the handkerchief's signifying function highlights the ways in which productions of Shakespeare at the Globe are engaged or influenced institutionally.

---

[4] There would have been a portion of the audiences for *Othello* in 2007 who would have had some working memory of the Globe Education productions, owing to the public resources and storytelling events that continued to develop and which enabled the image of the strawberry handkerchief to sustain a local as well as institutional familiarity.

Arguably, the handkerchief used in the production contained meaning, articulated widely or not, that was internally constructed by the Globe itself. Sofer's citation of Marvin Carlson is worth recalling here: 'at the same time, props are *retrospective*: in Marvin Carlson's apt expression, they are "ghosted" by their previous stage incarnations, and hence by a theatrical past they both embody and critique'. The handkerchief is 'retrospective' in this regard, recalling its recent previous embodiment in a performance that reinforced its exotic identity, enhanced all the more by Milam's contextual multi-locale setting and multi-ethnic casting.

Although, as Alice Rayner remarks, 'the touch of a shared object evokes intimacy, identification, and love' (81), handkerchiefs have lost their historical significance as love tokens, no longer objects traded between lovers signalling emotion and romantic intent. What enables an 'authentic' cognitive reception of the handkerchief, however, is the historical aesthetic of the theatre space itself, but more importantly, the network of relations that simultaneously undermine its rearticulation of early modern courtly discourse, including the play's transhistorical and prescribed function of the handkerchief as a symbol of specifically female sexual transportability rather than purely a temporal signifier or textile witness of the past meant to convey 'the Renaissance'.

Portraying the Moor

> Although this play is set and written in the past, it is
> very definitely about the present.
> (Eamonn Walker)

In his essay, 'Symbols, Emblems, Tokens', Stephen Hannaford distinguishes between properties that are called into action by the playwright and those that function as 'scenic devices', and that are not necessarily used as 'manipulable agencies' (468). Hannaford also suggests that 'many "symbols" in the drama are never seen on stage' (470). I want to turn our attention now to a 'prop' that is not 'actually' seen on the Globe stage during the 2007 production of *Othello*, but which is replicated through costume. The portrait of Abd al-Wahid bin Masaoud bin Muhammed al-Annuri (the 'Moorish Ambassador') (*c*.1600), which hangs in the Shakespeare Institute in Stratford-upon-Avon, commemorates the state visit of the Ambassador from Barbary to Queen Elizabeth I's court in 1600 and has in recent years become an icon amongst early modern scholars, indexing the debates surrounding the religious and cultural origins of Othello. Jerry Brotton characterizes this debate by suggesting that 'for an Elizabethan audience, the term "Moor" evoked a whole series of complicated, and often contradictory assumptions and prejudices, which Shakespeare was clearly aiming to exploit in his decision to put *Othello* on the stage' (5). The portrait was acquired by the Institute in 1956 and presents '"ocular proof" of what the Elizabethans saw as a Moor of rank' (Harris, 1958: 89). This portrait of the distinguished ambassador, wearing a turban, robes of state and a sword with a hilt fashioned from gold, has become emblematic, for early modern scholars, of the play itself. Seen as an alternative to the African Moor, the Arab Moor in the portrait offers the possibility that Shakespeare's text was engaged in a rich dialogue with the East and more significantly with Islam, and that this engagement is substantiated by the very fact of the setting, Venice: the cultural intermediary between East and West during the Renaissance period. Critics tend to argue now that Shakespeare may have encountered the Barbary Moor at court and that this encounter might have inspired his construction of Othello. According to Bernard Harris, 'to Elizabethan Londoners the appearance and conduct of the Moors was a spectacle and an outrage, emphasizing the nature of the deep difference between themselves and their visitors, between the Queen and this "erring Barbarian"' (97).

The portrait was shown to the Globe's company of actors performing *Othello* as a way of introducing the critical discourse on the play. Eamonn Walker was emphatic that he would not play the Moor as a 'bare-chested savage', as he had seen performed so many times before. Inspired by the 1600 portrait, Walker wanted to recapture the religious and cultural heritage of his Moor, though he was not deliberately intending to raise to the surface the wars in Iraq and Afghanistan and the current tensions between Islamic and Christian ideology (personal correspondence with the author). The designer, Dick Bird, reconstructed the Ambassador's outfit, including the turban and the sword and its elaborate hilt. This historicizing practice of reconstructing clothing seen in a portrait was briefly reminiscent of the 'original practices' approach to making clothing of the period (apart from the materials and method of making), and was another element of Milam's stringent approach to reproducing the visuals of history. The reconstructed costume enabled the production to invoke the portrait, but since most audience members would have been unaware of the portrait's significance to Shakespeare studies, a copy of it was also reprinted in the programme, thus allowing the portrait to 'ghost' its memory upon the stage and act as a prop in its own right. The portrait, therefore, existed within the system of signs in the theatre as at once iconic and indexical in its function.

Walker saw his costuming throughout as symptomatic or suggestive of his character's 'journey' through the play. As Captain of the Venetian army, it was essential for him to establish continuity with the rest of the characters within that army. He was 'Venetian' until he resorted to the cultural norms, as Walker saw them, of his heritage, which was fundamentally 'moorish': 'when Othello gets desperately lost in his jealousy and madness, he desperately attempts to find himself again by jumping back to what he knows, which is Islam, the Muslim side of him'. From his understanding of early Islamic culture, Walker determined that infidelity was dealt with punitively and his Othello then opted to 'resort' to Islamic costume, to the clothing of his native world, when he was to deliver the punishment for his wife's alleged crimes. Within the costume, Walker as Othello appeared a 'walking portrait', positioning himself into a type of authentic incarnation of Shakespeare's encounter with the Ambassador: 'I imagine Shakespeare watching Abd al-Wahid bin Masoud bin Muhammad al-Annuri, the Moroccan ambassador, who visited London in 1599, in the Elizabethan court and starting to wonder what it must be like for that man.' The invocation of the Arab Moor in Walker's portrayal was unintentionally provocative for the collective imaginary of the Globe audience, which would not have necessarily been able to separate the word 'Islam' from the images of misogyny and terror that *Othello* produces. A dangerously xenophobic discourse was at play in the choice to enact the final scenes in Islamic costume. However, Walker's Moor was also deliberately evocative of the dignity that the portrait of the Moorish Ambassador conveys, thus giving it a paradoxical complexity in the way it produces meaning for a contemporary audience at the Globe. To use Rayner's term, the portrait as prop becomes a type of souvenir insofar as it represented a fragment of 'one world lost and another yet to be played out' (75). Held in suspension between the past and the present, the East and the West, the portrait as prop, like the Egyptian handkerchief, is indelibly suggestive of the more complex and transhistorical racial and sexual narratives in the play, and a 'unidirectional/retrospective' theatre space like the Globe provides a conduit through which trans-temporal signifiers can simultaneously convey and erase historical meaning in production.

7
Talking Heads

Carol Chillington Rutter

For those of us who are interested in the stage life of the (mostly silent) objects that Shakespeare writes into performance, trying to see what they have to say while his extraordinarily clamorous characters fill the plays with 'words, words, words', certain events at the end of 2008 were gratifying indeed. For a fortnight in November the Shakespeare object triumphed over the Shakespeare actor when Hamlet's occupationally mute sidekick grabbed the media spotlight and upstaged the lippy prince.

In Stratford-upon-Avon that season the RSC's theatre poster publicizing David Tennant's *Hamlet* had cast him as Caspar David Friedrich's romantic *Wanderer above the Sea of Fog*. Except that, counting on Tennant's star power to sell tickets – he was, after all, then known primarily to anyone aged under 85 in England as the man with the sonic screwdriver, television's Doctor Who – the graphics department turned the wanderer's head to show us Tennant's face. But by the time autumn rolled around and the production was preparing to transfer to London, the poster-boy reverted to a more conventional – and iconic – pose, one surely leveraging brand recognition: Hamlet with Yorick, the King-his-father's jester whom the prince knew as a child, 23 years dead, now a skull, perhaps the world's most instantly recognized, quoted and parodied Shakespeare 'still'. Coincidentally, even as the new posters were being printed, in an interview Tennant let slip that the Yorick he had been playing with all season in Stratford, the Yorick in the London poster, was in fact not a fake cast in plastic, but a real skull. When that story broke, Yorick was

A longer version of this chapter was delivered as the 2010 Ropes Lecture, University of Cincinnati. I am grateful to Jonathan Kamholz for the invitation to contribute to this prestigious series and for giving me the opportunity to start thinking about this topic.

Illustration 7.1   David Tennant as Hamlet (dir. Gregory Doran, RSC, 2008)

suddenly headline news – and Hamlet got the elbow. Everyone wanted to talk to the skull. How long had he been playing Shakespeare? 'Yorick': that was a stage name, right? Who was he before? What was his history? What did this shocking disclosure mean for other 'Yoricks'?

Alas, poor Yorick: his celebrity was short-lived. As it happened, a fortnight later both he and Hamlet were out of the show. A back injury meant that Tennant's understudy had to take over the London run, and the difficulty in securing a licence to travel from the UK's Human Tissue Authority meant that a plastic stand-in replaced the human skull – which returned quietly to its box on Shelf 3C in the RSC's Collection store.[1] It is just possible to see the media's fascination with this skull as in some distant way mimicking Yorick's first appearance in *Hamlet*. If Roland Mushat Frye is right, Yorick was the first skull to appear on the early modern stage, trailing behind him, to be sure, a long *memento mori* tradition illustrated in portraiture, tomb sculpture, embroidery, jewellery and printing, where the skull motif, done in marble or gold or ink, bids the spectator *respice finem* (206; see also Sofer 89–100). But the thing itself, put into play: Yorick appears to have premiered the part and, ventriloquized by the Prince who turns the chop-fallen skull into a talking head, to have broached the unsettling matter that has challenged us ever since, to think about our own ends: 'Now get you to my lady's chamber and tell her, let her paint an inch thick, to this favour she must come' (5.1.178–9).

But if we find it disconcerting to imagine our familiar Yorick, the skull, a novelty on Shakespeare's stage, we might find it even more disconcerting to discover that heads – human or otherwise – certainly were not. An inventory of the properties owned by the Admiral's Men at the Rose in 1598 listed (among rocks, cages, tombs, a bedstead, hellmouth and 'the sitte of Rome'), an assortment of body parts ('Kentes woden leage', 'Faetones lymes') and the following:

iiij Turckes hedes

owld Mahemetes head

---

[1] See, for example, *Daily Telegraph* 25 November, 2 December 2008 and *Daily Mail* 25 November 2008. For the story of the man who would be Yorick, see www. andretchaikowsky.com/miscellaneous/skull.htm [accessed May 2011]. And for an additional twist to the tale, see *Daily Telegraph* 25 November 2009 where the director, Gregory Doran, claims that 'the company secretly used Mr Tchaikowsky's skull all along'. Not to my knowledge. When I saw André's skull, *Hamlet* was playing London, but it was very definitely resting in the archive. André's Yorick does, however, appear in the RSC filmed *Hamlet* released in December 2009. I am grateful to David Howells, curator of the RSC Collection, for giving me free access to its materials.

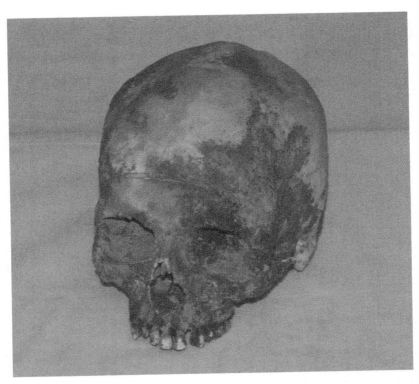

Illustration 7.2   Yorick, a.k.a. André Tchaikowsky (dir. Gregory Doran, RSC, 2008)

Argosse head

Ierosses head

j bulles head

ij lyon heades

j bores heade & Serberosse iij heads

Further on, it itemizes 'j frame for the heading in Black Jone' – a device, evidently, for an onstage decapitation (Foakes and Rickert 318–21).

None of these properties belongs to any of Shakespeare's plays, but, if one survived, the list of the heads he musters would be much longer: a minimum of six are needed in the *Henry VI* trilogy written at the beginning of the playwright's career; a 'whole heap' in *Pericles* at the end. In between, eight more plays put heads on stage – and a further five imagine them just off.

Illustration 7.3   Surplus body parts cupboard, RSC property workshop

To get some sense of what might have been itemized in that notional missing Shakespeare inventory, we can open the metal cupboard in the RSC's props workshop that is neatly marked 'severed heads; head moulds; face moulds, ear moulds' where the decapitated rest cheek by jowl, unceremoniously thrown together on standby for future casting.[2] These heads in the cupboard arrest my attention in a way that Yorick does not. Perhaps 'custom' has made Yorick 'a property of easiness' to me (as Horatio might put it). Or perhaps it is that, as Michael Bristol observes, there is an anonymity to bone. Without the Gravedigger's insider knowledge, could we even begin to identify which of the three skulls chucked out of soon-to-be-Ophelia's grave is 'the whoreson mad fellow' Yorick? The skull has 'no identifying features, no countenance that allows us to recognize individuality' (192). Yorick exited Hamlet's life 23 years back. Returning now, he operates as a bizarre mnemonic, strangely familiar (or, familiarly strange), both proxy king and surrogate

---

[2] I want to thank John Evans, Head of Property Workshop at the RSC, for all his help.

dad, a prompt to remembering Hamlet's childhood. But he's sightless, his eye sockets empty.

By contrast, Shakespeare's decapitated die with their eyes open. Their final scenario is violent death, execution, mutilation. Skulls are found objects. Heads are made. Typically, they have left the stage only minutes before as someone, a subject – call him Jack Cade or Quintus Andronicus. Returning, they re-enter as an object of almost too much 'countenance', appallingly recognizable, immediate in flesh, still warm, the 'not-quite-dead' (Aebischer 64), a 'self-thing', and what they return is the person spectacularly changed – the body, de-faced. In the immediacy of their deaths, these heads suture subject to object: they are messengers as message. They don't just remember, like other objects in Shakespeare. Indeed, their memories as objects are ludicrously short. Instead, they fix a wide-eyed, if glazed, gaze on their future history post mortem. They keep looking. Theirs is a gaze I want to meet and I am going to use this chapter to ponder the startling ubiquity of the head on Shakespeare's stage. I will consider some of the work it does there, how it 'means' in performance, its properties and its status as a theatrical property.

Directing my gaze is a question: do heads act like other props? Are they 'instructive object[s]'; 'charged signs'; 'improper properties ... embodied commentaries' (Bristol 187; Dawson and Yachnin 138; Aebischer 65)? If so, what do they instruct, signify, comment? Do they poison sight (*Othello*, 5.2.373)? Turn hearts to stone (*2 Henry VI*, 5.3.50)? Or, remedi-ally, make onlookers 'melt in showers' – like little Lucius, weeping in *Titus Andronicus* (5.3.160)? Can we usefully think about them in terms borrowed from the anthropologist, Arjun Appadurai, who writes that 'things ... , like persons, have social lives'; that, as they circulate 'in dif-ferent regimes of value in space and time' and move 'through different hands, contexts, and uses', they 'accumulat[e] ... biographies', follow 'careers' that are typically (in the theatre, *always*) fraught with evalua-tive, interpretative and processual difficulties such that their 'life jour-neys' get interrupted, blocked, diverted? Are severed heads the extreme case of Appadurai's 'diverted' 'things-in-motion', demonstrating the paradoxical register of value that makes the object both priceless – and price-less: that is, 'beyond price' and 'worthless' (3, 26)? Does this thing wrest from a completely different order of object – the luxury good – its status as 'incarnated sign' displaying 'semiotic virtuosity' (14, 38)? In my simple terms, does the head talk?

Seeing the head as a theatrical commonplace in Shakespeare, I want to pause briefly to consider first encounters and where it may have started to register as such. Long before he ever came to put any on stage, as a boy Shakespeare must have known a number of heads that impressed his imagination. In the Old Testament, there was Goliath's (with its thrilling story of David arming); in the New, John the Baptist's (a story of female revenge); in Ovid's *Metamorphoses*, a core text known to every grammar-school boy, snake-haired Medusa, whose severed head turns men to stone and who appears a couple of pages on from Pyramus and Thisbe; and, shockingly, the child Itys, the final victim in the rape story of Philomela. In the contemporary retelling of the medieval story, there is Sir Gawain who, by invitation, lops off the Green Knight's head, then watches, appalled, as the body retrieves it, *and it talks* – an episode remembered, perhaps, in Christopher Marlowe's *Dr Faustus*, where another decapitated body rises and speaks. And certainly, when Shakespeare began reading the chronicles of Edward Hall and Raphael Holinshed he met the heads of English history, traitors whose fate was to have their heads cut from their shoulders and set upon poles, a 'technology of punishment' that Michel Foucault terms 'monarchical' (23, 80), a peremptory display of 'heuristic' discipline – a discipline that Shakespeare's stage both represents and troubles.

Some of Shakespeare's earliest plays were histories, where he stuck quite closely to his sources; so to begin my survey of heads and their performances, I turn to the *Henry VI* trilogy, three plays that tell the story of England's first civil war (as Shakespeare makes it, the 'Wars of the Roses'), and to Queen Margaret, whose enterprise in decapitation offers an initial model of practice and repertoire of practices. Scorning her pacifist husband, herself taking up arms to command the Lancastrian army in a civil war that has split England, having hunted him to ground in his stronghold in the North, Margaret orders the summary execution of Richard, Duke of York. To the Lancastrians, he is a rebel traitor; to the Yorkists, he is the rightful heir to Edward III, the true King of England.

> Come make him stand upon this molehill here,
> That raught at mountains with outstretched arms
> Yet parted but the shadow with his hand.
> *(3 Henry VI*, 1.4.68–70)

'You ... would be England's king?' she grins, mocking him by setting a paper crown on his head. Eventually tiring of torture, she orders:

> Off with the crown, and, with the crown, his head ...
> [...]

Off with his head, and set it on York gates
So York may overlook the town of York.
                                      (1.4.71, 108, 180–1)

Later, escorting the king her husband into the city, where York's citizens are now humbly subject to Lancaster, she gestures, 'Yonder's the head': 'Doth not the object cheer your heart?' (2.2.2, 4).

Margaret's headhunting construes the paradigm, establishes its formalities. This trilogy obsessively puns 'crown' – diadem – with 'crown' – head – and suggests that as there is a royal monopoly on wearing the crown so there is a royal monopoly on taking crowns. The traitor who aspires to the 'golden round' will be punished not just with death but with laughter and humiliation, and made to enact a savage parody of elevation – climbing the great height of that molehill – and coronation – 'off with his head' – that, with a blackly comic sense of decorum, will be fixed to look perpetually on its crime, staring at the ambition that flattered with shadows mistaken for true substance. So, 'set it on York gates / So York may overlook the town of York'.

Elsewhere in the trilogy, in what we might take as parallel play, in Kent, a self-appointed crown deputy – his name's Iden, pronounced 'eden', and he thinks his walled garden 'a monarchy' – is dealing with another self-proclaimed king of England, one Jack Cade, supposed lost heir to the Mortimers, cradle-snatched at birth (*2 Henry VI*, 4.9.17). For Iden, though, killing Cade, the upstart leader of the rebel rout is a 'monstrous traitor' whose body he will drag 'headlong by the heels' and dump upon 'a dunghill' where he will 'cut off' Cade's 'most ungracious head' and 'bear [it] in triumph to the king' (4.9.63, 77–80). As in the case of York – York seeing York, York seen by York – recognition is important here. So are triumph and humiliation. Like York, 'monstrous' Cade decapitated is turned into a bizarre 'monstrance', from the Latin *monstrare*, 'to show'. That's what we do, making monsters: make shows, offer demonstrations.

Once again, headhunting falls within the 'jurisdiction regal' (as Cade ironically puts it; 4.7.22). And what it demonstrates ought to be persuasive, politically definitive: ought to stop emulous rebels in their tracks. But it doesn't work like that. The severed head turns out to be a Janus, not just inviting and repelling sight, but ambivalent in affect. Presented with the head of Cade, King Henry wants to see it: 'O, let me view his visage, being dead / That living wrought me such exceeding trouble'. And he wants to see it as a sign: 'Great God! How just art thou' (5.1.68–70). Pointed to York's head, however, the 'object' that Margaret thinks will 'cheer your heart', the King flinches from a 'sight' that 'irks my very soul'. He sees it as a sign of his unwitting perjury that will be punished: 'Withhold revenge, dear God!' (*3 Henry VI* 2.2.6, 7). The heuristic head – what does it instruct? For Henry, not vindication, but revulsion. And for the rebels, not submissiveness, nor conformity, but defiance. The Messenger who tells York's sons of their father's slaughter casts York as Hercules, as a one-man Troy withstanding swarming Greeks. When, in the telling, this epic narrative gives way to ugly farce, the messenger remembering the ruthless queen who 'laughed in [York's] face', and set his head 'on the gates of York' where 'it doth remain, / The saddest spectacle that e'er I viewed', we perhaps see a neutral turning into a partisan, new-made a terrorist recruited to the rebel cause (2.1.50–5, 60, 65, 66–7). Subversively, then, the head has the potential to turn the gaze, to make spectators look different. Authority cannot control its interpretation. In itself, authority doesn't know what to make of it. Moreover, as a sign, the ambivalent and portable head turns out to be two-faced in other ways. It is movable. So signification doesn't stay put. We see this when, arriving in York, the dead duke's sons bring down their father's head, restoring him as 'princely', 'noble', 'sweet'. Now he is 'The flower of Europe for his chivalry' (2.1.71), while it is Lancastrian Clifford, the man who beheaded him, the man they have just captured, who is the traitor. So 'Off with the traitor's head' and let it 'supply the room' on 'the gates of York' (2.6.85, 52–4). Handy-dandy, these wind-changing heads seem to say to civic spectators, which is the traitor, which the loyalist? Whose side are we on?

Officially, execution makes legible the state's absolute power. The monarch repudiates the traitor's attempt upon the head of state, upon the head of the body politic, by enacting on the traitor's actual body a symbolic inversion of the thwarted crime. In this ritualized parody, not the state, but the traitor, loses his head. In the *Henry VI*s, however, we discover that this power to represent power is not a royal monopoly, is not in control of the state; instead, can be improvised and anarchic, arbitrary and subversive. The first head to fall in the trilogy is an aristocrat's, the Duke of Suffolk's. But it doesn't fall to the state. It is struck off in an impromptu execution, crudely, 'on our longboat's side' by outlaws, pirates who, indicting Suffolk of crimes against the commonwealth (including waging costly wars that have impoverished the commons and cuckolding the King), enact their own parody, their own inversion. Suffolk's 'lips', they say, 'that kissed the Queen shall sweep the ground' (*2 Henry VI* 4.1.69, 75). The head 'that smiledst at good Duke Humphrey's death / Against the senseless winds shall grin in vain' (76–7). They dump the head with the mock that it shall lie there 'Until the Queen his mistress bury it' (145) – a mock that is gruesomely reiterated a couple of scenes later when Margaret wanders in to interrupt the King's council, talking to herself about 'grief' that 'softens the mind', discovering to their appalled eyes that what she is nursing on her 'throbbing breast' is Suffolk's head – even as they are discussing intelligence brought from the rebels who have vowed to take *their* heads (4.4.1, 5).

The killing of Suffolk changes politics. It teaches us that civil war in Henry's England is not just restricted business, royal house pitted against royal house, fought on a horizontal axis. It is also a contention between aristocracy and commons, the head and toe of the body politic, where the legitimacy the commons are defending is not pedantic and legalistic, an argument about precedent claims and inheritance – who should be king – but basic, about the legitimacy of their grievances. Beheading Suffolk, those plebeian insurrectionists usurp the notional royal monopoly, show how fragile is the hierarchical chain of being that keeps them in their place; show how easy it is to requisition the property of the elite and to appropriate its signifying systems. When Jack Cade comes up from Kent with his fake lineage and ragged-arsed, would-be class warriors, appropriation morphs into grotesque parody, the anarchist paradoxically as 'wannabe' king. Declaring that the 'laws of England' shall 'come out of [my] mouth'; that the 'proudest peer in the realm shall not wear a head on his shoulders, unless he pay me tribute' nor 'a maid be married, but she shall pay me her maidenhead ere they have it'; and that 'men shall hold of me *in capite*' (*2 Henry VI* 4.7.5, 110–15), Cade isn't rejecting the system. He is adopting it turned upside down, constructing its carnival inversion by imagining himself king – of misrule. And the sign of his authority is that he can execute traitors: men condemned as having 'most traitorously corrupted the youth of the realm in erecting a grammar school'; or 'caused printing to be used'; or who 'usually talk of a noun and a verb' (4.7.27–33). Beginning with Lord Say, Cade mimics the 'jurisdiction regal': 'Go ... and strike off his head presently; and then break into his son-in-law's house ... and strike off his head, and bring them on two poles hither'; 'with these borne before us instead of maces will we ride through the streets, and at every corner have them kiss' (4.7.99–103, 142–4). Taking heads for signs of magistracy, Cade constructs an anti-court, obsequiously loyal, full of nodding yes-men to his every insane reformation. This exhibition perhaps returns us to Margaret, shrilling for York's head. In the trilogy, as the story is told – one damn thing after another – we see Cade and his rabblement first. That is, his goon-show rebellion in *2 Henry VI* is the

Illustration 7.4 Jack Cade (Oliver Cotton) and his rebels in *The Plantagenets* (dir. Adrian Noble, RSC, 1988)

farcical curtain-raiser to the serious business of usurpation by York in *3 Henry VI* to come. But if Cade's inversion of crown execution anticipates Margaret's legitimate procedures in 'capital' punishment, does the memory of his 'illicit' trouble her 'licit'? Will we remember these jigging heads, summarily executed, when Margaret, perhaps remembering summarily executed Suffolk, summarily executes York? Will we see Margaret, usurping masculinity and her husband's part, as a kind of Cade, and England's body politic, post-Cade, as no-bodied?

Insistently punning 'crown' and 'crown', the *Henry VI* trilogy equally tropes 'head' and 'heart', the heart (in early modern understanding) being the birthplace of thought, the head giving expression to that thought. Treason, then, picks up on this emotive imagery of the body. Costing heads, it turns out to be a crime of the heart, expressed as an inexplicable betrayal of love of the monarch: a constellation of ideas we see worked out most poignantly in Shakespeare when the English traitors are discovered in *Henry V*.[3]

In *Titus Andronicus*, Shakespeare's earliest tragedy, written side-by-side with the *Henry VIs*, the recurrent trope that animates politics in fifth-century Rome connects 'head' and 'hand' – logically, because *Titus Andronicus* is Shakespeare's study of 'rhetorical man', and in Roman rhetoric (which Elizabethan schoolboys like William Shakespeare learned by rote, imitated and performed in the grammar school, so-called because what they learned there was Latin grammar), the hand is oratory's physical extension. The hand enacts eloquence. Talking heads need hands, are somehow dumb without them, for rhetoric, George Hunter reminds us, being 'a science (or art or *techne*) of persuasion, an art, that is of public activity', it 'is a science of *doing* rather than knowing' (103). So the hand acts what the head articulates. Gesture completes thought. Handlessness and headlessness: in Rome, one disability implies the other. In *Titus Andronicus* Shakespeare stages both.

Of course, what the play most notoriously speculates upon is the 'exemplary' or 'instructive' rape and mutilation of Titus' daughter Lavinia in the second act of the play. Her tongue is cut out, like Philomela's in Ovid's *Metamorphoses*. But that is not all. Her body is translated by abuse into a kind of academic joke. In Shakespeare, her rapists, clearly lads who have been to the grammar, who know their Ovid, know how the crime was exposed in Ovid by Philomela weaving her story into a cloth.

---

[3] I am grateful to my colleague, Paul Raffield, for sharing these ideas with me, which he elaborates in Raffield, 2010.

So they better their instruction. They cut off Lavinia's hands. Tongueless (symbolically, therefore headless) and handless, Lavinia persists in *Titus Andronicus* for the next three acts as a significant interrogation of 'rhetorical man', a (wrecked, even monstrous) physical allusion to its ideals, where 'allude', we recall, from the Latin *al-ludere*, means 'to play with, joke or jest at'. As we will see, this play traffics in black jokes. Savage laughter is produced by sleights of hand and tongue: 'hue' – colour – puns with 'hew', 'arms' with 'arms' and 'tears' with 'tears', while 'hand', the rhetor's instrument, morphs into stymied rhetorical practice when the orator is unable to 'handle' speech. That story of Lavinia's symbolic beheading, however, is one I want to fit into a bigger, overarching story in *Titus Andronicus*, a story of failed 're-heading'.

The play opens in a Rome that is headless. The emperor is dead. His two sons are competing for the election – electioneering set, as it happens, on the 'Capitol'. But Rome's senators choose neither, electing instead Titus Andronicus, war hero, returning home today, victorious after ten years campaigning against the barbarous Goths, bringing rich booty and royal prisoners – Tamora, queen of the Goths, and three of her sons; bringing home, too, corpses, the most recent of the 21 of 25 Andronici sons slain defending Rome in battle. Titus is appealed to, to stand 'candidatus' to 'set a head on headless Rome'. But he declines. He is too old, he says, addled: 'A better head her glorious body fits / Than his that shakes for age and feebleness' (1.1.187–8). He makes a catastrophic mistake. He appoints Saturninus – there's a clue in the name that Titus somehow misses – emperor. The rest of the play plays out the consequences of his refusal to head Rome.

So far, the play has been working in metaphors, but on Shakespeare's stage, metaphors habitually move from text to performance: the figurative gets enacted. Bodies do operate here as texts legible to interpretation: like Lavinia after the rape, metaphorically a 'map of woe' from whose 'martyred signs' and 'dumb action', says Titus, he will 'wrest an alphabet' to 'know [her] meaning' (3.2.12, 36, 40, 44, 45). But bodies don't remain in the space of the discursive. When Titus' four surviving sons demand the 'proudest prisoner of the Goths' for human sacrifice, to 'hew his limbs' and with his 'entrails feed the sacrificing fire', to 'appease' the 'groaning shadows' of their dead brothers who, 'unburied yet', need the blood-ritual to buy their passage across 'the dreadful shore of Styx', Titus agrees (1.1.96, 97, 144, 126, 88). He awards them the Goth's 'proudest prisoner', Tamora's eldest son. The mother kneels and weeps – and warns: 'Andronicus, stain not thy tomb with blood. / Wilt thou draw near the nature of the gods? / Draw near them then in being merciful' (116–19). But Titus refuses. His Roman sons 'Religiously ... ask a sacrifice. / To this your son is marked, and die he must' (124–5). 'O cruel, irreligious piety,' answers Tamora (130). This exchange articulates the core oxymoron – 'irreligious piety' – that structures 'civilized' Rome's 'barbaric', nay, 'gothic' rituals. And it proposes the reactionary logic, *quid pro quo* – son for son – that organizes Rome's civic narratives. Doing so, it lays out the coordinates that will map Titus' woe.

The human sacrifice of Tamora's sons happens in the play's opening scene. The middle of the play replays human sacrifice. By now, huge reversals have happened. Tamora is Saturninus' wife and Empress of Rome, and two of only three remaining Andronici sons are on their way to execution, on faked murder charges. As their cortège passes, Titus kneels, bowing his head to the earth. He prostrates himself, a headless Roman, using the dust for paper – to 'write [his] heart's ... languor' – and his tears – 'orators' – for ink (3.1.13, 26). His lamentations are interrupted – by Marcus, his brother, carrying in his arms 'consuming sorrow'. 'Will it consume me?' Titus demands. 'Let me see it then' – so Marcus hands over ravished, ruined Lavinia, as dead, a human sacrifice: 'This was thy daughter.' But Titus corrects him, turning the verb: 'Why Marcus, so she is.' And when Lavinia's brother Lucius reels from the sight – 'this object kills me' – Titus rails at him, 'Faint-hearted boy ... look upon her' (61–6). Just then, Aaron the Moor, master craftsman of the new brutalism as installation art, enters with an offer. If Titus will send the emperor his hand, that human sacrifice will ransom his sons' heads. Farce ensues, a family squabble, Marcus and Lucius arguing that *their* hands – that have done so much less for Rome – should go; Titus seeming to comply, then, when they're offstage, getting Aaron to 'dispatch ...', his hand chopped off (a gruesomely literal moment that we read also as symbolic) in front of spectators' eyes. When Aaron exits, Titus kneels, 'bow[ing] this feeble ruin to the earth' even as, even yet 'rhetorical man', he keeps talking, 'lift[ing] this one [remaining] hand up to heaven' (205–6). The picture of ruin darkens as Lavinia joins him, amputation reducing her to the limited lexicon of tears. And it is as Titus is making them over metamorphically into a single, traumatically rhetorical body – his 'bowels' swallowing her 'woes', his 'stomach', only 'ease[d]' with 'bitter tongue ...', 'like a drunkard' 'vomit[ing]' her pain (229–32) – that a messenger from Saturninus enters with, as the First Folio stage direction has it, '*two heads and a hand*'. And a speech:

> Worthy Andronicus, ill art thou repaid
> For that good hand thou sent'st the emperor.

Illustration 7.5 Sequence from *Titus Andronicus* (dir. Julie Taymor, Blue Sky Productions, 1999)

Here are the heads of thy two noble sons,
And here's thy hand in scorn to thee sent back –
Thy grief their sports, thy resolution mocked,
That woe is me to think upon thy woes
More than remembrance of my father's death.
                                                                (3.1.233–9)

The dysmorphic body emblem presented here is as telling as it shocking. Amputated hand weirdly grafts onto decapitated heads in a joke
allusion figuring a new rhetorical 'techne' in a Rome now headed by the
barbarians who are writing the parts for Rome's bodies. The eloquence of
these heads is dumbing. The appalled reckoning inscribed in this 'speaking picture' turns Titus and his family 'even like a stony image' (257).
What reaction? Marcus the (suddenly lapsed) Stoic wants his brother 'to
storm' (262). But what does Titus do? He laughs. In Shakespeare's script:
'Ha, ha, ha!' (263). It is as though he gets the joke: 'these two heads do
seem to speak to me' (270) – and what they speak is 'Revenge'.

On the back of Titus' laughter comes the play's final human sacrifice.
Getting his hands on Tamora's boys, the rapists who made his daughter
handless (and who think that he's lost his head, that he's mad), he binds
their hands, gags their tongues, rendering them doubly mute, then
informs them how he 'mean[s] to martyr you': 'cut your throats', drain
your blood', then 'grind your bones to dust, / And with your blood and it
I'll make a paste, / And of the paste a coffin I will rear, / And make two
pasties of your shameful heads' (5.2.185–8) and feed this feast to their
mother. In Yukio Ninagawa's 2006 RSC production, in the sensational
denouement when Titus (dressed, bizarrely, as the First Folio requires,
'*like a cook*'), commanded to produce Chiron and Demetrius, gestured,
'Why, there they are, both baked in this pie' (5.3.59), he shoved his
hostess trolley at the mother whose dinner was suddenly sticking in her
throat. It smacked against the table. The pastry fell apart. And Tamora
was staring at what stared at her, the cooked heads of her two boys.
It was a sequence straight out of Ovid, where the rapist and unwitting cannibal, having just consumed his son, calls for the child, and
Philomela, his tongueless victim, 'her scattred hair aflaight', enters like
some Gorgon to answer by 'throwing the bloody head / Of Itys in his
fathers face' (Book VI, 833–4). Head, the one Titus refused to 'set a head
on headless Rome', somehow answers head in this play, like a figure in
rhetoric, like human anaphora.

But although the bloody banquet ends with three deaths in as many
seconds, with bits of body from the half-consumed pie spewed across

the table, the play itself, astonishingly, ends by attempting to reverse dismemberment, trying to put Rome back together, to 'knit again' a city imaged as 'scattered corn' into 'one mutual sheaf', its 'broken limbs again into one body' (5.3.69–71). Rome elects a new head by 'common voice', taking Lucius Andronicus in 'hand' (139, 137). Meanwhile, Aaron – the 'execrable wretch' and 'breeder of these dire events' – is sentenced (176–7). He is to be 'Set ... breast-deep in earth and famish[ed]' (178). That is, buried up to the neck, but vowing that his 'wrath' won't be 'mute' or his 'fury', 'dumb', he will be turned (sensationally anticipating Beckett) into a talking head.

Watching Titus watching *Titus Andronicus* I get a sense of what it must be like for Macbeth to watch *Macbeth*. The Roman, his eyes stunned by the latest atrocity, asks: 'When will this fearful slumber have an end?' (3.1.251). That is a line that might be taken as an epigram for *Macbeth*, where a sleeping man is murdered by a man who imagines he has murdered sleep, who thereafter sleeps no more but dwells in a nightmare world where 'terrible dreams' are his 'nightly' 'affliction', and where his wife walks in her sleep (*Macbeth*, 3.2.20–1). Every way he turns, Macbeth faces spectacles that appal. Not the 'strange images of death' that he himself makes on the battlefield where, in defence of his king he can 'bathe in reeking wounds', 'unseam[]' the traitor Macdonwald 'from the nave to the chops' and 'fix[] his head upon [Duncan's] battlements' (1.3.95, 1.2.39, 22–3). Those images aren't unsettling. They are the stuff of Macbeth's daily working life. They are the stuff he makes. What appals are images that weirdly materialize as objects embodying his unconscious: a dagger; a ghost. Are they real or imaginary? What appals are images that suddenly start up across his field of vision, like those three 'fantastical' creatures, those 'imperfect speakers' who suddenly appear on the 'blasted heath', stopping his way with 'prophetic greeting', with 'strange intelligence' (1.3.51, 68, 75–6): are they bodies or bubbles? But what appals most of all are the images that *unmake* Macbeth, arriving uncalled for, unsummoned in his head: 'horrible imaginings', 'fantastical' 'thought', 'murder' (1.3.137–8).

Like *Titus Andronicus*, *Macbeth* is framed by severed heads. At the beginning, there is the traitor's, Macdonwald's; at the end, the tyrant's, the 'butcher', Macbeth's. Macduff holds aloft 'the usurper's cursed head' which he himself has taken, to declare 'the time is free' and to restore the crown – the 'kingdom's pearl' – to the right head (5.11.21–2). These severed heads, then, are meant to work like the decapitations in *Henry VI*: trophies, instructive objects, heuristic parodies replaying thwarted ambition, mockeries provoking laughter. It is precisely this scenario that plays out at the end of Roman Polanski's *Macbeth* (1971) where the filmmaker, shooting the scene *through the eyes of the severed head* as it is jostled through the jeering crowd (seeing but not hearing the mockery twisting the faces that thrust themselves at it), captures one historically accurate detail of the early modern executioner's craft. The point of holding the severed head aloft was not primarily so that we could see it, *but so that it could see us.* The master craftsman in decapitation could get the head off and up before the brain stopped thinking, before the eyes stopped seeing. Ultimately, though, whatever official paradigm of capital punishment as public discourse it is meant to instruct, the head in this film works, I think, like York's earlier, subversively, to turn the gaze. As Polanski frames the scene, Macbeth's eyes see *us*, witness *us*, interrogate *us*, caught in an act of butchery, butchering the butcher. Is the effect to make Macbeth the victim of sanctioned violence – no longer the 'Hell-hound' or 'Hell-kite' but the 'bear' 'tied ... to a stake' baited by dogs (5.10.3, 4.3.218, 5.7.1–2)? If butchery perpetually answers butchery, making us the butchers, when will the revenge cycle we saw in *Titus Andronicus* be broken, 'When [indeed] will this fearful slumber [ever] have an end?'

Polanski's film forces that speculation – even overdetermines how we see the end of *Macbeth*. But I want to offer a different observation, that Shakespeare's astonishing theatrical achievement in *Macbeth* (and the extraordinary advance he makes on *Titus Andronicus*) is not that the play *takes* heads; rather, that it *makes* one, and makes it from the inside out. This play enters Macbeth's mind, bores through his cranium, occupies the interior and anatomizes the brain, sometimes imagining that organ as the seat of 'dull' forgetfulness; sometimes as 'heat-oppressed', 'diseased', 'full of scorpions'; sometimes as pulped, a baby's brains dashed against a stone (1.4.148, 2.1.39, 3.2.37). Probing inwardness, it uses Macbeth to meditate on the epistemological conundrum that structures all relationships in this play. How do we know what's on anybody's mind? How can we examine heads, read faces to know thoughts? How do we trust? Is there an 'art / To find the mind's construction in the face' (1.4.11–12)? And further, how do we save the mind from infection? How can we 'minister to a mind diseased'? Is there some 'sweet oblivious antidote' that will cleanse memory, 'Raze out the written troubles of the brain' (5.3.42–7)? Probing inwardness, this play studies Macbeth as a headcase.

We watch him thinking: 'Two truths are told ... This supernatural soliciting / Cannot be ill, cannot be good. If ill ... / If good ...' (1.3.126–33); 'If it were done when 'tis done then 'twere well / It were done quickly'

120

Illustration 7.6 Sequence from *Macbeth* (dir. Roman Polanski, Columbia Pictures/ Playboy Productions, 1971), with Jon Finch as Macbeth

(1.7.1–2); 'Is this a dagger, which I see before me?' (2.1.33); 'How is't with me when every noise appals me?' (2.2.56); 'If't be so, / For Banquo's issue have I fil'd my mind, ... / Put rancours in the vessel of my peace / ... and mine eternal jewel / Given to the common enemy of man' (3.1.65–70).

How very different is the quality of this thinking than, say, Hamlet's. If Shakespeare's soliloquies are machines for knowing the mind, Hamlet's soliloquies give us a mind working over the materials of memory ('But two months dead ...'); a mind processing stories ('What's Hecuba to him?'); a mind dealing with what has happened ('I, the son of a dear father murdered') (*Hamlet*, 1.2.138, 2.2.536, 561). These are soliloquies that work in performance as dialogue: he is always talking to us ('To be, or not to be – that is the question'; 'Who calls me villain?'; 'Who would fardels bear?'; 3.1.58, 2.2.549, 3.1.78).

By contrast, Macbeth never talks to us. He is always inside his own head – his soliloquies fantasizing a head with a crown on it; his soliloquies conducted as explorations of the hypothetical, a future conditional that seeks to know, to deal with what hasn't happened. Hamlet, thinking abstractly, is a materialist. Macbeth, thinking materially, is a surrealist. I know no better description than Antony Sher's of this mind as a headcase. Sher played Macbeth at the RSC in 1999 (back-to-back with Leontes in *The Winter's Tale*) – and he happens also to be an artist of impressive talent. Macbeth, he writes: 'stays alarmingly sane'.

> He never enjoys the wild, almost liberating oblivion that Leontes knows. Instead, Macbeth just keeps watching himself, increasingly appalled by what he sees. He's locked in a wrestling match within his own body; the limbs, the muscles of a man of action grapple constantly with the head, the great visionary brain, that gorgeous damaged imagination. A very different thing from what nests in Leontes' skull. I see Leontes' imagination as something painted by Bosch; it teems with horrid little sticky pink nudes. Macbeth's imagination is by Dali: elegant, epic pictures of lonely figures in empty landscapes – a newborn baby carried on the wind, one bloody hand turning the sea red, a queue of pointless tomorrows shuffling toward oblivion.
>
> (345)

Or indeed, a 'great visionary brain', a 'gorgeous damaged imagination' stranded on a bleak, storm-blasted, blood-scoured heath.

Like Titus facing those heads that 'seem to speak to me', Macbeth will encounter talking heads. When he visits the Weird Sisters seeking

answers to his future, they will offer him apparitions, constructed, mon-
strously, out of harvested body parts: 'eye of newt', 'toe of frog', 'nose
of Turk', 'Finger of birth-strangled babe' (*Macbeth*, 4.1.14–30). These
apparitions will rise out of the cauldron and speak – an armed head, a
bloody child, a child crowned – and appallingly, he won't even have to
question them, for they will 'know[] [his] thought' (85). They will be
'instructive objects': advising '"Fear not til Birnam Wood / Do come to
Dunsinane"'; 'none of woman born / shall harm Macbeth' (5.7.42–3,
4.1.96–7). But their true horror will not be their status as objects, what
they look like, whether or not Macbeth recognizes them, reads them
as signs. Rather, it will be how they enter his head, mess with his
mind, not so much optical illusions as psychiatric prostheses installing
'answer[s]' that will work to satisfy his need to 'know / All mortal consequence' (5.3.4–5) – and to make him invulnerable to such consequence.
But these 'truths ... told' that promise to 'keep ... promise' will turn out
to be double-speak, two-faced 'juggling', equivocations 'that palter with
us in a double sense', that lie 'like truth' (1.3.126, 5.10.19–21, 5.5.42).
These talking heads reframe the conundrum that has obsessed Macbeth:
how do we know what we know? They prompt in him the most human
of activities: trying to make sense of things. He can't help it. It's the
way the mind works. But as his mind gropes distractedly, clutching at
metaphor, imagining things by imagining other things that can only
be imagined by, paradoxically, unknowing them, another mind in the
play is literalizing this mental activity. How do we know what we know?
Walking, talking in that restless ecstasy that travesties sleep and that
breaks apart 'little hand' from 'hurt mind', Lady Macbeth becomes this
play's most terrible talking head. In the sleepwalking scene, we watch
the detached body performing the damaged mind.

Lady Macbeth standing in for Macbeth offers a segue to *Measure for
Measure*, a play that thematizes the stand-in, that makes standing in its
core theatrical activity, and that tropes decapitation as problematically
as *Macbeth* does.

In *Measure for Measure*, the truant Duke, Vienna's head, who has
failed to enforce the law for 18 years – the entire lifetimes of the youth
of his city – leaves town; leaves as a stand-in, a deputy, one Angelo,
a 'man of stricture and firm abstinence', a man so 'precise' that he
'scarce confesses / That his blood flows; or that his appetite / Is more
to bread than stone' (1.3.12, 50–3). That is the kind of substitute who
can clean up a Vienna that is not just morally corrupt, its stews boiling
with disease, but anarchic, a Vienna where 'Liberty plucks Justice by the
nose' (1.3.29). Angelo works fast. He targets offences: sex crime. Pulling

one 'biting' statute off the shelf, Angelo has a youth, Claudio, arrested for fornication. Although Claudio argues a technicality in marriage-contract law, to Angelo, it is clear that Claudio is guilty; his betrothed is visibly pregnant. Fornication is a capital offence. Claudio will be executed tomorrow – his head chopped off. Desperate for an appeal, Claudio elects a deputy, his sister, Isabella, who, that day, is entering the convent, imploring her to 'make friends / To the strict deputy'; to 'assay him'. 'For in her youth', says Claudio of Isabella, 'There is a prone and speechless dialect / Such as move men'; 'beside', 'she hath prosperous art / When she will play with reason and discourse, / And well she can persuade' (1.2.159–63) When Isabella confronts Angelo he's immune to her 'prone and speechless dialect'; it's her 'reason and discourse' arguing for her brother's life with passion, but also the rhetorical skills of an expert advocate that surprise the deputy with desire, rouse his blood with hot flushes: 'She speaks,' he says, 'and 'tis such sense that my sense breeds with it' (2.2.144–5). Going head to head with Isabella, Angelo finds he's committing a sex act. Obdurate, first, that Claudio is a 'forfeit to the law', that there is no way out, no 'remedy', he admits one: an elegant (or monstrous) *quid pro quo*, a ransom head for head. You can 'Redeem thy brother', he tells her, 'By yielding up thy body to my will' (2.2.73, 49, 2.4.163–4). You can buy his head with your maidenhead.

Measure for Measure is a comedy. It is going to find a way through the brick wall it hits in 2.4. It will produce a bed trick: a substitute to deputize for Isabella in Angelo's bed. But it will also produce a head trick, because the bed trick won't work. That is, although Angelo will believe that Isabella has kept the bargain, bought her brother's life with her virginity, his body with her soul, he will renege, conclude that Claudio must be executed and further, demand 'for [his] better satisfaction' that the youth's head be sent to him for inspection (4.2.113). What follows is gruesome slapstick. Angelo's command must be followed. The Provost must deliver a head. But the Duke, disguised as the Friar and staggered by Angelo's perfidy, really believing he would pardon Claudio once Isabella paid his price, cannot let the execution proceed. So what are they going to do for a head? Find a stand-in. A deputy. Substitute one condemned man with another who is meant to die. 'Call your executioner,' orders the Friar-Duke, 'and off with Barnadine's head' (4.2.188–9). Except that, summoned, Barnardine refuses to co-operate. So what are they going to do *now* for a head? Find another stand-in – Raggozine, who has helpfully accommodated the plot by dying that morning.

Measure for Measure makes a joke of execution – and the power of the state to regulate human appetite. Treason may deserve beheading.

But 'a game of tick-tack'? A man lose his head for 'the rebellion of a codpiece', for 'filling a bottle with a tun-dish', for 'putt[ing] a ducat in [a] clack-dish' (1.2.167, 3.1.358, 405, 369)? *Measure for Measure* stages a trial – that collapses when the accused, asked if prostitution is a lawful trade, makes a nonsense of the law by replying, 'If the law would allow it' (2.1.202). *Measure for Measure* goes inside Vienna's prison – and makes a nonsense of that system, too, by bringing on the common executioner, one Abhorson, who is going to do the job on Claudio in the morning. An assistant is needed. Plucked from the cells is one Pompey Bum, officially a tapster, actually, a bawd, his business, the flesh trade. 'A bawd?' roars Abhorson. 'He will discredit our mystery' (4.2.22). But there they stand, this regime's deputies, hangman and bawd, court officials. One man's commodity is heads, the other's, maidenheads.

What interests me is the way *Measure for Measure* brings those gendered heads into a terrible parallel predicament; the way it rhymes 'head' with 'bed'; sexualizes crime and punishment; but also theologizes both (not least, theatrically, by placing in the spectator's visual field one character dressed as a friar, another, a probationary nun). We first heard jokes punning heads and maidenheads in Cade's mouth in *2 Henry VI*. Sampson and Gregory, old Capulet's swaggering servants, conduct the same banter at the opening of *Romeo and Juliet*: 'I will cut off their heads'; 'The heads of the maids?'; 'Ay ... or their maidenheads' (1.1.19–21). Virginity is a joke commodity – as Parolles sententiously theorizes (or riddles) in *All's Well That Ends Well* where he advises that 'It is not politic in the commonwealth of nature to preserve virginity'; that 'Loss of virginity is rational increase' because 'there was never virgin got till virginity was first lost' (1.1.119–22). In *Measure for Measure*, however, for Isabella, the head/head exchange isn't a quibble; it is sacrilege. The pattern of redemption is Christ, ransoming mankind by giving his body for our souls. What Angelo requires of Isabella is a monstrous inversion, her eternal soul for a brother's oh-so-desperately-mortal body.

The last scene of this play plays out like a rewrite of the gospels, Salome performing before Herod and demanding the head of John the Baptist on a plate. The Duke has returned to Vienna. By a series of spectacular unmaskings (some, literally unhoodings that discover heads), Angelo's crimes are revealed. The Duke sends Angelo to be officially married to the woman who, technically his wife, deputized for Isabella in bed; then, immediately, to execution, condemning him to 'Measure ... for Measure', 'An Angelo for Claudio; death for death', 'to the very block / Where Claudio stoop'd to death – and with like haste. / Away with him' (5.1. 401–7). Away with him? Angelo for Claudio? Is the Duke so out of his mind with rage at Angelo's barefaced lying and hypocrisy, at his corrupting of authority and sleazy sexual blackmail that he has forgotten one crucial fact? Claudio is not dead. The Duke, sending Angelo to the block, is executing him for a crime he has not committed – which exactly reproduces Claudio's case (condemned for a crime he says is no crime at all) and puts the Duke (an ironic deputizing) in Angelo's shoes. If the sentence is carried out, the Duke, like Angelo, will have killed a guiltless man.

What happens next is a miracle. The woman who gave her head – her maidenhead – to save Angelo from the crime (or is it the sin?) of fornication kneels in the street and pleads for his head. Not once or twice but five times she interrupts the Duke, who says his decree is 'definitive': 'Never crave him'; 'You do but lose your labour. / Away with him to death' (419–21). Mariana argues, doggedly, 'labour' against 'sense' (420, 425), for Angelo's life – and implores Isabella to kneel with her. Once again, Isabella is faced with the choice: head for head? She could demand 'Measure for Measure', Angelo's head on a platter. But she does not. She honours Mariana's ransom, a body given to redeem a soul, and asks that 'this man condemn'd' be looked on 'As if my brother liv'd' (436–7). Is that the line that jolts the Duke back to his senses, produces the flurry of activity around the Provost and the sudden line-up of bodies fetched from the prison – one of whom, unhooded, re-headed, turns out to be a 'prisoner ... / Who should have died when Claudio lost his head' (481–2): Claudio himself, alive, giving life ('a quickening in his eye', 489), miraculously, to saved Angelo, redeemed not just by his wife but by the evidence before his eyes that he is not guilty of Isabella's head *or her brother's*?

But of course, neither Angelo's nor Claudio's is the last head to consider in *Measure for Measure*. It is Isabella's, troped in a marriage proposal that asks her 'ear' to 'incline' to a 'motion' that will, says the Duke, persuade her to 'Give me your hand and say you will be mine' (529, 486). The Duke wants her maidenhead – wants it, like Salome, on a platter. What should Isabella do? Return to the convent? Take the veil, consecrate head and (maiden)head to barren – but holy – privation? Or enter the mess and muddle of the world – where the good and the bad are cut from the same cloth, where only a 'pair of shears' goes between them (1.2.26)? In a profound way, if comedy as Shakespeare writes it is going to work towards its conclusion – 'Lovers, to bed' (*A Midsummer Night's Dream* 5.1.347) – women are going to have to lose their heads.

And that is an observation that alludes to the heads I have not talked about here – the heads men lose in comedy as love turns them into 'civil monster[s]' (*Othello* 4.1.61) that trope their erotic destinies: Falstaff, stewing in the grease of his own lust, tricked into appearing as mythical Herne-the-Hunter, wearing stag's horns that metamorphose him into a cuckold; Benedick, love's most 'obstinate heretic', capitulating, setting his head in the marriage yoke, and 'the bull's horns' on his 'forehead' (*Much Ado About Nothing* 1.1.191, 216); bully Bottom, translated into the ass that every other man is making of himself in that woods near Athens (and into the arms of the Fairy Queen). If, in the 'commonwealth' of Shakespeare's comedy, it is 'not politic … to preserve virginity', the truth of the matter is that love, in Shakespeare, costs everybody their heads.

Illustration 7.7 Snug's lion's head from *A Midsummer Night's Dream* (dir. Peter Brook, RSC, 1970)

That observation brings me to a final image, and returns me to the material theatre where I began. This head is Snug's. It appeared in Peter Brook's *A Midsummer Night's Dream* (RSC, 1970). The logic of this production, which honoured the 'rude mechanicals', those 'Hard-handed men' who are disparaged by Puck and Philostrate alike as plebs who 'work for bread upon Athenian stalls', who 'never laboured in their minds till now' (3.2.9–10; 5.1.72–3), meant that when Peter Quince sent Snug home to learn the Lion's part, Snug went to work not on words or even sound effects – the roaring he is assigned instead of a script – but on wood. For Snug is a joiner. He is a cabinetmaker. So *of course* the Lion's head is made from the materials of his craft, planed and pinned and returned and bevelled, and inlaid, and offering doors that open so that the roaring can roll forth and a human head can be seen – and so that the ladies of the court can be prevented from making a terrible mistake of identity that would have heads roll if Theseus decided to 'hang us all' (1.2.63). Snug's Lion's head reminds us that the heads on the early modern stage – the 'ij lyon heades', 'owld Mahemetes head' of Henslowe's inventory, York's head, Cloten's and Bottom's – like the heads on Shakespeare's stage today, were made things: of wood and leather, of rubber and silicone. It bids us to remember the craft of the theatre that makes things from the poet's makings, *making* Shakespeare.

8
Costume

Bridget Escolme

> I have a hunch that the politics of [*Julius Caesar*]
> emerge more, rather than less, clearly when it is played
> in authentic Roman costume. With period dress you
> also get a sense of historical perspective; for as Martin
> Wiggins points out in his excellent new Penguin
> introduction, the conspirators are 'not just republican
> liberators opposing an incipient monarchy, they are
> also young conservatives hostile to social and politi-
> cal change'. How often does that come across in a
> modern-dress production?
>
> (Michael Billington, *Guardian* 21 April 2005)

Having seen the production of Deborah Warner's *Julius Caesar* to which
Michael Billington refers here, I have some sympathy with the notion
that 'modern dress' in Shakespeare production does not necessarily
clarify for a current audience the political, or indeed the emotional, stakes
and relationships encoded within a 400-year-old play. Warner's was an
excitingly staged, powerfully acted and very well-received production
of *Julius Caesar*, in which around one hundred supernumeraries, taken
partly from each of the local communities in which the production
played (London, Paris, Madrid, Luxembourg), performed as the plebeian crowd. A scene of postmodern political and aesthetic fragmentation
was created from truncated classical columns, surrounded by police
incident tape and backed by perspex gates and a bright yellow backdrop.
Politicians in suits 'pricked down' those who were to die on their laptops.
The Iraq War was clearly referenced via desert fatigues in the second half
of the production and through photographs in the British programme.
In the second half, Cassius (Simon Russell Beale) wore suit trousers

128

and a cardigan to confront Brutus (Anton Lesser) in his camouflage gear. It was as if, despite the pair's spat over who was the better soldier (4.3), Russell Beale's Cassius was not a solider at all but a modern politician who sent men to war but played no risky physical part in it himself. I have argued elsewhere (2007: 173) that the highly individualized costumes of the plebeians produced the sense of a spoiled, fickle bunch of postmodern consumers rather than the highly motivated, sometimes violent but sometimes intelligent and discursive mob of the play. It seemed that at points in this production, costume decisions emerged from a desire that the play should speak modern politics. Warner states in an interview that '[i]n a time of crisis, we go to the strong texts – well, I certainly do. This is not a time for television-style documentaries about politics. We need insights, important truths about the human condition' (*Observer* 10 April 2005). Though elsewhere in the production costume worked differently, as we shall see, here Cassius' costume read very much as part of a television documentary-style commentary on the relationship of modern politicians to war, one which bore little relation to the risks Cassius takes in the play that finally leads to his death.

On the other hand, I am at something of a loss to discern how Billington's preferred 'authentic Roman dress' would have allowed an insight such as Wiggins's (that the conspirators 'are also young conservatives hostile to social and political change') to emerge at all. How would the semiotics of the toga work in this respect? Billington is presumably suggesting that because, in his ideal production, the conspirators would be wearing the traditional dress of the Roman patrician, it would be clear to the audience that they are no more radical in their thinking about society's hierarchies than Caesar himself. It seems to me, however, that what togas produce for a modern audience is a general sense of Romanness, and that modern audiences would not necessarily be inclined to interrogate the politics of a Brutus or a Cassius just because they were wearing patrician garb – they would, more likely, simply assume that that is what all Romans wore, whereas a recognizable conservatism is surely evoked by a certain kind of modern man's suit and tie.

This chapter explores the ways in which costume makes meaning in Shakespeare production. It argues for a particular kind of conscious theatricality in costume design, the purpose of which is not merely to 'set' the play in a particular period, be that Shakespeare's, our own, or another, but to demonstrate the ways in which 'man' (or woman), to recall *Measure for Measure*'s Isabella, 'is dressed' in the 'little, brief authority' (2.2.141–2) – or the class, or the gender – society ascribes to him or her. I am going to discuss the meanings produced by both 'period' costume and 'modern dress' and the ways in which a consciously theatrical costume aesthetic of either sort might draw attention to the exciting or puzzling differences between Shakespeare's period and our own. The most obvious work that costume does on stage is to create a cultural and historical world for the play that makes sense for the audience. But costume can also highlight the socially and theatrically constructed nature of that world, the class, gender and racial relations within it and the ways in which we are always in the process of producing and reproducing the past.

It is significant that there has been very little published theorization of the ways in which costume produces meaning in the theatre. Until Aoife Monks wrote her exceptional *The Actor in Costume*, scholars and newspaper critics were inclined, to borrow from film theorist Stella Bruzzi, to look *through* rather than *at* clothes on stage (36). Costume is often figured in writing about performance, particularly performance of historical drama, as a part of the more general period setting of a play rather than a material factor in the semiotic and phenomenological production of meaning in its own right. Thus Billington assumes that 'authentic Roman dress' (and Shakespeare) will offer the audience an unproblematically transparent window onto the politics of ancient Rome, rather than draping the actors in layer upon layer of constructed past-ness, recalling other versions of the ancient past, from Mankiewicz's Hollywood Rome, to decontextualized museum displays, to any number of past productions of Shakespeare's Roman plays.

However, there is a different kind of 'authenticity' that can be aimed for when working with 400-year-old plays and costume design than the one Billington suggests is most desirable. *Julius Caesar* is, of course, based on Roman historical sources. But it also contains one of Shakespeare's best-known anachronisms, the clock that Cassius says has 'stricken three' (2.1.193), and a cobbler who would have been more at home in early modern London (1.1). For the early moderns, classical literature produced analogies for the political dilemmas of its own time. On stage, major figures in the Roman plays might have been given props, armour and costume pieces such as the laurel wreath, cuirass and fabric drapery indicated by the much-cited Peacham drawing of *Titus Andronicus*. This is the only extant contemporary image of a Shakespeare production available to us – or at least, our only image of a production imagined by a contemporary.[1] In this drawing, Tamora pleads for the release of

---

[1] As Reginald Foakes (50) and others have pointed out, the drawing, the original of which is in the collection of the Marquis of Bath at Longleat, is not an accurate

her sons to a Titus dressed in these Roman signifiers, while other characters stand by in a mix of what Martin Holmes (150–3) has suggested
is a mix of plausibly Roman-looking armour and contemporary dress.
In a detailed analysis of the armour in the drawing, Holmes argues that
the reason why the 'general effect' of the mixed-period costumes 'looks
somehow quite right' (153) is that Titus' Roman sons' recognizably
English dress on the left of the drawing makes them

> look like the audience's ideas of St George in a pageant, or recol-
> lections of Essex in the tilt-yard or Ralegh coming home from an
> expedition abroad. It is less important that they should look like real
> Romans than that they be recognizable at once as national heroes,
> and such modern or near-modern armour as was available would
> therefore be appropriated to them.
>
> (153)

Whether this eclectic costuming is intended to read as Holmes suggests,
or is simply suggestive of the mix of costume items the playing company owned at the time, this is both Caesar's Rome and Shakespeare's
London, a world both alien and familiar to its audiences and one
whose alien and familiar elements are offered up for comparison and
contrast.

Stage Roman-ness in Shakespeare's theatre might, then, have had
more in common with the way in which Warner dressed her Roman
patricians for the death of Caesar (in modern suits with toga-like drapery attached and swept about the shoulders) than with the Roman
costumes that the Victorian antiquarian, or Billington, might have
appreciated as 'authentic'. Jenny Tiramani, the costume designer for
Shakespeare's Globe under the artistic directorship of Mark Rylance, at

---

depiction of the lines it is seemingly there to illustrate (Tamora's plea to Titus,
a version of her reply, from 1.1, and a speech of Aaron's from 5.1). I am convinced by G. Harold Metz's and Jonathan Bate's arguments that various moments
from the play are emblematically represented in the drawing. These are usefully
summed up in June Schuleter's article on the drawing (174–5), in which she
suggests that the drawing is not of a production of Titus at all, but of a German
play, *A very lamentable tragedy of Titus Andronicus and the haughty empress*, 'a play
performed in Germany by English actors which survives in German, in a volume
published in Leipzig in 1620' (171). This is a fascinating argument, but not one
that contradicts the idea of this being a recalled or imagined early modern production; Schuleter quotes from Holmes on this (174–6), as I do below.

the time when that theatre was most interested in experimenting with the materiality of 'original practices', described, her costumes for the theatre's millennium *Hamlet* as 'Modern Dress circa 1600' (in Bessell 7). Shakespeare's audiences would have seen and heard not only ancient Rome or medieval Denmark on the Globe stage before them, but actors dressed like themselves and their social 'betters'. The next section of this chapter considers the effects of this kind of recognition of the contemporary on current audiences. How might audiences today make meaning out of a 400-year-old play spoken by actors in clothing that is recognizably of their own cultural milieu?

Shakespeare and 'modern dress'

Why dress Shakespeare in our own clothes? The reason is obviously bound up with drawing parallels between Shakespeare's work and current concerns. 'Modern-dress' productions might also suggest to an audience that Shakespeare has something 'universal' or 'timeless' to say to audiences of any period, a problematic kind of essentialism discussed by W.B. Worthen (1997: 65–6). Barry Jackson produced the first British modern-dress Shakespeares at the Birmingham Repertory Theatre in the 1920s. Since he advertised his London *Hamlet* as 'Hamlet in Modern Dress' as if, as Peter Holland suggests, to warn his audiences of the shock of contemporized Shakespeare (2001: 202), proving Shakespeare our contemporary via clothing has become something of a theatrical commonplace. It is important not to generalize about the effects of this costuming choice, however. Modern-dress Shakespeare productions have ranged from the heavily localized and period-specific to aesthetics more generally suggestive of a theatrical present shared by actors and audience. Compare two productions directed by Steven Pimlott during his time as an Associate Director at the RSC. For *Richard II* (2001), with Samuel West as Richard, Sue Wilmington dressed the actors in contemporary haute couture; in a white-box studio setting lit partially by fluorescents, the 'modern' costumes in rich jewel colours and highly textured fabrics gave the impression of decadence and conspicuous consumption without linking the generalized 'modern' period of the production to a particular contemporary political system or national power base. Pimlott's *Hamlet* (2000), however, also with West in the lead but designed by Alison Chitty, used costumes with modern touches that anchored the play to a very specific 'now'. The Danish court was peopled by officials with conference badges; Hamlet was a sulky adolescent in a black hoodie. It is not that Hamlet was supposed directly to represent an anti-globalization protester outside the 2000 G8 summit, but this Denmark certainly recalled a very recognizable modern bureaucracy.

I would argue that the former, theatrical 'present' of *Richard II* was the more multivalent and resonant costume design. The white-box studio with its lit auditorium seemed to invite the audience into a theatrical here-and-now, in which a civil war was taking place about which they had to make decisions, take sides. *Hamlet*'s costume design was in danger of suggesting links with the present too specific to be productive: a Hamlet set in a recognizable bureaucracy invites, I would argue, easy judgement rather than challenging involvement. Where the first production invited the audience to make links between 'then' and 'now', the second suggested those links had already been made.

While there is an inevitable, and often fascinating, disjuncture between Shakespeare's language and a modern setting, highly specific modern visual references can, paradoxically, seem to suggest that this disjuncture can be erased through allegory, limiting rather than opening up possible meanings in production. In Cheek by Jowl's 2008 *Troilus and Cressida*, Helen of Troy spoke the Prologue in her off-the-shoulder white ball dress and long gloves, suggestively fingering (as a number of reviewers commented) the swords of the Greek and Trojan soldiers, who stood in frozen line along the traverse stage. She and Paris were Posh and Becks-style celebrities; several reviews commented on their posing for photographs as if for *Hello!* magazine, the soldiers dressed in what looks like American football gear. Returning home from battle in 1.1, with Cressida and Pandaras looking on, they 'resemble a cross between big-headed American sport stars and Action Men dolls as they parade on and lap up the applause' (Paul Taylor, *Independent* 2 June 2008). Both the sport and Action Man similes were taken up by more than one reviewer; the costumes gave a sense not so much of a theatre as of a catwalk of war, where the powerful pose for the public but, like fashion shows with a military theme, were only playing at battle. The Trojan War, of course, starts because Helen looks good, and Helen herself in Shakespeare's play is notorious for appearing bland and shallow in her one scene. The problem, however, is that these armies are not 'only playing' at war. There is more at stake here than in a game of football or Action Men between spoiled celebrity children: Greeks and Trojans die for Helen, whereas I am assuming no one went to Iraq for Victoria Beckham.

The use of costume to comment on the perceived superficiality of our own culture was in danger of disregarding the complex layering of versions of masculinity and power that can emerge from this play. It is interesting that in this production, when plotting the fixed lottery which will result in Ajax rather than Achilles fighting Hector in the duel of 4.5, Ulysses handed out compromising photographs of Achilles and Patroclus, adding a visual narrative of corruption and scandal to the play's own. In *Troilus and Cressida*, Hector wants to prevent Achilles taking part in a show fight with Troy so that, win or lose, the Greeks can say they never fielded their best man (1.3.368–87); in Cheek by Jowl's *Troilus and Cressida*, Hector was additionally smearing Achilles' name by spreading sexual scandal about him. Postmodern celebrity culture and the concept of reputation that is so central to Shakespeare's version of the ancient world were linked here – but superficially, I would argue, and in a way that does not really illuminate either. How our own culture persuades itself to go to war might be foregrounded in a certain kind of modern-dress production – but it would be a production that heightens the rhetorical acts of political and self-persuasion in *Troilus and Cressida* that would do this most successfully, rather than one that tells us that Shakespeare's Greeks and Trojans were just like us.

Having made this criticism of Cheek by Jowl's allegorical costuming, my own recent performance-research projects have taught me that a limiting visual allegory can emerge in excess of one's own intentions. One of these pieces was a staged collage of *Measure for Measure*, its source texts and adaptations; another was a promenade version of *Coriolanus*. In each, a 'found' costume aesthetic was intended to heighten the act of imagination and cultural construction performed in the production of a 400-year-old text. For *Measure for Measure*, the basic costume over which other items of clothing were worn was a motley collection of glamorous underwear over jeans. The only actor who did not get to wear under-wear over his trousers was the Duke Vincentio figure, who spent the whole piece endeavouring – and often failing – to control an exuberant collage of source texts and adaptations by pulling us back to *Measure for Measure* and Shakespearean authority. Wearing 'foundation garments' as dressing-up clothes put their constructed sexiness in quotations in ways that I think worked for the piece when it was performed in Leeds, but seemed to make too obvious a point when the piece was performed at a theatre festival in Amsterdam. In Leeds the costumes seemed fluid and playful, in Amsterdam a tired and tiresome commentary on the tourist-oriented displays of the sex trade there.

With the arts company Flaneur Productions in Minneapolis, we made two versions of *Coriolanus*, both promenade experiments with site-specific Shakespeare. The first version was a workshop performance made over two weeks that took place in two art-gallery spaces – costume was limited to rehearsal gear, colour-coded to differentiate Romans from

Volscians. The second performance was a fuller production, staged all over and around a theatre building. We decided that we wanted to make it very clear who fought in this society and who did not. The pre-production, theoretical discussion of the effect of wearing camouflage combats for a production of *Coriolanus* in the USA during the Iraq War failed to predict the intense effect of empathy for Martius produced by this decision – especially when teamed with the brightly coloured Good Old Boy plaid shirt (in the first production) and rainproof jacket (in the second) he was made to wear by Menenius for his appearance in the Gown of Humility. The use of practical items of clothing like these suggested that Rome – and by analogous implication the current American administration – could appropriate anything and anyone to signify ideologically. Ironically for a company far from sympathetic with the warmongering outlook of a Caius Martius, what the audience's laughter at this moment seemed to signify was many of the spectators' recognition of a George Bush-like politician's attempt to appear as a man of the people – and Martius' disgust at having to make such an attempt; Martius became highly sympathetic in his refusal to be Bush. He became yet more so in his army-combat costume, his warrior's working gear. His desire to put his 'nervy arm' (2.1.115) into action rather than have it put on display positioned him outside political machinations of both patricians and tribunes in a way disturbingly close to the ways in which the American – and indeed the British – army is placed out of reach of political critique today (we may disagree with a war, but we must Support our Troops). When Martius returned from battle to tease his wife for weeping, he entered from the real street into a real bar surrounded by audience members, any number of whom might have been waiting for just such an event themselves. It was easy to forget Martius' patrician snobbery and join in the welcome home.

Modern dress, then, shifts its meanings depending on physical environment and cultural context, and powerfully serves the need to read 'now' into 'then'. It can be used to insist on Shakespeare's 'relevance' and, simplistically, suggest that the cultural and political concerns of a Shakespeare play are identical to our own; or it can provoke nuanced comparisons between historical periods. It can be an easy universalizing trope or produce challenging disjuncture and distanciation.

Period costume

A different range of rewards and challenges arise from period costume. Setting a play in a period between now and Shakespeare's is a popular move on a substantial costume budget and makes an instant statement about a play via current concepts of the period in question. It is difficult to say whether the S-bend corsetry, bustles and stiff collars of Edwardian Shakespeare, for example, alert us to, or lead us to invent, the repressions and coercions beneath the psychologies and politics of the Shakespearean world being designed. Through the iconography of the film costume drama, this costume favourite has provoked questions of gender, class and colonial power structures that are perhaps more easily recognizable and critique-able than Elizabethan ones. The literal and metaphorical state of being buttoned up in a stiff Edwardian collar fits a post-Freudian understanding of a repressed Angelo perfectly (Trevor Nunn's RSC production of 1991, designed by Maria Bjornson and with costumes *c.*1900 by Sue Wilmington, even included what one reviewer assumed to be Freud's couch as part of the *mise en scène*; *Times* 19 September 1991), or offers the place of butler to Malvolio, in a domestic and class structure immediately comprehensible to viewers of television costume drama. Setting a Shakespeare play in another period in this way can smooth out the awkward differences between two historical periods – Shakespeare's and our own – by imposing another that we think we already understand. If Angelo is a repressed Edwardian, we can put aside the startling suddenness of his declaration of love for Isabella and the differences between what the word 'love' might mean for an early modern audience and for the spectator today; we can even explain away Duke Vincentio's decision not to reveal himself and damn Angelo earlier than he does, in terms of a society that, in the costume drama of restrictive buttons and laces, favours the maintenance of outward appearances over the exposure of inner corruption.

I might seem to be moving instead, then, to historical reconstruction. Can the kind of clothing that Shakespeare's actors might have worn produce the sense of historical otherness I appear to be privileging here? Or does 'authentic' late sixteenth/early seventeenth-century costume simply produce another set of easy-on-the-eye (and on the critical faculties) system of signs, this time a pageant of Elizabethan merry England? After all, in one sense, watching actors wearing clothing styles from the past is far from a historically authentic experience. As we have seen, and as Tiramani points out (58–9), Shakespeare's own audiences would most likely have seen their own clothing and those of their social superiors on stage at the Globe or the Blackfriars, unmediated by a sense of the past, except where it was explicitly foregrounded, as demonstrated in the Peacham drawing.

Original practices costuming at the Shakespeare's Globe, under Rylance and Tiramani, endeavoured not just to re-create an accurate *impression* of historic clothing but the materiality of the thing itself: the dyeing methods, the stitching and the fastenings were reconstructed and experimented with to varying degrees of excitement and irritation among the academic and acting community. Whatever you thought of Elizabethan underwear, these practices foregrounded all kinds of social performances within the plays for the performers – about covering and uncovering the head, what it means to wear a sword, how close one can get to a friend in a farthingale. The Globe experiment offered the possibility of interrogating not just a history but a social phenomenology of costume. The encoding of social status in the wearing, doffing and replacing of hats, for example, can suggest a social system succinctly and rapidly to an audience not familiar with it (see Ryan, 8–9). Period costume offers a sense of how the Elizabethans and Jacobeans constructed gender through clothing. The gendered shapes produced by men and women's clothes, the sense of distance created around an aristocratic woman in the wide farthingale of court dress, the ways in which clothes encourage or permit men and women to sit, stand, run, greet one another, all these can be felt by actors and audience today.

Of course, it is impossible to reproduce the quotidian normality of seeing and wearing Elizabethan/Jacobean dress and the innate understanding of the social world encoded in such dress. Some aspects of the materiality and the layers of social significance of costume as it is encoded in the plays are lost even to the scholar of costume history, and certainly to most audience members. I would also argue that at the point in theatre history when Shakespeare was writing, a degree of what we might think of as dramatic realism, has erased the obvious costume symbolism of earlier dramas, as least insofar as that is evident to us in the play-texts. For example, in the source play for *Measure for Measure*, George Whetstone's *Promos and Cassandra* (1576), direct references to clothing figure heavily; reading the play, one feels the weight of it, materially and symbolically. The rambling, unsophisticated dramaturgy of this two-part play and Whetstone's lack of a relationship with the professional theatre suggests it was never performed. But the highly specific stage directions that inform the imagined actors when they must be ready to enter and give instructions for the kinds of props and scenographic devices that a stage production would need show that Whetstone is certainly imagining a performance as he undertakes his gentlemanly exercise in playwriting. In this play, clothing and properties function within a simple iconography that denotes political, moral and familial status. The early version of *Measure's* first scene, the conversation between the Duke and Angelo in which the latter is urged to 'take [his] commission' (1.1.49), is a ceremonial tableau in *Promos*: Promos, the Angelo prototype, is given a Sword of Justice, the city's keys and the King's 'Letters Patent' which must, according to Whetstone's stage direction to the imaginary props maker, 'be fair written in parchment, with some great counterfeit seal' (1 *Promos and Cassandra* 1.1 SD). Lamia, the courtesan, who features much more prominently than Mistress Overdone, has a number of songs in which she flaunts her ill-gotten gowns (she exhorts herself to 'all avaunt now flaunt it, brave wench cast away care'; 1.2.1) and is threatened with a 'blue gown' of correction for her illicit trade in her own extravagantly dressed body. Paulina, the pregnant lover in this version, first enters in that same shameful blue gown, and Cassandra herself, who does agree to Promos' suggested means of saving her brother (no bed trick in the early play), enters, once she has lost her virginity, in a blue gown to denote her moral fall, trimmed with black to signify mourning for the brother she thinks Promos has killed.

Clothing is foregrounded materially in *Promos*, in a soliloquy in which a hangman expresses delight at the 'nine and twenty suits of apparel' (2.5.2) he gets to collect from the bodies of the dead, the quality of which has mightily improved now that the new, strict rule of Promos as deputy means no rich man can bribe his way out of punishment. This is a play with a residual morality play aesthetic in which clothing is part of a clear and simple visual economy. Clothing in *Promos* is pay for Lamia and the Hangman and a means of displaying authority, correction and status for the state.

The play-texts of Shakespeare do not offer us quite the transparent semiotics of clothing that an earlier work like *Promos* does. In Shakespeare's version of this story, *Measure for Measure*, it seems to have dissolved into metaphor. Angelo is 'dresst' with the Duke's love (1.1.19), and, for Isabella, in 'a little brief authority' (2.2.119) rather than adorned with symbolic sword and keys; the 'destin'd livery' (2.4.145) Angelo urges Isabella to put on is not a blue gown of shame but a metaphorical figuring of her position as woman in his eyes (2.4.137). *Measure for Measure* reads as a modern play in comparison to *Promos*, not only because of its more sophisticated, suspense-driven plot but because it is concerned with reading beneath the surfaces to discover 'what these seemers be' (1.3.54); in *Promos* the characters tell the audience what they are, through expository speeches and symbolic clothing.

If we are looking for what the plays of Shakespeare tell us to wear and how to wear it, there is a certain amount of decoding to do that might not be entirely transparent to current audiences, despite Tiramani's assertion and my own that we can read social relationships in the clothing of the past. Does it matter, for example, if we know what items of clothing Margaret in *Much Ado* is referring to when she says she prefers the 'other rebato' and the 'tire within' to the ones Hero is trying for her wedding? *Rebato* and *Tire* sound like *robe* and *attire*, so we can imagine any number of garments rather than the stiff collar and headgear that the text refers to. The 2011 production at Shakespeare's Globe, for example, once the home of Tiramani's original costume practices, has Margaret refer to an underskirt Hero is wearing as a rebato. Also lost to most current audience members will be the likelihood that the 'tire within' is a headdress with false hair attached. Margaret thinks that the headdress within would suit Hero even better if 'the hair were a thought browner' (3.4.13), and many recent Margarets have made gestural reference to Hero's hair on this line, as though the colour of the headdress she is thinking of would better go with browner hair than her mistress's. But it is likely the comparison of the hair on the headdress with Hero's own that is being made here. At any rate, this scene can read oddly on stage in a 'modern-dress' production, given that a modern bride getting ready for her wedding is unlikely to have a number of alternative tiara/band-and-veil arrangements (the modern equivalent of the headtire, 'tire' still being the word referred to by purveyors of wedding gear today) in another room, with false hair or otherwise. The iconic modern wedding garb would have been chosen long before the scene in which Hero and Margaret try to decide which of her 'attires' would be 'best to furnish [her] tomorrow' (3.1.103).

The Hero wedding preparation scene offers a clear opportunity to read clothing culturally. What does the onstage construction of wedding-day Hero with rebato and headgear to go with the basic canvas of her gown of 'fine, quaint, graceful and excellent fashion' (3.4.20–1) signify? The donning of these pieces of clothing can be read as a highly ironic creation of an innocent bride, when the audience has had Don John's plot revealed to them in the preceding scenes. Hero's toilette might be, simultaneously, the construction of the whore that she is to be accused of having become. After all, she is getting dressed with Margaret, not Ursula, whom she originally invited to pore over 'attires' with her (3.1.104) – Margaret, who as we already know has been set up to behave whorishly by looking out of Hero's bedroom window and talking to a man at night, while supposedly looking exactly like her. In the early modern period the vocabulary of women's costume is bound to the misogynist discourses of seeming and falsehood in women, and is inventoried by fictional courtesans such as George Whetstone's Lamia in *Promos and Cassandra*, flaunting herself in clothes given to her by her many lovers, or Gervase Markham's *Famous Whore or Noble Curtizan*, who lists 'Perfumed gloves, gowns, kirtles, vascaies, muffes, / Borders and tyers, rebatoes, falles and ruffs' (Markham, n.p.) amongst the gifts bestowed upon her in addition to her courtesan's 'monthly pension'. However, the wearing of a head-tire or a rebato is the prerogative of any relatively wealthy woman rather than the sign of loose morality per se, and Hero's dress is 'fine, quaint, graceful and excellent' in comparison to the Duchess of Milan's gown ('cloth o'gold, and cuts, and laced with silver, set with pearls, down sleeves, side sleeves and skirts round underborne with a blueish tinsel'; 3.4.18–20) with which Margaret, perhaps unwittingly, teases her. The conversation about these articles of clothing does construct Hero as part of the visual economy of female-on-display, always ambivalent in its sexual morality in the eyes of men, as is demonstrated by the ease with which Don John's plot comes off. Even her hair can be put on, falsified. On the other hand, while Hero seems momentarily dismayed by the idea of the gown that 'excels' her own, she insists on a rebato of her own choosing, not that of Margaret, the lover of finery above her station (3.4.5–7).

Perhaps Hero could be both 'fine, quaint, graceful and excellent' *and* signify women's easy slippage into false 'bravery', immoral display, at least for early audiences. The references to possible different rebatoes suggest that Hero is standing in her shift in this scene, as woman's dress in this period is constructed over her shift once the collar or ruff has been attached. That she is about to be 'put together' by the addition of skirt, bodice and sleeves, tied and pinned separately, and possibly crowned with false hair, would be known by the early modern women in an audience and any man who had seen one dress or undress. She is being constructed for her downfall on the one hand – and perhaps reminds the audience that Margaret would have been similarly constructed to look just like an unchaste version of Hero for Don John's Trick; she is taking part in an ordinary domestic ritual on the other.

Bill Alexander's Caroline RSC production of 1991, set in a period during which stiff rebatoes gave way to lace collars, is one in which Hero stood in her shift, her lace neckwear giving a sense of the magnificence of the wedding wear to come. Over stands and frames hung the foundation garments that go to construct the particularity of this early modern English female form. Alex Kingston's Hero looked small, frail and vulnerable in her shift and stockinged feet against the swathes of pale curtaining that made for a far-from-intimate boudoir. She had a number of collars tried on her, then the bum-roll upon which her skirts were to rest was tied around her waist by Margaret, and an underskirt and overskirt pulled down over her shift. At the end of the scene, when it was announced that the menfolk had come to bring her to church, she was still asking her cousin and her waiting woman to help her to dress: there is much construction still to come.

A not dissimilar sense of a woman constructed by foundation garments was produced in Cheek by Jowl's Edwardian-dress production of 1988. In this version of the scene, Hero stood in drawers, corsetry and black stockings, that particular combination of white and black, innocence and sexiness that such a get-up connotes for a modern audience. The ways in which foundation garments produce the female form are perhaps most familiar to us via the Victorian crinoline and the Edwardian S-bend corset. Shifting Hero's wedding-preparation scene into this later period produced an aesthetic that exoticized, sexualized and, I would suggest, was simultaneously in danger of condemning the past for its constructions of the female: poor Hero, look at what the oppressions of the past are doing to her. What this might achieve is a smoothing-over of the historical and material similarities and differences between getting ready for a wedding Then and Now. It offered the audience neither the historical specificity of early modern cultural or stage practice, nor a way in to thinking about our own ways of doing or representing weddings – but rather a generalized costume drama of the past, safely gorgeous and easy on the eye – but equally easy on our cultural sensibilities, because reassuringly past in its obviously repressive sexual politics. Such a clear signal about the construction of the female does nineteenth-/early twentieth-century fashion supposedly give, that even in Di Trevis's RSC production of 1988, designed by Mark Thompson, where the women in earlier scenes appeared in wide late 1940s/1950s skirts with Elizabethan-inflected bodices, Hero's wedding dress was Victorian in style: a giant crinoline and enormous hat and veil swamped her in constructed virginity.

The problem with all this is not so much that Hero is so often constructed in costume as a vulnerable innocent being prepared for a failed display of consumable virginity. Indeed, I would argue that this is a highly plausible reading of the dressing and the aborted wedding scenes. My concern with these visions of Hero in her dressing room is the iconography of pastness that is produced here, the instantly recognizable clichés of repressive corsetry or anachronistic white wedding-cake dresses that simultaneously condemn the past and titillate the present, where the scene in its own period might have suggested a more nuanced set of possible readings between innocence and 'bravery'.

When costume is used to 'set' Shakespeare in the past, then, a range of historical and theatrical negotiations come into play that are sometimes erased by costume's role in an overall design. In considering period dress, I am far from denigrating a consistent period aesthetic and would argue for a variety of means of allowing the spectator, as Stella Bruzzi would have it, to look at clothes rather than reading though them. I have been suggesting that it is worth paying attention to the ways in which clothing signifies in theatrical and cultural history, not in order that we can make better historical reproductions but so that the analogies and other meanings we make with clothes on stage can at least be constructed with political, historical and theatrical consciousness, rather than in a naturalizing spirit that suggests that war or prostitution or marriage are the same for all time. I want to suggest that the most engaging and provocative costume designs allow that construction to come to the fore at points during the audience's experience of a period drama. To conclude, I turn to two productions, one a theatre piece, one a television series, which exemplify the ways in which costume can productively foreground itself, drawing to the audience's attention the ways in which clothing produces gender, class and the past itself.

It is significant, of course, that the examples that follow are not Shakespearean ones. They are not productions of plays from the past, they are reconstructions of the past by contemporary writers. Perhaps there is more room here for acknowledgement of, and experimentation with, the fact that when we costume the past, we reconstruct it rather than simply reflect it; the burden of telling a timeless truth about history is less apparent than in Shakespeare production. The costume designers for the productions explored next were working with less cultural baggage, less of an expectation that their work should reflect the universal meaning of a sacred text. To permit Shakespearean costume design to take from work like this would be to acknowledge that Shakespeare production is doing similar work of theatrical and historical construction.

Reading clothing and the production of the past

The RSC's programme of new writing at Wilton's Music Hall in London in 2008 included *The Tragedy of Thomas Hobbes*, by writer Adriano Shaplin, who was 'embedded' with the RSC for two years; he observed rehearsal for the Histories cycle and, as was much quoted in the press, acted as an 'agent provocateur' within Michael Boyd's company (Susannah Clapp, *Observer* 23 November 2008). The title suggested that the play would tell the story of philosopher Thomas Hobbes, though it was more clearly focused on the empiricist scientists against whom Hobbes rails. Science in this play, as Clapp remarks in her review, becomes the new theatre in Shapiro's interregnum, as the scientists perform sensational experiments before royal and intellectual elites. The play was not generally well received by the critics, who found it ill-constructed and overly long. My own view of the piece coincides with that of the only British broadsheet critic who was relatively positive about the play and production, Michael Billington. The *Guardian* theatre critic, whilst admitting that *Thomas Hobbes* is a rambling piece packed with far too many ideas 'fighting, like ferrets in a sack, for prominence', found it to possess a 'reckless vitality' (19 November 2008). Though he does not mention it himself, costume is a significant means by which the qualities Billington appreciated emerged.

The first impression of costuming in *Thomas Hobbes* was one of period: long frock coats over tight breeches and boots. Images from the production in newspapers where it was reviewed uphold this impression; they show neither the rough, scaffolding stage erected within the romantically dilapidated mid-Victorian building, nor the fact that the breeches worn by the male characters were in fact the drainpipe jeans that had made an almost ubiquitous fashion revival amongst young people as 'skinnies' around this time. One of the more negative reviews of the production lamented the fact that Stoppard or Frayn had not been given this RSC new writing commission, as they would have been better able to 'explain the science ... make links to our own time' (Charles Spencer, *Daily Telegraph* 19 November 2008). The jeans did something slightly different. They were not the most prominent aspect of costuming; the audience was introduced to this brilliant, competitive, narcissistic group of men, then, perhaps later, realized that the impression of period dress had been created using both period reproduction and contemporary clothes. What this costume design foregrounded was the constructed nature of the past in the play and in culture: the fact that this version of the Dawn of the Enlightenment is inevitably speculative and that the links we make to our own times are invented ones, however illuminating. When Charles II enters in louche, bright red frock coat, jeans and tumbling curls, we see a contemporary construction of the theatricality of the Restoration strut across the stage. This is a Charles of our century's own making, and I would argue that this combination of rock-star and costume-drama fetish take us a step further than the comparisons made in Cheek by Jowl's *Troilus and Cressida* between 'then' and 'now', provoking questions about patronage, fashion and the circulation of ideas. Where Cheek by Jowl set *Troilus and Cressida* in a vain celebrity-obsessed here and now, the RSC sets this play both 'then' and 'now', provoking comparison rather than insisting on similarity.

Interestingly, as Clapp points out, this production ran concurrently to the television series *The Devil's Whore* (in her review of *Thomas Hobbes*, Clapp refers to the setting of the two works as 'the newly media-friendly civil war period' and asks, 'will the credit crunch and *The Devil's Whore* make puritans of us all?'). This is a costume drama with a significantly different take on period nostalgia from the novel adaptations usually associated with the genre. It is inhabited by the historical figures of Oliver Cromwell and his associates and the fictional heroine Angelica Fanshawe, a proto-feminist who questions the right of her childhood friend and husband, Harry, to govern her sexual desires (he demands that she is symbolically silent during sex and fears that her enjoyment of it demonstrates a lack of chastity) and political life. The series follows her across the history of the English Revolution, pursued by her nemesis Joliffe, whose friend she kills in an early episode, after an attempted rape.

The lighting in the series departs from the conventions of television realism, producing a painterly effect of seventeenth-century chiaroscuro, reminding us that the characters in this piece, like the paintings they recall, are artistic creations, rather than people that might exist today, only in better frocks. The satin of the Royalists' costumes, particularly the women's dresses, are rendered particularly lustrous here and make a great deal of rustling noise. Angelica (Andrea Riseborough) is laced up in her corset in the very first sequence by her waiting women, as if to foreground audience expectation of the titillation/disapproval binary outlined in the analysis of *Much Ado* above. Angelica, however, defies our patronization of the past by seeming to enjoy being constructed as bride enormously. The series hints strongly that she is not the 'whore' the men in the play have constructed of her, insofar as she has not had the sex before marriage of which her naïve young husband suspects her, but rather someone who falls under patriarchal suspicion for enjoying a sensual life. Of course, this particular television production of pastness has its own clearly feminist agenda. I am not suggesting that the actress playing Hero in *Much Ado* should clearly revel in the thought of her wedding night when what she says is that her 'heart is exceedingly heavy' (3.4.16). But the sensuality of costume in this costume drama is in excess of costume-drama conventions in the way that it draws attention to the genre's own excesses.

In *Thomas Hobbes*, an RSC production of a contemporary take on the past, and in this costume drama, we have two examples of an interrogatory foregrounding of costume that I want to suggest provide useful ways of thinking about costume in Shakespeare production. I am not suggesting that costume should constantly alienate its audiences from the fictional world of the Shakespearean drama. I rather want to argue that, like the plays themselves, costume can do the job of pulling spectators in to another world, then reminding them that they are having to work at constructing the past in our imaginations, along with the actors and design team. The question of what the text seems to demand of the body – how it might stand, move, hide or display itself – might well elicit the help of the costume historian or reconstructor of historical costumes, and can be answered by way of detailed attention to a play's dramaturgical structure and performance history. But theatrically conscious costume asks not only how clothing performs *in* the Shakespearean text but how it *performs* that text in each new production. In considering these questions, the plays might throw into productive relief our own sartorial displays, restrictions and commodifications, without having to insist that we are what Shakespeare was talking about.

9
Fighting

Stuart Hampton-Reeves

They fight is one of Shakespeare's most used stage directions, but what kind of stage action is he directing when he adds these words in the margin of the text? A stage fight is thoroughly predetermined: every step, every blow, every punch, every sword thrust, will have been painstakingly rehearsed, choreographed in slow motion, and practised diligently before every performance. The risk is pure illusion. The paradox of stage fighting is that the moment when the stage seems the most disordered, when the actors seem most out of control, is also the moment when the actors are in most control, when their safety depends on their fellow actors knowing exactly what each other will do and when.

Although professional stage-fight directors insist that there is no real connection between actual fights and play fights, at least part of the pleasure of watching a stage fight may be, for some, the voyeuristic desire to see a planned fight go wrong. This happens more often than it should. In his preface to William Hobbs's authoritative manual for stage combat, Laurence Olivier mischievously lists the number of wounds he received in his career, including broken bones and 'untold slashes including a full thrust razor-edged sword wound in the *breast* (thrilling)' (10). He remembers more gruesome injuries inflicted on other actors, including the time when Geoffrey Toone was hurt so badly by Olivier in one of the fights in *Romeo and Juliet* that he had to leave the cast for several weeks 'on account of his thumb *hanging by a thread*' (10). That so many tutors feel the need to insist that stage fighting should never be genuinely dangerous, to the point where this has become a maxim that virtually defines the profession, perhaps indicates the extent to which either audiences *presume* or actors *hope* that such fights might deliver a more authentic experience. Having myself witnessed numerous stage fights from the front row, I find it both uncomfortable and, as

146

Olivier puts it, thrilling to be so close to two actors chasing after each other, grappling with each other, slicing at one another, even throwing things across the stage. However carefully rehearsed such action is, the moment of performance brings its own energy, and its own commitment to authenticity. As Olivier shrewdly observes, stage fights offer 'the actor a unique opportunity of winning the audience, as great almost as any scene, speech or action' (9).

Olivier bluffed his way through fight scenes. Modern stage fights presume to a more advanced approach to the representation of fighting, but perhaps they do not take fully into account the possibility of real violence, which makes watching a stage fight (and perhaps being in one) genuinely exciting, as a moment where reality and illusion come together. Theatre always carries with it the danger that a pretend fight could become real, that a punch thrown in play could make a connection, that a stage dagger might get mistakenly exchanged for a real one, that an actor playing dead might actually be dead.

When Shakespeare added *They fight* to his script, he did not just indicate an action, he effectively created a space for a different kind of theatre, and a different kind of performance tradition, to take the stage and impress upon textual drama its own way of conveying conflict. In this chapter, I want to start by excavating the ancient performance traditions which underlie stage fighting and signal the dissonances between that tradition and (early) modern textual theatre. By looking at other performance cultures which have given a higher priority to martial arts, we can approach the representation of fighting in Shakespeare as a complex and sophisticated performance form. I will then go on to describe the martial-arts culture of Elizabethan England which Shakespeare would have drawn on and participated in. The chapter concludes with detailed studies of the work of contemporary stage-fighting directors, who make a much larger contribution to theatrical meaning than is usually accounted for.

A gamble with death: theatre and martial arts

Every year, the evening peace of an area of the Alleppey district of Kerala in the south-west of India is broken by the sounds of trumpets and kettledrums. In answer to this clarion call, men and boys from each house come out to a gathering point, all dressed in a spectacular costume of red, white, silver and gold. They gather together as two armies in a courtyard in front of a temple, greeting each other with elegant dance moves. As Chummar Choondal puts it, 'the players prance like spirited steeds and jump and dance about and around' (63). Some men twirl small shields in time to the discordant mustering music. These are episodes of single combat, a challenger from each side displaying his skill with the sword and shield. Finally, one side is declared the victor, and the losing side runs up the temple steps.

This ceremony, known as Velakali, is a community performance of fighting which displaces the memory of battle into mime and dance. Like many performance cultures around the world, Velakali integrates martial arts with what is essentially a theatrical performance. Even though the performance takes place in public, at a temple, and there are no lines to speak, the martial displays are framed by a set of actions already plotted in advance, and the whole spectacle is witnessed by an audience. This may seem at first sight a long way removed from Shakespeare's fight scenes, but performances such as this remind us that fighting displays are part of the ancient raw materials of performance, that they have their own histories and own claim to an audience–actor relationship.

The emergence of martial arts into textual theatre has taken a very different course in cultures around the world, with modern Western stage practices being perhaps the most removed from a sustained tradition of martial arts. Nevertheless, Shakespearean martial arts share with the Velakali a distant memory of the battlefield. Wherever martial arts end up, they begin as a communal re-creation of war. The Velakali makes a performance out of violence and so commemorates the crucial relationship between any social grouping and the violence it needs to enact in order to protect its territories and way of life. Although gaudy and entertaining, the Velakali is approached by its participants with complete seriousness. The players undergo a rigorous training regime in the Indian martial art Kalarippayattu, and the performance itself enables them to display their proficiency in this demanding body art. Phillip B. Zarrilli's definitive performance ethnography uncovers the ancient link between performance and fighting in the etymology of the word Kalarippayattu, which (to paraphrase Zarrilli's more detailed account) combines the Malayan word for 'place, open space, threshing floor, battlefield' with a word for 'fencing exercise' (1998: 25). The disjunctive presence of the battlefield in a domain which is otherwise performative hints at the primal memory of war hidden in the highly sophisticated exercises used to develop proficiency in Kalarippayattu.

There is a striking parallel with the way in which Shakespeare's contemporary, Thomas Nashe, chose to characterize theatre as a place where battlefields are literally brought to life again in his 1592 pamphlet, *Pierce Penniless, His Supplication to the Devil*. Not only are past heroes 'valiant acts ... revived', but 'they themselves raised from the grave of oblivion, and brought to plead their aged honors in open presence'. Nashe gives as an example the then recent performance of the English hero Talbot in Shakespeare's *1 Henry VI*: 'How it would have joyed brave Talbot', he writes, '... to think that after he had lain two hundred years in his tomb, he should triumph again on the stage, and have his bones new embalmed with the tears of ten thousand spectators at least ... who in the tragedian that represents his person imagine they behold him fresh bleeding.' Nashe directly echoed a similar defence of playing made by Sir Philip Sidney, who guessed that the roots of theatre lie in the ritualized recounting of past battles reported in the *areytos* of Central American natives (502–3). Sidney has a claim to being the first performance anthropologist. In the twentieth century, Victor Turner and Richard Schechner produced copious evidence that points to the close relationship between theatrical performance and the community rituals of pre-literate societies (see Schechner, 1985, 1988 and Turner, 1982 for an introduction to this important area of performance studies). For performance critics, the nature of 'play' as something which is purely physical, pre-textual, instinctively pleasurably and yet potentially lethal rubs against what we have come to expect as the scene for Shakespeare performance. Play fighting not only precedes text, it precedes any ability we have to understand or produce text. All human cultures have ways of turning play fighting into highly developed cultural, ritualized forms from martial arts to sports, which are highly regulated ways of displaying a body's physical prowess. Stage fighting represents a particular and uniquely Western iteration of this prehistoric performance form, which emerges restlessly into the contained form of the textual play.

Shakespeare seemed to realize that fighting is intensely theatrical. The rules and rituals of fighting dress the physical act in artifice in ways which ensure that the outcome of the fight is understood. It is not essential but common for fights to have an audience, much like the audience which watches Orlando and Charles the Wrestler fight in *As You Like It*, or Peter Thump and his master in *2 Henry VI*. An audience gathers ready to watch a fight in *Richard II* that the King calls off, and *Hamlet* draws attention to the similarity of play and fighting by having the same audience gather for *The Mousetrap* and the duel between Hamlet and Laertes. Audiences can be arranged for a planned fight, as in *Hamlet*, but even in those fights which happen spontaneously, such as Mercutio, Tybalt and Romeo's fight, spectators quickly gather and choose their sides without crossing the invisible threshold which defines the space of the fight.

What is true of small fights can also be true of pitched battles and full-scale wars. The performance anthropologist Greg Dening looks at war as a kind of performance through an analysis of the Battle of Valparaiso (1814). He notes the lengths those involved go to in order to normalize acts of killing:

> In this deepest of deep plays that battles are about, in this gamble with death that men undertake in fight for honour and a goal, in this ultimately asocial or anti-social act of killing one another, they maneuver with one another to make a common social stage on which they can do the totally unacceptable in an acceptable way. Battles are filled with play to make the totally irrational proper.
>
> (84)

The term 'theatre of war' perhaps discloses more than it means to about the performative nature of fighting and war. Wars can be thought of as theatrical if we bear in mind all those elements which make a war aside from the acts of violence which they produce: the displays, the speeches, the attempt to define the values at stake, the organization of territory into war zones, the uniforms and music and war cries which give war a visual field and a sound all of its own.

It is useful to contrast the highly contained and textualized use of martial arts in Western drama to other cultures, in which theatrical forms equally as sophisticated (and in some cases, contemporaneous) with Shakespeare have arrived at a completely different negotiation between fighting and play. In parts of Asia, particularly in China, Taiwan and Japan, martial arts are dominant forms in traditional per-formance. In Beijing Opera, for example, actors are trained from child-hood in both martial and performance techniques. Beijing Opera actors learn the specialist martial skills associated with a stock character which they will later play, usually exclusively, in their adult career. In Taiwan, where the form now flourishes, the institution was closely aligned with and sustained by Taiwan's military academies (see Huang, 2012). For Western audiences, Beijing Opera seems balletic, with the actors' move-ments heavily stylized.

Wu Hsing-Kuo's *Kingdom of Desire* (1986) was a Beijing Opera ver-sion of *Macbeth* in which fighting was represented through spectacular acrobatics and outlandish military costumes. In 2007, Ninagawa set *Coriolanus* as a Samurai play, drawing heavily on Samurai displays to create a play-world rooted in the fetishization of the warrior. Ninagawa, having cast Toshiaki Karasawa, an expert sword-fighter, as Martius, remarked to one British interviewer, 'He's also very good at sword-fighting. British actors don't do sword-fighting very often, do they?' The production was noted for its intense physicality, which set it apart from standard, text-centred performances of the play. Both Ninagawa and Wu used martial arts to create a much more sensuous and physical kind of theatre for Shakespeare. Here, fighting is not a simple piece of stage business, but a deeply learned skill that is at the heart of a fully developed performance aesthetic. Zarrilli describes how martial arts actors engage their 'total being' in a 'psychophysical process'. Character is created 'not in the personality of the actor but as an embodied and projected/energized/living form between actor and audience ... the actor and spectator co-create the figure embodied in the actor as "other"' (1990: 143–4). This shows a different kind of contract between player and audience to the one Olivier imagined when he cheekily boasted that success in a fight scene was a way to win an audience.

When Shakespeare instructs actors to fight in his text, he captures and contains an alternative tradition of performance which in many cultures has priority over textual drama. This is a form which locates theatre in a different place, somewhere between blood sports and military drills, where the rules of engagement are different, where the definition of success lies not in the ability to move an audience through character, but to stimulate an audience through the exertions and skills of the body. At the same time as circumscribing this form of performance within words, narrative and character that together predetermine the outcome, Shakespeare nevertheless refuses, or fails, to prescribe how his stage directions are interpreted. This leaves a space for martial arts to re-emerge, and subvert the structures of textual drama.

A palpable hit: *Hamlet* and stage-fighting manuals

They prepare to play. Shakespeare exploited the metatheatrical tension between performance and reality in martial arts when he set the climax to *Hamlet* in a fencing match, which begins with this stage direction. Fencing is a highly refined martial art. The weapons are thin and blunted, the participants wear protective clothing, and the rules of fencing are precise. Everything about the set-up focuses the event of fencing on the display of competitive skill at sword-fighting with none of the risk of a real duel. Rather than write, 'they fight', Shakespeare signals each bout of the match with 'they play'. There is no fighting, only play.

The scene – and *Hamlet* – turns on the moment when ritualized fighting turns into real violence. The ambiguity is there at the outset, because we already know that Laertes, prepped by Claudius, intends to use the match to kill Hamlet. As this 'play' is overshadowed by their scrap over Ophelia's grave, the match is already being used as a way of deflecting real anger into sport.

They play. There are two plays in *Hamlet*: this one, and *The Mousetrap*. In both, the court gathers to watch a spectacle, and the focus of the scene moves between the performance itself and the onstage audience, who interject with comments on the action. Both are covertly re-scripted to trap one of the key players. In *The Mousetrap*, Hamlet interpolates extra material into an existing play to make the players' work pointedly political; in the fight scene, Claudius spreads poison on Laertes' blade. And in both the victim of the trap – first Claudius, then Hamlet – subverts it by breaking the structure of performance (an audience watching a spectacle) and dissolving its fictional, ritualized world. Both scenes start with the formality of performance, with its clear division between audience and players, but end with confusion. Both plays also, through collapsing, allow truths to emerge: Claudius' guilty reaction in the player's scene foreshadows the revelations that tumble out at the fencing match's conclusion. The moment when play collapses into reality defines crisis moments: when Claudius dissolves the performance with his guilty conscience; when Laertes hacks at Hamlet, breaking the rules and causing uproar in the audience. The stage directions avoid using the word 'fight' to describe the action: *LAERTES wounds HAMLET; then in scuffling, they change rapiers, and HAMLET wounds LAERTES.* It's that simple – and yet, in performance, these few words require a great deal of choreographing. How does Laertes wound Hamlet, and where? Is it played as an accident or, more likely, does Laertes suddenly become angry? They have to scuffle, but why scuffle when they have swords, and why change swords? They have to drop them at some point, but how do the actors make it clear to the offstage audience, who carry the secret knowledge that one of the rapiers is poisoned, which sword is which?

By disguising this fight as a fencing match, Shakespeare simultaneously signals the latent performativity of fighting and the implicit potential violence of performance. Dening identifies a continuity between the battlefield and the gentlemanly act of duelling, which likewise contextualizes violence within codes and rituals: 'Precision about the boundaries of honour and even greater precision about the circumstances in which one could kill and be killed were the essence of dueling … The dueling code, even nicer than parlour etiquette, defined class and group membership powerfully' (83). A fencing match is an extension of this code into a formal game, a play, in which it is essential to observe the etiquette of the duel without the actual violence. However, in *Hamlet* at least, the fencing match is haunted by the ghost of the battlefield. Both the audience and the players formally acknowledge the conventions of fencing with their interjections but, as the fight grows more physical, and the stage more disordered, this initial contract between audience and performer is broken.

Shakespeare's audiences would have brought their own deep knowledge of fencing culture to bear on their understanding of this scene. They were, as Richard Lane puts it, 'connoisseurs of swordfights' (2). Stage fights engaged with an established culture of fighting which many of them participated in and respected. Audiences would have been quite capable of evaluating the authenticity of these pretend fights, and there is evidence that some at least saw through the illusion. In his play *Every Man in his Humour* (1598), Ben Jonson, who killed a fellow actor in a duel and claimed to have killed when he was a soldier, mocked Shakespeare's attempt to represent the Wars of the Roses with 'three rusty swords' (Prologue 9). The following year, Shakespeare seemed to acknowledge the insult in *Henry V*, when the Chorus apologizes for representing Agincourt with 'four or five most vile and ragged foils' which would be 'right ill-disposed in brawl ridiculous' (4.0.50–1). This culture was fuelled by numerous fighting schools and fighting manuals. Soldiers returning from European wars found they could cash in on their experiences with military pamphlets, of which there was an epidemic in the 1590s (Charles Edelman discusses this at length in his definite work on the subject). Italian immigrants were able to exploit a raging fashion for fencing by establishing themselves as sword masters. Fencing schools and military academies used the London playhouses to stage fighting displays, so sharing the same cultural space as players.

One of the most important martial artists in Shakespeare's time was George Silver, whose influential *Paradoxes of Defence* was published in 1599 by Edward Blount (who would later publish Shakespeare's First Folio). Although Silver's main thesis seems narrow (essentially, he argues that short swords are, paradoxically, better to fight with than long swords), the volume includes on its title page a revealing admonishment to all Englishmen to 'take heed, how they submit themselves into the hands of *Italian* teachers of Defence ... and to beware how they forsake or suspect their own naturall fights', concluding with a short celebration of the 'noble science or exercising of arms'. Silver had broader ambitions for his short manual: to professionalize Elizabethan martial arts and protect the profession (and those seeking to learn how to fight) from bad teachers. Most Elizabethan men carried a sword, which meant that the market for students wanting to learn how to use their sword properly was potentially very lucrative. Silver's intervention, which he clearly thought was necessary to make, suggests that fighting skills were being seen as a marker of a gentleman (as Silver calls himself in his signature). To fight well, to learn the 'noble science', was to put oneself ahead of the crowd.

Silver was keenly aware of the theatrical power of sword-fighting and, like Claudius, saw the spectacle of a sword-fight as a way to settle a score. He recounts one anecdote of a public fight played at the 'Bell Savage upon the Scaffold'. The Bell Savage was an Inn in Ludgate Hill, London, with a cobbled courtyard often used for entertainments including fighting displays and plays (including a performance of *Doctor Faustus*).[1] Silver had heard two Italian sword masters disparage English fighters as slow-witted. Indignant at this insult to his national pride, Silver and his brother Toby challenged to 'play with them' over a number of rounds with 'the single Rapier, Rapier and Dagger, the single Dagger, the single Sword, the Sword and Target, the Sword and Buckler, & two hand Sword, the Staff, battell Axe, and Morris pike'. Silver's language is interesting to compare with the stage directions in *Hamlet*. He did not want to fight them but to 'play with them'. Their display was 'to be played' on a scaffold erected in the inn courtyard, elevating the fighters so that they could be seen clearly by the spectators. The Silvers wanted this display to demonstrate how the cunning English were superior to the arrogant Italians. The fight had a pre-scripted narrative with a clear sense from the outset about who the 'good guys' were in the combat. This was pure theatre. Silver posted over a hundred 'bills of challenge' which he put up right across London to publicize the event. In the end, the fight did not take place. The Italian fencers refused to come, even though

> many gentlemen of good accompt, carried manie of the bils of chalenge unto them, telling them that now the *Silvers* were at the place appointed, with all their weapons, looking for them, and a multitude of people there to behold the fight, saying unto them,

---

[1] For more on the Bell Savage as a venue for drama and fence play, see Berry, 2006.

now come and go with us (you shall take no wrong) or else you are shamed for ever.

(66–7)

The play was all the more effective for not happening: national honour was saved, and the fashionable Italians humiliated. For Silver, more was at stake than simply challenging a jingoistic insult. He wanted to affirm the supremacy of the English style over the now 'shamed' Italians.

The fencing match in *Hamlet* is Italianate, for Hamlet and Laertes fight with the rapiers that Silver despised. Such cultural codes are lost to modern audiences, for whom fencing is a specialized sport. Nevertheless, the fighting display that Silver recounts and the fencing match which Claudius sets up share a common dependency on the performative nature of the event. Both are kinds of traps: the Silvers did all they could to rig the fight by conditioning the audience to think of the Italians as the 'bad guys'. Play fighting and real fighting vie with each other for audiences to ascribe victory and defeat, but both script audiences by carefully managing the structures of performance. For Silver, everything goes to plan, but then he has the benefit of being the victor writing history, and he had a shrewd business interest in disparaging his Italian competition.

In *Hamlet*, the performative structure of fighting, of a stage divided between audience and performed, is hollowed out by the memory of real violence. In the narrative of the play, this is the memory of Hamlet's murder, the primal scene on which the story hangs. In the ancient performance culture of fighting, it is the primal scene of the battlefield which haunts the gentlemanly display of arms, a savage violence which tugs at the formality of show, and finally erupts and destabilizes the match, transforming a ritualized display of martial skill into a stage full of bodies. When Fortinbras discovers this carnage, and sees Hamlet dead, he commands four of his captains to carry his body 'like a soldier, to the stage' and orders 'soldier's music and the rites of war' to 'speak loudly for him'. He orders all the bodies removed, because the spectacle 'Becomes the field, but here shows much amiss', before ordering the soldiers to shoot, their peal of ordnance closing the play. Through Fortinbras, Shakespeare underlines the extent to which the ghost of the battlefield has possessed the chivalric codes of the fencing match. In opening his play to an alternative performance tradition rooted in martial arts, Shakespeare was able to recover its ancient violence. Hamlet the scholar finally becomes his father, clothed in imagined armour, his body borne up on to a scaffold where Horatio will tell his story.

Pure motion: the modern stage-fight director

The modern fight director is an integral part of Shakespeare performance. Reflecting on the impact of this role, Richard Lane, who has the
enviable job title of 'Executive Director of the Academy of the Sword',
notes the extent to which modern Shakespeare theatre is made through
the heightened choreography of stage fighting: 'When two characters
fight on stage, the conflict that has motivated them in the story escalates
beyond words. What was before left to dialogue, stage direction, and
voice inflection now becomes the province of pure motion. Audiences,
too, become more focused during a fight' (2). Lane advocates a practical approach to fighting which imitates the commitment of actors to
the text and the creation of character by arguing that actors need to
'get inside' the fight. This is an aspect of theatremaking that rarely gets
outside again. When a fight scene becomes part of the analysis, we usually ascribe its artistic success to the performance's director. I have been
guilty of this omission in my own work. In an earlier book, I devoted
a chapter to Jane Howell's BBC production of Shakespeare's first tetral-
ogy. In order to make sense of the four plays' many battles, Howell
convened a second company to work exclusively on the fight scenes
under the direction of fight director Malcolm Ransom. The result was a
bifold performance with two companies working together to produce a
hybrid of a stage play and a martial arts play, with the increasingly dire,
traumatic battle scenes acting as an ironic counterpoint and an emotive
undertow to the play itself. The text's many appeals to chivalric hero-
ism and providential history contrasted with bloody, desperate scenes
of men being killed in battle. In analysing these scenes, I referred only
to Howell as the guiding artistic voice realizing this anti-play – but I was
always aware that Ransom's role in the creative process needed more
explaining (Hampton-Reeves and Rutter 114–33). As we have seen,
although Shakespeare left it to actors to decide how to play a fight, in
a number of his plays the outcome of a fight drives the story – and if
the fight comes at the end of the play, as it does in *Lear*, *Hamlet*, *Richard
III* and *Macbeth*, then the way in which the fight is staged can have a
massive, even definitive, impact on the performance's rendering of the
text. In other words, the fight director has the gift to influence the story
that the performance tells.

Fight directors rarely talk about their work, or about their relationship
with actors and directors. When they do, or when actors talk about how
they worked with them, it is clear how much they contribute to the
performance itself. In his co-authored manual on stage fighting, John

Waller includes as an appendix a remarkable account of his staging of Richard's final fight with Richmond for the Royal National Theatre's *Richard III* (1990) with Ian McKellen playing an Oswald Mosley figure. Although McKellen wore 1930s dress for most of the performance, for the final fight, the director Richard Eyre wanted him to wear medieval armour. Waller started with the idea that Richard was not an invalid, but a 'highly mobile mounted figure' (Ducklin and Waller 187). To get a feel for the part, McKellen even rehearsed in a replica steel harness of the kind worn during the Wars of the Roses. Through working together, a shared interpretation of the fight emerged which coloured McKellen's performance. Waller explained, 'I believe that Richard's deformity should be seen less in physical terms, and more as a symbol of the character's failure to accord with the medieval and Elizabethan image of the *parfait* knight, the warrior who was physically and spiritually perfect' (188). This is an insight which reflects Waller's interest in martial arts, but it is nevertheless an interpretation which contributed to the performance. In choreographing Richard's movements, Waller deliberately played against Richard's own remarks about his deformities. But not only was this Richard capable of being very agile, he was also a deformed version of what it meant to be a martial artist – a twisted, corrupted version of the spiritual as well as physical character of the warrior. Waller introduces this idea as his own – although it was agreed with Eyre and McKellen, possibly even influenced by them, in introducing the reading Waller does not defer to them or distance himself from the idea. He could have written, 'Eyre believed ...', so relegating himself to the role of a backstage hand, who does what he is told and serves to fulfil the director's vision. Waller is quite clear, however: 'I believe ...', he starts, as he elaborates the guiding thoughts and readings behind his choreography.

Waller's notes to the actors elaborate this point, to the extent that Waller went further than simply notating a series of fight moves, and included directorial interpretation. For example, he prefaced his notes by instructing the actors that during 'the fight everyone should be aware that RICHARD is like a wild boar surrounded by hounds waiting for the hunter to finish him off'. Waller gave other actors on stage the latitude to develop their performance in their own way within this framework, so long as they understood that Richard was a cornered, vicious animal. He continues: 'All keep tense – when RICHMOND is in danger close in to help; when he recovers, back off; change postures during fight – adopt different aggressive stances' (188). By defining the rules for the other actors on stage, Waller ensured that Richard was always the centre of attention, and always alone. Richmond receives aid; Richard is the target of aggressive stances.

The rest of the notes are very precise, and reveal the extent of Waller's contribution to the performance. The following extract provides a flavour of them:

IAN Cuts down at C's head

COLIN Defends, sword point left, elbow right

IAN Thrusts at C's groin (aim upstage)

COLIN Beats aside, blade down right

IAN Backhand cuts left to right across C's stomach, then forehand cuts to stomach right and left

COLIN Jumps back both times, then cuts down at I's head

IAN Steps into attack, blocks with sword, point left, elbow right, takes C's sword down right, barges C with left shoulder

COLIN Staggers back stage-left

(188)

Each line is an instruction for the use of the blade, and the position of one or both actors' bodies. Taken together, the fight is structured around the physical interplay of body and weapon. By fragmenting the body of the *parfait knight* into head, elbow, groin and stomach, Waller enacts in note form his core interpretative idea that Richard is a failed knight. However, Waller's notes say more about what this looks like than how the illusion of fighting should be created. Presumably C (Colin Hurley) did not really cut down at I's head, nor did I actually barge C with his left shoulder. The notes describe the fiction of the fight rather than capturing the underlying pretence. This would have been achieved in rehearsal, where Waller worked directly with the actors to help them realize his narrative into a convincing stage fight. The notes present their own kind of performance.

Waller's approach contrasts with that of Terry King, who puts much more emphasis on working with his actors to build a performance layer by layer. King's work with actors usually begins early on in rehearsals, and although directors will have initial meetings with him, most of

King's work is done without the director present. Speaking to the BBC, King said, 'usually your initial talk is with the director, and very often the director will be in the fight rehearsals maybe for the beginning, but to be honest, most of them get bored quite quickly, because it is slow'. Videos of his work in rehearsal on a production called *His Dark Materials* (2004) posted on the Royal National Theatre website (www.stagework. org.uk) show the extent to which the work of the fight director overlaps with and even substitutes for the work of the director. In one video, of a fight scene between two bears played by actors holding (rather than wearing) a bear mask and a single bear paw, King controls the space while the director sits at the back quietly observing. King plans the movements and takes the actors through the script for the fight, but he then builds upon that layers of expression and performance which texture and interpret the fight. He pushes the actors to develop their performance and even (like many directors) demonstrates what he wants them to do by jumping into the performance space and doing it himself. He intervenes in the performance without interrupting it, the actors continuing to circle in battle mode as he narrates the performance. Although King is not on stage for the actual performance, the actors will be expected to internalize his commentary so that, for the actors at least, King is present when they fight, his narration of the fight an invisible part of the performance that the audience sees.

King brings to his work the skill to turn a fight script into a multi-faceted performance. In one of the accompanying interviews, King explains that he does not regard stage fighting as 'combat' at all, but as 'co-operation' between two actors. Actors have to work together to make the fight believable. King acknowledges that sometimes real animosities between actors can manifest themselves in stage fights; however, he feels that, ironically, such fights rarely have the same impact as one in which the actors are working together. The conflict should be between the characters, he insists, not between the actors. These are shrewd points, but they are also, crucially, interpretative points that reveal King's ability to contribute to the artistic achievement of the performance. His stage fights are often highly psychological, and bring out dramatic character conflict in ways which enhance, and sometimes even define, performance interpretation.

Terry King designed the fights for Gregory Doran's 2008 RSC *Hamlet*, when the line between play fighting and real fighting was mapped onto the production's aesthetic split between an Edwardian aristocracy and a modern working class. Hamlet's melancholic dissonance is often signalled through costume, but instead of putting Hamlet in mourning weeds, Doran dressed the actor David Tennant in a blue parka, black cap, jeans and Converse trainers. It was only in the play's final scene, with its multiple layers of artifice, that Hamlet started to behave more like the stately courtiers that he despised. Through blocking, Doran had already established a sharp contrast between Hamlet's impish restlessness, as he darted about the stage never wanting to be defined or contained, and the stately, still world of the court. A large, cracked mirror that dominated the rear of the set in the Courtyard Theatre signalled the flaws in Elsinore's cut-glass world, but it was through Hamlet's fencing duel with Laertes (Edward Bennett) that this fault line finally tore that world apart. Doran established Laertes as a character who could almost be Hamlet himself, jumping into Ophelia's grave and pulling her body from it with passionate anguish, her head escaping from the shroud she was wrapped in. In this earlier scene, Laertes attacked Hamlet viciously, grabbing him in a headlock (echoing the way he held Ophelia, played by Mariah Gale) and then clutching Hamlet's throat in an attempt to stop him speaking. Hamlet tried to reason with Laertes, but he refused to listen and lunged at Hamlet mid-speech like an animal diving on its prey. Just as Claudius (Patrick Stewart) could not bear Hamlet's excessive grief in Act 1, now Claudius was equally worried by Laertes' uncontainable anger and grief. Through the duel, Claudius was able to find a way to contain this frightening excess breaking into his careful, ordered world.

Hamlet and Laertes' costume signalled their different attitudes to the fight. Hamlet wore a fencing shirt with jeans and trainers, only paying lip service to the formality of the occasion. He overplayed the show, refusing to take any of it seriously, but he could also, and suddenly, be deadly serious. Laertes, by contrast, was in full fencing gear and he approached the fight seriously, sullenly. The psychology of the fight was established before a blow had been struck. Hamlet still subversively refused to play the game in any way except his own. Laertes did everything right, wore the right clothes, played the right moves, but was also doing little to conceal (from Hamlet at least) his determination to use the play for revenge. Hamlet was suddenly serious when he put his mask on, as if inhabiting a role, but he then went further, posturing, bending his knee, leaning forward, rocking back and forth, in a parody of a fashionable fencer, in front of the disdainful Laertes. The scene hovered between fight and play from the moment they put their swords together, stroking each other's blades, building up tension by sounding steel against steel, waiting for the signal to start the fight. As soon as Osric put his hand down, Hamlet leapt forward and hit Laertes on his rump. Doran called this a 'cheeky jumping in': Hamlet was not just fencing, he was playing. In the prompt book, this action is added on a

Post-it note, as if put in as an afterthought, with the line 'Hamlet taps Laertes on bum'. Laertes protested indignantly but Claudius, amused, allowed the point. Hamlet's 'palpable hit' was nothing more than a boyish prank. At this point, the director and fight director have to work together as part of the narrative play seeps into the fight. Claudius needs to get Hamlet to drink the poisoned wine. Hamlet needs to refuse it, the wine needs to make its way to Gertrude. Here, Hamlet was too irritated by Laertes' attempt to cheat to pause for a drink, so he called for another bout, brushing the drink away.

This time the temperature of the fight was raised. As they touched blades waiting for the signal to start, Laertes raised his other hand aggressively. Hamlet put his hand behind his back, mocking Laertes, and he kept his hand back as they fought. He won his point with his hand literally behind his back. He was showing off. For the next bout (played just after Gertrude drank the wine), Laertes refused to wait for Hamlet to get ready and lunged at him before Hamlet had a chance to put his mask on. Now the fight became furious, Laertes spinning to give his blows extra force. Hamlet was on the back foot, and had to fight hard just to avoid being hit. King's choreography made it look like this action was unscripted, the formal rules of play giving way to a fast, energetic, even desperate chase around the stage, with courtiers fleeing as Laertes rushed through the onstage audience. Their 'play' became physical as Laertes grabbed Hamlet. Hamlet broke free, but Laertes broke the rules of play again by attacking him from behind. Even though Hamlet began the fencing match acting by not taking it seriously, King made sure that it was Laertes who transgressed the rules of play and forced Hamlet into a fight.

King took an unusual approach to Hamlet's wound. This is often just a small nick in the arm, since Laertes only needs to draw a little blood to make sure that his poisoned blade works. This Laertes drew his sword fast across the back of Hamlet's neck. Hamlet winced and felt his neck, then looked at the blood on his hand disbelievingly. Fencing swords are meant to be blunted, but Hamlet realized that Laertes had unblunted his rapier. He put down his foil and ran at Laertes, grabbing him in a headlock. All pretence at play was gone. This was the moment that King was able to arrange for the two swords to be switched. Having wounded Hamlet, Laertes had already put his sword away when Hamlet attacked him. When they disengaged, Hamlet ran to get Laertes' sword and swiped it viciously at his unarmed opponent. He was furious. This was a key moment for the performance. Doran had put the interval in the middle of 3.3, with Hamlet poised to kill Claudius as the lights went down on the first part. When the audience returned, the scene continued with Hamlet backing away from Claudius. Hamlet's failure to respond then was recalled and released as Hamlet swung his foil around the stage. The Courtyard Theatre has a thrust stage, so those in the front rows were very close to the actors and their blades, close enough to feel threatened. The fight concluded with Hamlet giving Laertes exactly the same wound (and, without realizing it, with the same sword). This was revenge, this was retribution. Laertes seemed to accept the wound. He stood for a moment before Hamlet struck, able to step away, and seemed about to flinch. His shoulders sank, he tightened the muscles in his face, but he did not move as Hamlet pulled his blade sharply across the neck.

Bennett, Tennant and King worked on the fight together for some time before they brought their work into rehearsal. To begin with, the fight was plotted out in small sections at an extremely slow pace to make sure the actors understood and internalized the moves. Doran and King had initial meetings at which they developed a 'really specific storyboard' (in Doran's words) to structure the fight. Unlike Waller, King does not seem to have written down a narrative description of the fight. Instead, the prompt book records a series of moves which skeletalize the fight, as in:

> La attacks Hamlet
> Osric pushed SL
> Ho x SL
> then Ham faint, shoulder, hip, hip, model
> Ham x CS
> Circle parrie [sic] (L) shoulder, hip shoulder
> Turn (L) pushed DSC
> Shoulder, hip, hip, shoulder grab wrist section
> La clips back H neck as he walks away[2]

These notes recall Waller's only to the extent that they focus on parts of the body, which are here dismembered into percussive lines that sound like the instructions for a country dance: 'shoulder, hip, hip, shoulder'. The prompt book may not be the only record made of the fight, since

---

[2] The prompt book uses standard abbreviations to denote places on the stage: SL (stage left), DSC (downstage centre), CS (centre stage). Other abbreviations indicate character names.

fighting directors' own notes are often not archived. They script physical action, but it is through performance that its narrative emerges. In an interview for the BBC, Bennett explained that the fight was more physically taxing for him than for Tennant because so much of the emphasis is on Laertes and his wild attempts to injure Hamlet: 'Terry King … very carefully plotted in to make sure that Laertes was always on the attack, and only when Hamlet finds out that the sword has been unblunted does he go on the attack, so it's very carefully scripted'. (Videos of the making of Gregory Doran's *Hamlet* are available online at http://www.bbc.co.uk/hamlet.)

Keith Osborn, who played Fortinbras, recalls that their object was to create a fencing scene that 'gets wilder and more out of control as it evolves' (97). Creating a sense of disorder required meticulous planning and training. As well as working separately with King, Bennett and Tennant were required to rehearse their fight moves before every performance. When the fight was brought into the rehearsal room, Doran started to build up a performance around it. Osborn puts this in a revealing way: 'Doran layers on the acting and reactions of the court' (101). He *layered* acting onto the fight. Osborn has chosen exactly the right word to describe the critical relationship between fight director and acting director. King created the fight with the actors, and it seems that Doran then added layers of performance to it to help create a sense of chaos on stage. Through their reactions, their panic, the other actors were able to create a sense of disaster which made the intricately planned fight seem as if it were out of control. The fight was subsequently restaged and filmed. Although the production had ended six months before, Tennant and Bennett went through exactly the same moves again for the film version. The film is a good record of the movements and psychological undertow that King, with Doran, developed for the production. However, the film does not capture the visceral experience of watching a fight. It does not capture the danger and the thrill of feeling the actors' physical presence as they rushed across the narrow thrust stage of the Courtyard Theatre.

Conclusion

The stage fights in Shakespeare plays are a fundamental part of the ways that his works made and continue to make theatre. Shakespeare wrote for a culture expert in sword-fighting and other forms of combat, for whom the spectacle of fighting was as important as the story itself. We do not know the extent to which Shakespeare attempted to meet that level of expectation, and certainly he was not shy of apologizing for theatre's inability to reproduce the realities of war. However, Shakespeare exploited the dramatic potential of fighting. In doing so, he opened textual drama to an ancient performance tradition of martial arts. He contained this radically different form of theatre within words, characters and stories, but he also seems to acknowledge the inability of the written word to ever fully contain the physical energies of fighting, or the visceral pleasure of watching two people fight. The work of modern stage-fight directors has returned to the stage a level of sophistication that demands critical attention and challenges the resources of Shakespeare-performance criticism to find a way of engaging with the nonverbal, physical theatre that they have rediscovered.

10
Audiences

Sarah Werner

The subject of this chapter is at once both utterly obvious and baf-
flingly inexplicable. While on the one hand it is a commonplace that
theatre needs, at minimum, both performers and audience, on the other
hand, there is rarely sufficient questioning of what it is that audiences
do. What does the presence of an audience bring to the dynamic of a
performance? In Jerzy Grotowski's words, theatre is 'what takes place
between spectator and actor' (32). But what is it that actually takes
place? Consider the list of questions we could ask about that relationship between spectator and actor:

- Are audiences passive receptacles for a performance's meaning, ide-
  ally infused with the sense of the actors' performance but in danger,
  on the flip side, of utterly failing to understand what the performance is telling them?
- Or does an audience participate in a performance, bringing their own
  reactions and sensibilities to bear upon the meanings that are created
  in performance? Are they makers of meaning rather than receptacles
  for it?
- Is an audience a collective body, something of which we can speak
  in the singular?
- Or are audiences collections of individual bodies, an aggregation of
  many different responses that should more accurately be described
  in the plural?

This chapter will not answer these questions definitively – these are
questions that cannot be answered definitively, and it is not the purpose
of this book to theorize the reception of theatre. Rather, I want to
foreground these questions in order to think about how assumptions

about the role of audience might affect how Shakespeare is made in the theatre.

In exploring the role of audiences, I focus on today's audiences in today's theatres. Other scholars have speculated about early modern audiences, but such work is not only speculative (if it can be difficult to know what today's audiences are doing, it is even harder to ascribe responses to past audiences), but also often unproductive for today's practitioners. If early modern audiences were rowdy, does that mean that today's audiences should be? And if they are rowdy, are they being so in the same way that a 1590s audience would have been? To focus on today's audiences does not, of course, completely eliminate a consideration of early audiences. Whether they are the same or not, both audiences are responding to a script that is approximately the same and both audiences watch their own contemporaries performing that script on stage. And, indeed, those scripts make clear that audiences are often centrally involved to the performance of a play. When *Hamlet* opens with the question, 'Who's there?' the answer is not only Francisco and Bernardo, but also that we are always there. As Bridget Escolme (2005) has argued, the moments of audience address in Shakespeare's plays are the moments that give shape to the characters on stage and to our attitudes towards them, moments that raise fundamental questions about how and who we are. But audiences' interactions with a performance are shaped by extra-textual matters as well: playhouse architecture, performer interactions, the personal lives of spectators (see Knowles for a persuasive account of the myriad factors shaping audience reception). All these elements come together in affecting the two-way interactions between audience and performance.

Many (though not all) of the performances I discuss in this chapter are not typical of Shakespearean productions, especially in their conscious efforts to highlight the interactions between actor and audience. But if they are atypical, what seems different about them showcases more effectively those elements of making theatre and making audiences that are true for all productions.

Audience address: in text and on stage

The most obvious place to start thinking about audience is in those moments where they are clearly being addressed. Roles like that of the Chorus in *Henry V*, Gower in *Pericles*, Time in *The Winter's Tale* and Rumour in *2 Henry IV* exist to present the play to the audience; they speak directly to the spectators, influencing their perception of the story. As their names indicate, they are less characters than roles, appearing not so much as fully-fledged people than as windows into the play. They are not, of course, necessarily transparent windows. Rumour identifies his bias from the start, but leaves unsaid what the connection might be between the rumours that he tells us are being spread and the action that follows – what is the connection between history and theatre and rumour? The Chorus is even more slippery, presenting himself as a neutral master of ceremonies who will help the audience imagine the real story behind the actors' fictions, addressing the audience in order to encourage them to 'Piece out our imperfections with your thoughts' (*Henry V*, Prologue, 23). But is his the only point of view in the play? Compare his speech at the start of Act 3 extolling the heroics of all Englishmen, 'For who is he, whose chin is but enriched / With one appearing hair, that will not follow / These culled and choice-drawn cavaliers to France?' (3.0.22–4), with the scene 45 lines later, when Nim, Bardolph and Pistol expressively refuse to follow Henry once more unto the breach at Harfleur. The Chorus might directly address the audience, but the play stages actions that present an alternate point of view, one that is less boosterish of Henry and more cynical about his motives and actions.

We are, of course, generally taught that Shakespeare's characters do not lie to the audience, or to themselves: when they speak in soliloquy, they are speaking what is true to them. In the opening scene of *As You Like It*, after Oliver has fought with his brother Orlando and set him up to lose in the wrestling match, he speaks alone on stage and confesses:

> I hope I shall see an end of him, for my soul – and I know not why – hates nothing more than he. Yet he's gentle; never schooled, and yet learned; full of noble device; of all sorts enchantingly beloved; and, indeed, so much in the heart of the world, and especially of my own people, who best know him, that I am altogether misprized. But it shall not be so long.
>
> (1.1.139–45)

The speech is, in part, plot information. The audience is likely to be wondering why Oliver treats Orlando as he does; here Orlando explains it. He hates Orlando because everyone else loves him, though he also insists that he does not know why he hates him; there both is and is not reason for that hatred, but the speech emphasizes that hatred is at the heart of Oliver's actions. There are other addresses to the audience that have the same effect of commenting on a character's actions. In *The*

Taming of the Shrew, what is Petruccio up to in refusing to let Katherine eat? He tells us in a soliloquy midway through the play:

> My falcon now is sharp and passing empty,
> And till she stoop she must not be full-gorged,
> For then she never looks upon her lure.
>
> This is a way to kill a wife with kindness,
> And thus I'll curb her mad and headstrong humour.
> (4.1.171–3, 189–90)

And now we know what Petruccio is doing: he is taming Katherine, just as one might train a falcon.

The question to ask about these moments of direct address is not why the character is saying these lines, but why is the character saying these lines to the audience. If the purpose of moments such as these is to provide plot information and explanation, then why not have the character explicate his actions to another character on stage? Could Petruccio not divulge his strategy to Grumio? The last lines of Petruccio's speech help us understand what is lost if it were delivered to another character: 'He that knows better how to tame a shrew, / Now let him speak. 'Tis charity to show' (4.1.191–2). The speech does not simply state information but draws the audience into the situation, making the audience complicit in Petruccio's actions, or at least making them question their relationship to those actions. Delivered to another character, the challenge of Petruccio's last lines stays within the fictional world of the play; delivered to the audience, the challenge expands to us all. The inclusion of the audience also shifts the responsibility for a character's actions. By including us in his strategy, and by staying silent when questioned, do we become complicit in Petruccio's treatment of Katherine? Escolme, in her study of the effects of audience address, argues that when a performer shares his or her process with the audience, speaking to them and involving them in the performance, a spectator becomes invested in that character. In her account of watching Antony Sher's Macbeth, Escolme wonders at her inability to pass judgement: 'I can't judge Macbeth because I feel partially responsible for the figure he becomes in the act of performing to me' (2005: 4). (See the next section for more on audience response to Petruccio's soliloquy.)

If it seems obvious while reading the text that Oliver's and Petruccio's lines are addressed to the audience, other moments in Shakespeare's plays are less clear-cut. When Lear finds himself arguing with Goneril over the behaviour of his retinue, he expresses his outrage over the insult:

> Does any here know me? This is not Lear.
> Does Lear walk thus, speak thus? Where are his eyes?
> Either his notion weakens, his discernings
> Are lethargied – ha, waking? 'Tis not so.
> Who is it that can tell me who I am?
>
> (First Folio, 1.4.191–5)

Within the fictional world of the play, these are questions addressed to the other onstage characters, with the fallacy of his outrage punctured when (in the First Folio version of the play) the Fool answers his final question: 'Lear's shadow' (1.4.196). But in performance, are those questions that also take in the audience? Does Lear turn to the audience to include them in his address? Does the audience consider themselves addressed even if Lear does not look at them? If we are addressed, how is our relationship to Lear and to *Lear* affected?

The moments in which a character explicitly or implicitly addresses the audience are moments that obviously create space for a production to speak to its audience and for the audience to speak back. But it is helpful to remember that unspoken moments can invite the audience in; problems in character motivation, for instance, can create a gap that an audience fills with its own sense of consistency. Leontes' outsized jealousy often proves a stumbling block in *The Winter's Tale*: why is he so convinced that his wife is having an affair with his best friend? How can he dismiss her and their infant daughter so quickly? The script does not provide words to obviously answer these questions, but that absence need not be a block for the audience. In the 2009 production I saw directed by Sam Mendes for The Bridge Project, those questions were not answered explicitly, but were called attention to by the production's repetition of the haunting lullaby that Leontes hummed when tucking his son in at the start of the play and instinctively reprised when he briefly comforted his infant daughter before putting her aside and turning away. That soundscape, in drawing on the audience's own experiences of parenthood (ticket prices and venues meant that the audiences in Brooklyn and London included many adults of parenting age), used those audience memories to generate a sense of both of Leontes' loss in refusing his baby and of investment in that baby's welfare. What is left blank in the text is filled in in the production by the audience's emotional response. (See Hartley, 2010 for an exploration of the phenomenology of theatre that makes both possible and necessary such responses.)

These examples have all been focused on the connections made with audiences by looking at the text for openings to invite them in. But it is also important to look at the theatre into which you are inviting them. How will the auditorium and the surrounding space shape the audience's expectations and experiences of the performance? The theatre in which I saw *The Winter's Tale*, the Brooklyn Academy of Music's Harvey Theater, was built originally as a playhouse, then converted to a cinema in the 1940s, and abandoned in the late 1960s. The Academy converted it back to a theatrical space in 1987, renovating much of the performance space while leaving remnants of the theatre's faded past visible in the architectural details and peeling paint. The result is a space that is both grand and faded, one that lends itself to a privileged nostalgia and that helped create the sense of longing that pervaded that production of *The Winter's Tale*.

Responding to the past: the Globe's reconstructed playhouse

Reactions to moments such as those I have just discussed depend in part on what other cues an audience is picking up on their relationship to the performance and on how performers conceptualize their relationship to the audience. For while there can be signs in the text of direct address, there are no signs of how an audience might respond and no guarantee that an audience will react the way in which a performer expects. In her Shakespeare in Production edition of *The Taming of the Shrew*, Elizabeth Schafer records a range of performance strategies that have been employed for Petruccio's taming soliloquy, discussed above. As she explains in her note, 'This is a crucial speech which will affect how the audience feel about the treatment of Katherina' (180). But her edition also records the resistance that audiences can put up to what they see and hear on stage. In the archival video of the 1978 Shakespeare in the Park production in New York, when Petruccio paused after 'He that knows better how to tame a shrew, / Now let him speak', a woman in the audience is recorded 'shouting out and suggesting Petruchio [*sic*] try a little tenderness'; the actor playing the role, Raúl Juliá, 'suggested that would be less dramatic but added "I thank thee for thy advice"' (183). This anecdote is revealing in many ways: it touches on the place of gender equality in the late 1970s, on the popularity of Otis Redding, and on the star appeal of Raúl Juliá. But it also reveals how audience response is shaped by the nature of the performance; most observers would agree that it is rare for a spectator to shout back at a production, but observers would also agree that audience behaviour at a free, open-air perform-ance is different from that in a mainstream, indoor theatre.

Shouting back at a production is extreme, but other indications of audience response are not, and thus might be more suitable to exploring what factors shape the reception of a performance. To that end, I want to consider a moment in a 2008 performance of *King Lear* at Shakespeare's Globe Theatre in London.[1] This moment comes late in the production, in the last act. By this point in the performance, the audience has seen the division of the kingdom, riotous knights, naked wretches mingling with the audience during the storm scene, and – most horrifyingly – a sexualized blinding of Gloucester, in which the plucking out of his eyes turns into an act of foreplay for Cornwall and, especially, Regan. Cordelia has reappeared in the story, dressed in a modest grey dress with a wimple-like head-covering, and has been reunited and then captured with her father. Goneril and Regan have battled for Edmund's attention, Regan has been poisoned by Goneril, and Albany has discovered Goneril's love for Edmund and their plot to kill him. After Edgar's defeat of Edmund, Goneril laments, 'Thou are not vanquished, / But cozened and beguiled' (5.3.143–4). At this line, Albany turns to her with his response, 'Shut your mouth, dame' (144), and the audience laughs – not a chuckle, or a murmur, but a full-throated laugh, accompanied by cheers and applause.

Why does the audience laugh? What is funny about this moment? I don't recall that the actor playing Albany set up this line as a laugh point. Nor do I recall this line in other productions getting such a reac-tion. So what is happening here? One possibility is that the line is funny because it sounds so very modern, so very much like how we talk today. It doesn't use words like 'cozened' or even 'vanquished', there's no 'thy', there are no metaphors about names being 'By treason's tooth bare-gnawn and canker-bit' (*King Lear* 5.3.112). Instead, 'shut your mouth' is something colloquial and accessible, something an angry person today might say to someone who has betrayed them.

One possible understanding of this moment, then, is that 'shut your mouth' can provoke laughter in the shock of its familiarity. It is also possible that the audience laughs because they are relieved that Goneril

---

[1] I saw an evening performance on Wednesday, 23 July 2008, seated in the Lower Gallery.

is finally getting her comeuppance. She's been plotting against Albany and planning not only his death but those of her father and sisters. Is this the moment the villain gets caught, and good triumphs? It can get a laugh not necessarily because it's funny, but because it is a moment of release from the tension driving the accumulation of bad deeds, an audience endorsement of Albany's judgement against Goneril. But this is also a deeply gendered moment in a text that is full of slanders against women and in a production that flattened out any nuances of female behaviour; in this *King Lear*, Regan and Goneril are especially evil, and Cordelia is especially good – a dynamic that does no favours to the audience appeal of any of them. The laughter and applause of the audience at this moment seem not only directed against Goneril, but against Goneril as a woman, a woman who has been held up by Lear and by this production as emblematic of all women's unkindness. Edmund's revelation as a villain is not greeted nearly as enthusiastically as Goneril's as a villainess. Much of that is due to the dynamics of the playscript; those dynamics are further exaggerated by the choices of this production.

In the early years of the Globe, journalists reviewing its productions tended to judge its audience as having the wrong response, looking down on them as tourists jollying up their London visit by pretending they were at a Disneyland experience rather than appreciating the theatrical importance of Shakespeare (see Prescott). It can be tempting, from the perspective of a Shakespeare or theatre scholar, to feel that an audience fails to appreciate a performance; Helen Freshwater provides many examples of the sort of tensions and disdain that can run these lines (42–55). The moment I have described could certainly be seen as the audience failing to get what was happening in the play; it could equally be described as a failure on the production's part to get what Shakespeare was trying to do. But neither explanation addresses the ways in which meanings accrue in a performance through a variety of routes.

For instance, in exploring this moment of audience response, ought we to consider the impact of the reconstructed playhouse? In a theatre building that prides itself on its Renaissance construction, how much of the audience response is shaped by how it conceives Renaissance culture? What sort of cues are audiences getting from the playhouse (and its description in the programme) that might allow for this response? Might the acceptance of the play's nasty stereotypes of women be licensed by what the audience imagines is the appropriate 'Renaissance' response?

A second moment of laughter from a Globe production is helpful to consider here, this time focused on Rosalind in a 2009 performance of

As You Like It: 'Do you not know I am a woman? When I think, I must speak' (3.2.227–8).[2] Unlike 'shut your mouth', this line is obviously intended to be a laugh line. What I found surprising was that it got such *big* laughs, and applause, too. I don't recall that the actor playing Rosalind hit that line any harder than any of her other laugh lines. And I don't recall other productions getting the same huge response at that moment. In the same summer's RSC production, at the performance I saw, the line got some laughs from the audience, but scattered laughs, mixed in with some mutters of disapproval (which seemed to me to be directed not towards the actor, but towards the audience's laughter at the stereotype). And in the 1998 Globe production, the same line also got only scattered laughs. At the 2009 Globe performance I saw, however, the audience response was enormous, so much so that it reminded me of the *King Lear* that I saw there the previous summer.

As You Like It, of course, has a very different gendered dynamic than *King Lear*. It has its misogyny, including the slanders against women that Rosalind voices in the persona of Ganymede-as-Rosalind. But it is not generally a play that encourages a black-and-white view of women. Why, then, such an enthusiastic audience endorsement of the stereotype of the woman who cannot hold her tongue?

The answer, I think, lies in part in the contemporary note that I noticed in 'shut your mouth'. This *As You Like It* was a version that played up the comedy with plenty of anachronistic mugging from Touchstone – at his entrance into Arden he does a sarcastic, but recognizably modern, arms-in-the-air victory dance (a dance that went sour when he stepped in some shit). And when Jaques explains the meaning of 'ducdame' (2.5.53), he gestures so that the fools called into a circle are not the foresters (as is typical), but the Globe audience. In these ways, and in others, the production encouraged a participatory identification, setting up a dynamic in which the audience moves back into a Renaissance frame of mind, but moves back through the presentness of the play, through moments that are recognizably familiar. Jokes such as the seeming stumble Touchstone made when talking about 'Your "if" is the only pacemaker – peacemaker, not pacemaker' (5.4.91–2) reinforce the immediacy of the performance both by letting audiences feel the thrill of thinking they saw a mistake by

[2] I saw a matinee performance on Friday, 26 June 2009, seated in the Lower Gallery.

the performer and by reminding them that this is a twenty-first-century
actor playing to twenty-first-century spectators.[3]

These anachronistic moments help the audience see themselves in
the play. But they might also give licence to a politics in the audience
that is not set free in other venues. What attitudes do audiences bring
with them to reconstructed theatres, and how might those politics play
out? If a theatrical space that looks early modern – that sells itself as
being connected to original practices – is a safe haven for at least some
audience members to give voice to anti-feminist sentiments, what does
that mean for actors and directors who might not intend those politics
to come into play, or who might wish to counter those politics? I want
to emphasize that I am not insisting that the plays need to be staged as
feminist, or through any particular political discourse. But an awareness
of audience responses is a necessary part of creating a theatrical event.
And for performances in reconstructed theatrical spaces, the question of
what assumptions an audience brings to that space – and how their gender politics are shaped by that space – needs to be further explored.

Foregrounding spectatorship: the Toneelgroep's *Roman Tragedies*

So far I have been considering how audiences shape the meanings
they find in and take from performances. But it is also possible to
see audiences as more immediately being part of a performance. The
Toneelgroep Amsterdam's production of *Roman Tragedies* is one example of how audiences can become part of a performance in ways that
complicate both what they are watching and the act of watching.
Roman Tragedies is a six-hour performance of *Coriolanus, Julius Caesar*
and *Antony and Cleopatra* that toured internationally in 2009–10.
Directed by Ivo van Hove, and featuring a cast of actors as well as stage
technicians who video and project live action and recorded clips, the
production also centrally involved audience members who are invited
on stage, where they can sit on sofas to watch the live performance and
the video playing on monitors, and where they buy and consume food
and drinks. (Christian Billing's review of the production, which he saw

---

[3] I refer to this as a seeming mistake because another spectator at a performance
on 13 June describes the same joke on Peter Kirwan's blog, *The Bardathon*. For
more on why a performer would want to pretend to make a mistake, see Nicholas
Ridout's compelling analysis of audience responses to failure (129–60).

in its London venue, provides a detailed and thoughtful description of how the performance worked.)

It might be tempting to describe this as participatory theatre, the sort of communal, empowering enterprise that is often associated with Augusto Boal's Forum Theatre (see Freshwater 55–76 for a history of this theatre movement and a thoughtful critique of its limitations). And many of the reviews and buzz surrounding the show had to do with the movement of the audience, which was treated, correctly so, as a novelty for Shakespearean theatre. But the effect of this audience movement situated spectators not as participants in the drama, but as fractured consumers of it. Audience members did not interact with the actors, even when seated next to them. And much of the time, especially for those seated on stage, spectators preferred to watch the videos playing on the screens in front of them, rather than the live actors next to them. Even when occupying the same space, audience and actors did not share the stage.

One effect of this was to highlight the ways in which all spectators see different performances. Even in traditionally designed theatre, one individual audience member will react to and understand a performance differently than another audience member. In *Roman Tragedies*, each member of the audience experienced the production from a different perspective, whether that perspective came from where in the theatre or stage they were sitting or from which monitor they were watching. (Of course, spectators were not required to move around during the performance, and there were certainly people who chose not to do so. I was one of those: when I saw the production in Montreal, I stayed in the same seat in the auditorium for the whole six hours.)

While highlighting the multiple perspectives of the audience was one result of the audience staging, a more prominent effect was to situate the audience as passive consumers of the spectacle and politics being played out in the performance. For even while the audience moved to and from the auditorium to the stage, they did so at the behest of the production: loudspeaker announcements urged audience members to come on stage after the first twenty minutes and shooed them back to their seats for the final hour of the performance. The audience's movements were both encouraged and circumscribed in ways reflecting the production's larger themes. In reshaping Shakespeare's plays for his *Roman Tragedies*, van Hove not only updated the *mise-en-scène* to a modern world of politics (complete with power suits, Senate hearings, and omnipresent media broadcasts), but he cut out all the scenes of the plebeians: there were no citizens listening to Coriolanus' plea, no murdering Cinna the Poet, no guards querying Antony's effeminization by Cleopatra. Any direct addresses to the citizens in Shakespeare's plays were staged as being spoken to television cameras, videos that were then broadcast back to the audience on monitors. That offstage citizenry was replaced by the onstage bodies of the audience, but rather than talking back or rebelling in any of the moblike ways that Shakespeare's plebeians do, the audience of *Roman Tragedies* remained silent and docile, consuming food, news and spectacle. By bringing the audience on stage and into proximity with the actors, van Hove and the Toneelgroep emphasized how removed we are from political centers of power today, and how much we have ceded our voices and actions to the lulling comforts of mediated watching. The presence of the audience is a crucial part of how *Roman Tragedies* makes its meanings, but it works by striking a balance between staging the audience to itself, both incorporating them into the play's *mise-en-scène* and keeping them at arm's length from the action.

It is possible, in my description of this production, to see its treatment of the audience as slightly hostile, as if the production were using the audience against itself. But that would misunderstand how central the audience was to the performance's success. There was nothing underhanded about how the production worked; there was no expectation that the audience was participating in the action of the play, that there was room for spectators to shoot back as plebeians. And if the production created a passive audience as part of its deliberate exploration of politics and culture in the early twenty-first century, it also forged strong connections with the audience. Part of those connections resulted from the duration of the marathon performance: the six hours spent in a shared space as part of a shared experience yoked together performers and audience. That joint effort was highlighted when, in the final play, the actor playing Enobarbus unexpectedly left the theatre to agonize in public (on the street outside the theatre in Montreal, in the Barbican car park in London) before returning to the theatre to commit suicide. With a videographer trailing him and catching the confusion of bystanders, projecting both the actor and the real-world spectators for the theatre audience to observe, the moment separated those who were within the fictional world from those who were not. Those real-world spectators walking down the street did not know what to make of the man weeping to himself in Dutch. The theatre audience did, or thought they did, but how different were they from the outside spectators? How much do we know what we are seeing, whether we are inside the theatre or out?

Conclusion: making and being made

I began this chapter by listing some of the questions that I was going to leave unanswered. Do audiences receive meanings or make meanings? Should we think of audiences as a collective body or as discrete bodies? What is it that takes place between spectator and actor? The different moments in plays and productions that I have highlighted suggest different answers. The laughter in the Globe *King Lear* and *As You Like It* seems to me not created through a partnership between performer and audience but through external factors that impose their conditions on both. On the other hand, the audience's proximity to and absence from the action of the Toneelgroep's *Roman Tragedies* was deliberately fostered by the performers in order to create their production's meaning in cooperation with their spectators. In all those performances, my individual response and position as a member of the audience separates my discrete self from responses of other audience members; at the same time, the sense of a collective enterprise shaped my reactions to the performance and the other spectators.

I have, in these examples, spoken specifically of my reactions to these performances: I did not find anything to laugh at in Goneril's or Rosalind's lines, I did not move around the theatre to explore the angles from which I might have approached *Roman Tragedies*. I have tried not to assume what others have thought or felt, raising questions rather than making statements about their possible responses. But as insistent as I have been about this, it remains a difficult rhetorical strategy to put into practice: the temptation to speak authoritatively about how an audience reacted or what they felt is a strong one. And there are some good reasons for this desire to speak of the audience as a collective body rather than a gathering of discrete persons. One of the hallmarks of live theatre is that we experience it collectively: as a collective of performers and a collective of spectators. The difference between seeing a performance as part of an audience, as opposed to on your own, is obvious to anyone who has spent time seeing both films in a cinema and on a screen in their living room. The presence of other spectators and their audible responses shapes how we, in turn, respond, whether our reactions are the same or different from those surrounding us. Performers, whether actors, musicians, dancers, comedians or politicians, speak of audiences on a particular night responding differently than on other nights – laughing at different moments, bringing a different energy, being more or less responsive, more or less engaged. Given this collective nature of the audience, we cannot entirely dismiss their generalized experience, even as we must also remember that no individual spectator will have the same response as another.

Given the number of examples I have provided from productions that, in their foregrounding of audience awareness, might seem to be atypical of Shakespearean theatre, I want to share one more instance from a more traditional production style, one in which the stage is lit and the audience watches from seats in a darkened auditorium. In this 2006 production of *Measure for Measure* at the Folger Theatre in Washington, DC, the linchpin of the production came when Mariana begged Isabella to join her in asking for Angelo's life to be spared. It is a moment that is often perplexing. Angelo has betrayed and disdained Mariana at every turn; were he to be executed after their marriage, as the Duke has planned, Mariana's honour and wealth would be restored. Isabella, in turn, has no desire to help Angelo, who has shamed her, betrayed her and killed her brother. In most productions, I have experienced this moment as yet one more instance in which the two women are made to jump through hoops to satisfy the Duke's own needs. But in this performance, something shifted for me. The moment was staged with Mariana on her knees facing the Duke and the audience. When Mariana reached out her hand to Isabella to join her, the blocking made that moment register as an invitation to the audience as well: the success of the play hinged on Mariana's convincing us to move beyond bitterness and revenge towards the hope of love and redemption. It is the only time in which I have felt Mariana to be the emotional centre of the play, and in a production that was consistently strong and interesting, it is the moment that has continued to stay with me. Part of its success is how it was staged: it created an opening for the audience to see itself as part of the action and resolution of the play. It also drew on a powerful performance by Michele Osherow in the role of Mariana, one of the few characters in the production who was at all likeable; Osherow was also the play's dramaturge and a friend of Aaron Posner, the director, extra-textual roles that might have helped create the dynamics that allowed her to take a central role despite the small amount of time the character is on stage.

But I also know that part of the success of this moment came from the specifics of my place as spectator. When I saw this production, my father was dying and I was struggling with that pain and loss. It was a time when a message about learning to move forward into the future with love and hope would have been particularly resonant for me. In thinking about how audiences are made by performances, and how performances are made by audiences, I cannot separate the two dynamics here. The difference between what this performance of *Measure for Measure* staged and what I saw in it perhaps cannot be delineated. And that is the greatest challenge of thinking about audiences and making Shakespeare. Each makes the other, and whether we are performers or audience, we will not have the last word.

11
Sound

P.A. Skantze

> The search for the manner in which seventeenth-century performance works begins here with the assumption that sensual apprehension occurs in the wake of movement: that is, in its immediate aftermath, as if the movement were an originary vessel cutting through the air and leaving behind waves that lifted and plunged the receiver. This image reverberates in the province of sound, described as moving in waves, but also makes room for the kinetic consequences of movements made by the actors and perceived by the audience.
>
> (Skantze 23)

> Sound is produced when a body's motion is transferred to the surrounding air, creating an 'audible species' … . In the case of the audible species, these forms or images are perhaps best described as representations of the motion of the sounding body.
>
> (Folkerth 53)

Like explorers climbing one upon the other to gain access to the top of the wall, since the beginning of the twenty-first century critics have stood on each other's shoulders to peer over the wall separating us from the noisy early modern past. Whooping and stomping and thumping and oomphs of air can be perceived, barely, from our side. What's happening over there, on the other side, where the kinetic cannot be untethered from the thinking, where something about sound in its arc in time means everything to the world in motion on the stage, and

180

thus everything to the richness of the graphics we are left with on the page? To read Bruce Smith or Wes Folkerth – who themselves cite the shoulders of those engaged in acoustical history and theory on which they first stood – and then to write, is to clamber up on their shoulders with one's muddy feet, longing to get that much higher, that much closer to experiencing the noise, to experiencing the moving bodies in performance. In her book *Voice in Motion: Staging Gender, Shaping Sound in Early Modern England* Gina Bloom argues that 'a history of materiality is a history of things in motion, things moving through time and space' (100). Citing an early modern text by Kenelm Digby, Bloom suggests a perspective on sound that was commonly articulated by early modern theorists: that motion and sound are 'one and the same thing', a theory Digby supports by his investigations with subjects who are deaf, where the movement of objects 'make a like motion in his braine' to sound without 'passing through his ear' (102).[1]

Attention to this alchemical process of sound, motion and the performing body reveals how the performance becomes the argument in and through sound; how in fact, Shakespeare's peculiar 'capaciousness', as Folkerth suggests, manifests itself in the performing body as a kind of perpetual improvisation, words primed to become themselves again in performance, again and again and again.[2]

To engage in theory as a practice, to make a performance and, in doing so, to manifest acts of research, is to surrender to duration and time. This surrender is brought home if we pay attention to sound in its oscillating movements as duration, creating time. The route of surrender and patience that is 'making' has its alchemy in experimentation: in multiple attempts and in a keen interest in the failure of those attempts. I suspect Shakespeare and his company of craftsmen inhabited their roles as what we might call today 'theatre practitioners', not unlike the role explicated by performance critic Susan Melrose when she writes of the Théâtre du Soleil director Arianne Mnouchkine. Mnouchkine, who has directed several celebrated Shakespearean productions, describes for Melrose the way her practitioner intuition works: Mnouchkine 'will recognize what she wants [from the actors] ... but cannot identify it

---

[1] Digby's experiment, according to Bloom, 'investigates the phenomenon whereby a deaf man may perceive music by touching his teeth to a stick that lies on a musical instrument' (102).

[2] Folkerth's term 'capaciousness' signals the larger world of gift exchange operating in many levels in Shakespearean and early modern theatre texts, in reception and in performance (Skantze, 2003).

in advance of their producing it' (131). As a director I know just how unsatisfactory this kind of 'wait and see' attitude is to those who want to 'know what to do', and as a spectator of performance and a reader of Shakespeare's plays, I know how gratifying are the rewards of not knowing.

While Shakespeare studies over the centuries has provided rich sources for lively discussion about text, often the practitioner or scholar who seeks to understand the work in performance finds help in works by critics from allied performance fields, in dance or in music. In my earlier work on seventeenth-century theatre (Skantze, 2003) the key to understanding motion on stage came from early modern dance studies, where the theorists could not return to a close-reading model because there was no 'text'; anyone working in early modern performance studies is aided by studies where the authors remember that the word 'door' in the text still needs a body to push it open if the performance is to proceed. As with motion, so with sound. I have found that Fred Moten's writing about sound, music and performance in his *In the Break: The Aesthetics of the Black Radical Tradition* converges in what at first might seem an odd comparison: in a startlingly brilliant juxtaposition of Amiri Baraka's essay on Billie Holiday ('The Dark Lady of the Sonnets') and Joel Fineman's writing on Shakespeare, sonnets and subjectivity, Moten records the thing that happens that can't happen, the withholding that ends with a revelation in excess of the promised end. If in the following quotation, we substitute spectator and performance where Moten writes reader and sonnet, his formulation offers us a way into sound as improvisation even in those works that appear composed and finished:

> Shakespeare produces certain effects, then: a continual figuring of the position of the [spectator] and the dynamics of [performance] along with foreclosure of the possibility of a pure epideictic response that simultaneously produces that response and reproduces the demand for that response by demanding that we respond to him and allowing us to do so. He continually does that which upon closer analysis he proves he cannot do. And in so doing he forces us to accomplish the same feat … . For the myriad of effects contained in a given sonnet [performance], its multiple facets, when counted, added, collected in literary analysis, never add up to the sonnet [performance] itself.
>
> (112)

Moten reiterates what Folkerth and Smith urge us to see and hear: that sound employed in performance through text but as much through silence and sighs invite a response, as if in the moment of making, the completion of the give-and-take of the production must pass through the body of the listener every time a play is performed. To offer this process as an embodied making – think of Mnouchkine's practising presence where she must pay close attention to what is happening in rehearsal in order to 'know', to identify what she wants, what works – we might, with Moten, revisit and revise a dichotomy whose reign in traditional academic work has caused a separation that serves not only to blind us and deafen us to the power of the plays but has also serves to cast race, gender and all manner of living, moving difference into false categories. We must commit ourselves to

> the emergence of an art and thinking in which emotions and structure, preparation and spontaneity, individuality and collectivity can no longer be understood in opposition to one another. Rather the art itself resists any interpretation in which these elements are opposed, resists any designation, even those of the artists themselves, that depends upon such opposition ... [the philosophical and cultural] oppositions of improvisation and composition and black and white.
>
> (129)

What this chapter suggests, by inviting the reader to navigate the waves of performed sound through theories of contemporary performance makers, is that practice as research can begin on the page with the reader experimenting sonically, imaginatively, in a manner not unlike the performer or director who pays attention in order to know, to identify, to put into motion the printed record of a play or an actor's instruction manual from the sixteenth century or a critical text on sound. Keeping such improvisation and composition in mind as a kind of collaboration and ensemble work, I explore two examples of sound as and in performance in this chapter: I explore how the sound works as fuel and power in *Antony and Cleopatra*, and in the Wooster Group's production of *Hamlet*, I offer two instances of how practical choices can reorientate our ideas about familiar sound and seemingly static sights and meaning. Throughout I advocate the privileging of live performance; this book champions a conscious release of assumptions about what we think we know or thought we knew by sight and/or by sound. To hear is one thing, to listen collectively is another; these explorations originate in my experience as a listener in a collective body of listeners as well as in a practitioner/scholar.

Saving Cleopatra through sound

Sharp critical theory on *Antony and Cleopatra* notwithstanding, many performances and receptions of Cleopatra as a character in a book and on stage tend to find her unforgivable. Alluring and flighty, sultry and pouting, imperious and lying, she struts her hour on the stage too often in a girlish fashion, the princess queen. Such dismissive responses, I would suggest, rest on bad hearing, an acoustical fault in performer and receiver. To separate Cleopatra from the soundscape of the play mars the orchestration, embedded throughout the text, of a world conjured by motion, injured by the stops made in doubt and fear, reanimated in the performers' ability to improvise in extremity. The entire play could be scored – and Pat Parker and Wes Folkerth have trained our ears to hear the play differently – but let me limit myself here to a few examples, sound samplings, of the larger acoustic project of the play. East/west national identity appears in an instant through a director's use of sound; think of the cartoon versions of the 'national' at play when a hokey bit of music accompanies a cardboard costume of national dress. Nowhere is this more true than in the clichéd musical evocation of Egypt, as arms make right angles, the front one up, the back one down, while the head is rhythmically thrust forward and back. So a director who wants to use sound and music to subtly influence the ear geographically faces a complex task. How can you give Cleopatra's court a languorous feel acoustically without reiterating the most reductive of associations? 'Time immanent', to use Folkerth's distinction based on Schutz, seems patently to be the polythetic ground on which Egypt rests in the play, in clear opposition to time transcendent and the monothetic Caesar (21).

In an RSC production directed by Gregory Doran, exported to London from Stratford in 2006, the musicians sat visible to the audience in a small square section of the stage, sometimes a part of the playing, sometimes not. When I saw this production, I heard non-miked sound, a choice on the part of the makers that changes the affect of sound and motion on the performing and receiving bodies. I also 'saw' the musicians, a sensual trigger from eye to ear that affords a different form of listening than that of hearing invisible sound. Reception is exponentially different when the sound emanates from moving bodies on stage. Both the quality of 'live' – done now – sound and the motion of hands and mouths and lungs visible to the players and audience create a very different acoustic field than that of sound filtered directly into a mike, a sound requiring less physical propulsion, and received in the ear only from specific points in the performing space depending on the placement of speakers. Not only does live sound have a different acoustical weight in both the production and the effort necessary for the production and reception, but live sound makes the actor's body move differently. Live sound, at times measured as much by inaudibility as in audibility, makes the listener's body hear differently: it affects cognition.

Thus the particular sound of particular musical instruments (ones that seemed to have natural amplification, as the sound was not extracted by mikes and reproduced from only one or two points in the theatre) also tuned the audience's ear to the particular sound of the actors' particular vocal instruments. While we heard the setting we saw floating swathes of material laid upon the ground, signal for the swaddled East, a signal tuning us to hear the interaction between the gypsy and the man who uses his breath, his loud and prodigious breath, to be 'the bellows and the fan' beating out lust. Both principals wore copious amounts of material: Patrick Stewart in long, loose white pants, chest bare, chest heaving, lungs expanding as he speaks; Harriet Walter, moving fluidly in her classic garment fashioned after ancient sculptures of women.

The swathes of cloth, like the group of musicians, functioned as a visual metaphor for invisible sound. The twisting, floating and time-bound world of cloth in motion makes for no doubt an unconscious but no less potent sensual trigger to the receiving body; sound works like that in our ears, curling around the corners, floating on top of small scilla, making measured vibrations. Voices echoed all this swirling, visible and invisible. Stewart spoke in a sensuous growl to Cleopatra; in a hail-fellow-well-met homoerotic banter to his followers. Walter floated her voice up and down depending on intent, desire and playful calculation; as queen, imperious and shrewd; as lover, tantalizing and changeable.

'What makes Shakespeare "not for an age, but for all time" is his genius as an artist of sounds, not his ability to create memorable characters. That is the province of actors' (Smith, 1999: 278). If, as Smith suggests, the ability to create characters is an actor's job, I would say we as scholars do not pay enough attention to the intersection of the playwright's soundscape and the actors' reanimation of it.[3] Elsewhere I delineate

---

[3] My instinct is that the plays of some playwrights – Middleton comes to mind – sometimes suffer in revival from the short, sharp and particular sound of topical references no longer acoustically intelligible in the same ways. The danger in this of course is to reinscribe Shakespeare as universal and to find in others a 'lesser' power. Instead I think of Webster, and how in his plays sound propels action in his works in a different key, but reminiscent of those of Shakespeare.

how aesthetic attention to the collaboration of stillness and motion feeds performance as well as other cultural productions in early modern England and on into the present moment. This is a collaboration not only of sound and motion, but a corporeal representation of the collaboration through sound and the performing and reception of it: sound is indeed the bellows and the fan for the sensual drive of theatre, that which makes the fire burn.

Sound comes to the listening ear through our sense of the volume – loud enough, too soft, just right, but also along the continuum of fullness of sound; *Antony and Cleopatra* seems to me to perfectly illustrate Smith's suggestion that volume in early modern performance 'was not only a function of narrative line but of subject matter, acoustical space, date of performance and the age of the actors' (1999: 225). Sound plays both conveyer of and the signal for abundance in *Antony and Cleopatra*. From the opening match of pledges of love we hear Antony counter Cleopatra's conjured object of an abacus of sounded love, 'if it be love, tell me how much', by suggesting there 'is beggary in the love that can be reckoned' (1.1.14–15). And yet if it cannot be reckoned it cannot be exchanged, since the Old English verb underlying the meaning of 'reckoning' is 'to narrate'. So the pleasurable circle of denying a limit, out of all reckoning, depends upon reckoning, the telling-out in sound of the tale of immeasurability. At several points in the play's action – and for the first time here in the first scene, the motion of the building sound carries bodies across the space to each other, carries the gestures of enthralment and play rejection – the crescendo meets a satisfying end: 'Let Rome in Tiber melt, and the wide arch / of the ranged empire fall ...' (35–6).

Just as sound 'melts', according to Francis Bacon, not all at once – as he muses on the sound of a bell or percussion – but over time, so to this image of the melting city, decaying even as Antony's voice calls the image to our ears (quoted in Folkerth 54). This impossible pledge foreshadows a play of melting, reverberating sound reanimated into solidity and passion only to melt again. All loved things are thus, the play seems to show: the sound of the beloved's voice lost and regained, remembered and scorned, the power of the beloved country, formed into defendable image only to melt when challenged by a stronger sound/image. The ruler's job involves reanimating love of country with her voice and her presence, much as a lover must remind by sending messages substituting for her voice, her presence. For Cleopatra these roles clash, as when she swears while he is gone that everyday Antony will have 'a several greeting' or she will 'unpeople Egypt' (2.1.76–7).

Performance and performers in the Shakespearean soundscape always make things anew because this lesson never sticks. Nor is it supposed to. The whole pleasure of the lovers before us, no longer in their salad days, comes from sense embedded in the play of the years of their performing together, a sense conveyed as we inhabit our role as participating hearers. The play is shot through with aural nostalgia, tales told of past greatness. Haunted by sound, players reinvoke that haunting by resounding the words of the stories told and the story unfolding. The players' aural past comes alive in our listening present; it is redone for them and for us. Smith quotes Stephen Handel, who suggests 'listening is centripetal; it pulls you into the world. Looking is centrifugal; it separates you from the world' (1999: 10). Recently, Jonathan Sterne and others, developing theories of sound, have questioned this stark binary; however, the motion of the push and pull, even moderated by an understanding of how some will receive one form of address to the senses more powerfully than others, depending on our ear/eye training, still attests to a receiver's corporeal participation. Thus if we take this formulation into performance, the listening of the audience when sounds bring us along into motion means we can be pulled into the world made by words before us. This experience, when it works, is never one of being pulled back into an old world of a long ago-performed *Antony and Cleopatra*, though memories may occur; instead, if the performers do not use their voices to move through their bodies towards the conjunction of cognition and reception for the audience, then and only then do we fall back on looking, on observing what has not come to sounded life.[4]

Clues abound in the soundscape of the text, clues that offer not a bit of logical security about the stable things of the world: the delicious 'discandy'/discandying (3.8.165) – say it aloud – places us at the crux of the fabricated, the sweet and the melting, training us to receive the performance in a tantalizing taste/hearing collision. In her paper for the Resounding seminar at the 2007 Shakespeare Association of America Conference, Shannon Ciapciak explores what she calls the 'aquatic sonority' of the sea sounds in *The Tempest* and concludes that Sebastian's 'standing water' (2.1.975) vision of self is thermodynamically

---

[4] In fact some revivals go wrong precisely in the desire to create a centrifugal experience where the play offers a centripetal one. This seems particularly the case with the question of showing violence: the sound of the language that foreshadows and then describes great violence makes it inescapable where sometimes the sight of the violence played graphically before us leaves us more detached than the sound of the language of the play demands.

contrasted to Antonio's imaginary frozen, 'candied' twenty consciences that must 'melt ere they molest' (2.1.308). To dehydrate, or melt, the self, Ciapciak argues, would free the flow of tears for Antonio that might prepare him for a recognition of guilt, and thus rebirth.[5] The candied and the discandied seem to sound out a relation of frozen and melting that enacts a collaboration of the still and the moving, as well as propelling bodies out of a frozen and restricted confusion, fulfilling the narrative's momentum through the action.

If sound propels bodies it also transmits meaning through the air. In *Antony and Cleopatra*, the echoes of how sound carries meaning, how it carries character and carries the working-out of ideas are audible in the performance, the embodied manifestation of power. The RSC's production helped me to understand what had been at the back of my reception of this play for some time: the energy of the performers to continually reinvent themselves in a succession of triumphs and losses. For the first time I received and therefore understood power as primarily an act of improvisation, and in contrast I heard the incredible frustration of Caesar that he was conscious his acting was wooden, was bad. He lost his breath, he sounded stilted; his form of power involved silent strategizing to Antony's ruinous but appealing, bellowing bravado. (When Antony goes to war by sea there is no strategy in it, though one could not say the plan grew the more by reaping.) Caesar calculates by show, not just what Cleopatra fears he will make of her in the end, the deflation of her powerful self, the sound of her voice distorted by some 'squeaking Cleopatra boy' (5.2.218), but what he describes in 3.6 as the show they make to the 'public eye' which Caesar, ever a dismissing leader, calls 'the common showplace' (3.6.11–12).

Antony and Cleopatra, however, make their motion match their voices, so that when wearied they exhibit a loss of breath, and thus breadth. When they must rekindle themselves, they do so in speaking, in sound that extends to the sense of the listeners. It is no accident that Enobarbus' catalogue of wonders that is Cleopatra in Act 2 ends on the note that he did see her 'hop forty paces through the public street / And having lost her breath, she spoke and panted' (2.235–7). What would in most people, never mind rulers, be received as a weakness, the speaking difficult and punctuated by laboured breath, becomes in Cleopatra,

---

[5] I am grateful to Shannon Ciapciak for unpublished correspondence which elucidates these arguments, which she presented to a seminar at the 2007 Shakespeare Association of America conference.

according to Enobarbus, the ability to 'make defect perfection', and from this Cleopatra exhibits abundance where scarcity is expected: 'and breathless, pour breath forth' (2.2.238–9). The desire for Cleopatra extends to her sister soundmaker the air, who longed to rush out to see/experience Cleopatra, except it would have 'made a gap in nature'. Such a potential disordering of the natural world has an intriguing analogue in Bacon's description of the force of magnified sound. Folkerth cites Bacon's recording of the folk tale in which a loud song 'broke' the air 'that the birds flying over have fallen down, the air not being able to support them' (55).

In contrast with the stunning portrait of Cleopatra made literally in the air by Enobarbus, Maecenas counters with a pat emblem of goodness, a show that Octavia will provide, 'beauty, wisdom and modesty' (2.2.245). Like her brother, Octavia dwells in the world of sight, a world this soundscape often renders as a cold one, if one that also belongs to shows of power. Unlike the women characters in Shakespeare who, Bloom argues, persuasively employ silence as a form of agency, Octavia suffers from the too few words allowed her and the too much invoked sight of her as sister-cum-statue and valuable chaste property to create the gaps of silence that might demand she be noticed. For many spectators, we remain breathless, and as we long to see defect made perfection in the devil-may-care performance of hopping forty paces, perfection and chastity have nothing to overcome. The potential nonsensicality of Cleopatra's reported action, hopping forty paces, and the subsequent breathlessness, might also convey a sense of the otherness of Egyptian Cleopatra's sound that Smith finds in the sounded language of characters like Morocco in *The Merchant of Venice* or Caliban in *The Tempest*. Sound and the making of subjectivity here would counter to some extent Dymphna Callaghan's assertion that, in postcolonial terms, Cleopatra cannot be a 'subject of representation' but only an object of analysis 'fantasized into existence' (53). While Cleopatra's shifts from commanding ruler to giddy playmate also reinforce her place on the eastern edge of the rhetorically created rational nature of the Roman world, it is not that she does not speak sense, but rather that sense is not the only purpose in or of the sounds she makes.

Into this reverberating maelstrom of theatricality come constant reminders of other sound carriers: messengers ventriloquizing the voices they import. Messengers being mistaken for, nay treated as, the voices they articulate. But report doesn't only come bodily from West to East; a more subtle, infinitely powerful form of reporting occurs for the receiving audience in the moving images of the famous characters reiterated constantly, orally re-embroidered for the ears of the audience. Who could live up to such report: Antony's soldierly prowess, he whose heroic actions Caesar piles one upon the other, to the 'strange flesh' he willingly ate, that 'some did die to look on' (1.4.67–8); or Cleopatra, by age unwithered and unstaled? And yet the report functions in sound as a kind of speaking image larger than life. Folkerth's 'deep subjectivity', the sounding-out of the self that manifests itself in the 'efflorescence of language', the materializing of the self through sound, seems to me to work here in the context of the public persona made not only by the subject but also by the watching/listening audience to the performing subject, who creates an imagined image of a subject in motion (26). The luxurious descriptions function beyond the assessment they first might seem; they overdo for the audience's ear, creating in their impossible extravagance of sound, and thus of sensible sound, a theme against which the performers play.

This agreement between audience and player to up the aural ante allows both Cleopatra and Antony to lose themselves, lose their voices ('report that I am sudden sick'; 1.3.5), lose their tempers, lose their efflorescence, their sounded understanding of themselves ('here I am Antony / yet cannot hold this visible shape ...'; 4.14.14–15). That the degrees of sensation create an arc from fullness to emptiness means that the fierceness of abundance contrasts directly with the moments of doubt and the shrinking of the triple-pillared world created by the actors moving and sounding before us. Thus performance, ready and primed by Shakespearean sound, shows how they can regain themselves in order to reinvent and rule again, in each others' hearts, over their soldiers and subjects. In London in 2006, Walter and Stewart played out with us the virtuosity of performing. Their bodies shrank when they had disappointed themselves and their followers; expanded when the duet of their power/love play created the world anew around them. While at any moment the words they were speaking could be found in every form of textual reproduction, like the Billie Holiday recording to which Moten refers, the preserved form of container, paperback, folio, tape recording hold that in suspension which in the mouth, on the stage, in our ears 'sounds like' it is being made in the moment, now, composed on the spot by exceptionally gifted sound artists/actors.

Walter's Cleopatra, imbued with the sound of the play, making the sound the body of her moving conjectures and betrayals, served to create a complex queen. In this performance, Cleopatra's voice and motion in the face of Antony's fury about her ships' sudden flight and betrayal brought with it the sound of confusion and a recognition of failure.

A recognition echoing in Antony's wearied voice when he re-created for the last time the revels now to end, addressing Cleopatra as 'day of the world' and cajoling her to join him in the last night's carousing, though 'grey do something mingle with' their 'younger brow'. (4.8.19–20). Cleopatra's final retreat, then, from his hugely sounded fury at her also made more sense because Stewart made the rafters quake with his yelling; the natural motion of shrinking from the sound of his (justifiably) outraged voice was shared by the audience.

Folkerth notes 1,466 changes in punctuation in the Arden edition of *Antony and Cleopatra*; these editorial interventions seem intriguing enough as proof of needing to stabilize unruly sound, but his noting of another 217 exclamation points cannot help but stand in for the whoosh of heightened sound and heightened feeling that is part, I would argue, of the vitality of the in-the-moment suddenness of strong, of loud, of amplified speaking (24). I wonder if these exclamation points might not also be an editorial response to accounting for such emphatic sound from a female character, since as Smith notes, Cleopatra's share of the lines in the play is unusually large, and throughout the play she 'maintains her aural command of the field of sound' (237).

Moten's discussion of Billie Holiday as a kind of aural theorist in her production of sound has an analogue in Cleopatra's compelling ability to make sounded defect perfection. Moten argues that Holiday's 'willingness to fail' – many criticized the ragged edge of her voice in late recordings and the logic of her making them – prompts a listening in which one can hear 'the reach for a note that implies the note she will not quite make and the note she manages to invent in superseding it'. This twentieth-century sound artist seems very good company for the Egyptian queen and her fallible consort. For as Moten reminds us, out of the practice that is the willingness to fail comes 'new coefficient[s] of freedom' (108). One of the most compelling parts of the score of *Antony and Cleopatra* is the oscillation between rueful recognition of being bound and acts that do even in their imperfection – not quite falling effectively on one's sword, as Caesar might, for example – develop in time into a sounded and staged freedom.

In the end, from her tomb, Cleopatra asks that Antony be lifted up so she may hear him, the echo of the weight of his body in the word weight used earlier for that 'happy horse' bearing him (1.5.21). But the sound is also of 'wait': at this point in the play Cleopatra will wait out Caesar, making it look like she obeys. The end of the play sounds remarkably soft. Egypt plays the quiet card, the power of silence in the face of Caesar's sudden loudness; his is the only voice now that those others have gone. A tragedy made in sound, performed out of sound and finally left to the loud and clanging sound of empire established in plain sight.

'Past acoustic events'

> The world is in motion and in chiaroscuro. We always see one side of things, always moving, always chang-ing. Their shape dissolves into shadow, sketches itself in the motion, loses itself in the darkness, or in the excess of light. And our attention is also in chiaro-scuro. It comes and goes from one object to another, and focuses successively on the details and on the whole.
>
> (Michel Chion 104)

Sterne, writing about sound reproduction in *The Audible Past*, reminds us that 'sound-reproduction technologies are artefacts of vast trans-formations in the fundamental nature of sound, the human ear, the faculty of hearing, and practices of listening that occurred over the long nineteenth century ... as there was an Enlightenment, so there was an Ensonicment' (2). Folkerth also takes his cue from this long neglected ensonicment by opening his book about Shakespeare and sound with a discussion of the wax recording of Henry Irving's Richard III which asserts that 'Shakespeare's playtexts record past acoustic events' (7). In practice, as one can so clearly hear from the cheeky tweaking of a line from Marlowe placed in the mouth of a Shakespearean character, performance practice and those engaged in it can be no respecters of periods or authors. If an innovative bit of play requires anachronism in terms of time or invention and discovery, then the work shifts to include it, the rules bend if something works, that thing we don't know we want until we recognize it/experience it. This chapter argues for a like practice in scholarly terms when insisting on a relation between sound – antique, live and recorded – Moten's discussion of Billie Holiday and the improvised nature of Shakespearean language and composition as in the making of black music, and the immediacy of the acoustic project of the plays. To practically and theoretically explore the nature of sound is to dwell at the crux of the recording of the past acoustic event and the sudden now of the sound sounding improvised, sounding contemporary, no matter how faded the paper on which the lines are printed.

For assistance in considering the practice of making such a world of sound and performance, no contemporary performance group seems more apt than the Wooster Group and their 2007 performance of *Hamlet*. Though it would be evading the technological attractions of our day to call this primarily an acoustic event, I suggest that the mix of moving bodies, sound and ventriloquizing that makes up this playing reasserts the primacy of sound, Shakespearean and primed for improvising play, by rendering strange the familiar habit of watching film. Improvisation would seem an impossible word for a production that imitates a 1964 film and for players who often have the voice of Elizabeth Lecompte over the earphones in their ears throughout the performance guiding and controlling them, but still the primedness of the sound of Shakespeare's language, the elaborate sound of *Hamlet*, adds the acoustic flourish of the immediate to this play upon play with the past.

In 1964 Richard Burton played Hamlet on Broadway; he was dashing and dark and troubled in all the ways that are delicious to the dated evocation of the anti-hero. And his voice! But what made this production extraordinary was that it was filmed live, using 17 different cameras for the specific purpose of creating a record of this acoustic/visual event that would feel like a live performance for the spectators. The film was distributed simultaneously in 2,000 cinemas throughout the USA over the course of two days, with the purpose of giving people outside New York a sense of attending together a live performance.

As I watched the Wooster production, I thought to myself that the cans in which the film had rested for all those years must have read 'to be opened by the Wooster Group in the twenty-first century'. This was a gift made in heaven for a group who constantly experiment with the live and the technologically enhanced, with the video artefact and the playing/speaking body. If Shakespeare's plays mark Folkerth's 'past acoustic events', this production was the Russian doll of past events, opening again and again to reveal the next mimetic sound/sight upon the next, upon the next.

The stage replicated the stage on screen, bare, the stage-right section slightly elevated, two stairs going up. A large screen, the width of the playing space at the back, was filled with a shadowy image. Like the hooting of an owl, the opening does more than cry out a 'who's there'; the 'who' is repeated by the body on stage just after the 'who' has been heard from the body on screen. In a sense, this echoing will be the soul of this production, a production about haunting, a production the Wooster Group suggests is about a haunted text that haunts Western culture, as it haunts Derrida and his ancestors in *Spectres of Marx*. And the contrapuntal nature of players on screen, players on stage, necessitated the performance of hesitation since, ostensibly, the performers watch the filmed performers to catch their cue. It is a rather dazzling technological feat, a proof of how practice theorizes in the making, to strike out of the form of playing a sounded emphasis on these two pivotal performed themes in *Hamlet*, haunting and hesitation.[6] Just as dazzling is the use of microphones as part of the argument of the way the work is performed. Rather than an obligatory choice made in acknowledgement of a population accustomed to a certain level of noise issuing from headphones directly into their ears at a volume they control, instead, the microphones serve, as they always do in Wooster performances, to hint at the distance between the 'lost' voice (actor or text), the surrogate voice making the sound and the borrowed voice of the film or recording.[7]

Since the three-and-a-half-hour performance deserves endless revisitation and reverie, I will consider just two moments in the production, to heighten how sound works as performed motion and how the physical play of the actors brought acoustical awareness to the 'silent' bits of filmed performance. Kate Valk, principal actor of the Wooster Group and, in my opinion, American national treasure, appears on stage, regal, hair up in a commanding style, dress long and flowing. She watches, moves in time to her double on the screen, and is silent until she echoes the words coming out of the 'dead' queen's mouth on film, encouraging her son to accept what the present performance mitigates against and/or reifies, the passage of time: 'Do not for ever with thy vailed lids / Seek for thy noble father in the dust / Though know'st 'tis common – all that lives must die' (1.2.70–2). Mother plays straight woman here to the tragicomic son; she sets up the echo for him and

---

[6] Elin Diamond (1997) writes of improvisation as mimesis with hesitation, the space between 'the stake and the shifting sands', as Derrida articulates a hesitation between doing and the object/model made. I might suggest that performance out of the aesthetic collaboration between stillness and motion foregrounds the hesitation, the moment held for a second where we see/hear what usually remains an inaudible/invisible transition, a revelation in hesitation, time to catch our breath.

[7] Nowhere is this more clear than in their recent production of *Didone*, where they mix Cavalli's seventeenth-century opera with an Italian film about space vampires. In this piece the 'vampirization' of sound, the literal sucking-out of the operatic music into the mouths of those speaking non-musical lines, is extraordinary.

he takes it: 'Ay, madam, it is common' (74). Meanwhile Richard Burton speaks under Scott Shepherd's voice, or Shepherd hesitates, and so they speak the line almost twice.

During the production the sound from the film will go in and out. From time to time the actors will stop the film, rewind and then do it again. All that can be played, be sounded again, can be resurrected and restructured to invite an audience to receive intent, thematic sound-ings, and the words themselves. The players on the screen, ironically, seem far freer than the players on the stage, who must be miked and watch that they are setting up the visual/oral echo before us accurately. Valk again gives her son his ranting cue, 'Why seems it so particular with thee?' (1.2.75). And like a mountain of sound down which his ire can slide, Hamlet begins his descent: 'Seems, madam ...' (1.2).

The sound of Valk, the hyper-awareness of her doing and imitating, at once heightens the gendered nature of the sound in Hamlet. First a feast for the eyes on the arm of her ill-chosen consort, then a little bit of speech, cajoling, sounding out in small-syllabled words the text for her son to emblazon. What creates an even more powerful understanding of sound in performance and the way sound constructed character is the Wooster's choice to have us see Valk undo the false front of the dress she is wearing to place another over it, cover her head with a wig of cascad-ing locks and re-enter as Ophelia. (The trouble this makes for later on in the play is a Wooster group specialty, commenting while moving on the stage, discussing how 'we can't do that scene' because the Queen and Ophelia are both in it, deciding to have another actor stand in the Queen's place while Ophelia does her herbal catalogue.)

Women don't just often speak hesitantly in *Hamlet*, they sound hesitant and stilted. But the commonality of women in the play, the commonality of their voices, becomes visually and aurally reinforced by Valk playing both supposedly tarnished mother and spurned adolescent innocent. The before and after of the female condition comes readily to our spectatorial ear and is reinforced by Valk's voice not changing from one to the other, nor does it really have to because both extreme scenes of sound, the Queen's 'closet' and the 'mad' girl at Court, harbour the same mix of anguish in a minor key. I don't mean to belittle the anguish, but the language is not grand enough to raise it to the grieved outbursts of the male characters in the play. The soundscape we hear teaches us interpreting skills as we listen; such interpreting also relies on who we hear first, whose tragedy engulfs by sound another's.

Like race and age, gender is a species of sound; not simply in that many women's voices are higher, or lighter, but that on the few occasions women are allowed to rage and rule, the words of their part change, allowing the speech to build. Cleopatra certainly employs tympanic speech, as does Queen Margaret from the *Henry VI* plays and *Richard III*, but the sound carrying the female bodies in *Hamlet* often conveys the bounded nature of the space they can take up. Neither Gertrude nor Ophelia inhabit a space either historically or fictionally in the play from which they might reinvent themselves; in fact, the pressing of Ophelia into the two-dimensional scopic realm of representation when her father and Claudius give her instructions to become a silent trope common in sixteenth-century painting, a virgin with devotional book in hand, leaves her bereft of further vocal command. However, some directors have insisted on an agency in her silence, something Bloom (2007) argues forcefully for, by giving weight to her waiting on stage, abandoned by all but us, the watching audience.

The second collision of sound and sense and performance that the Wooster group production presents echoes not an aural moment from the film but a scopic one. Caught performatively in what Folkerth, quoting Jay, calls the 'tyranny of the scopic regime' (27), the players set up their scene and then do something acoustically strange to present audiences' ears: they move their chairs. It took me fully half the performance to 'get' that this was not a bit of performed percussion – the rolling of the wheels on the stage, the squeaking of the sudden stop to push the brake down on the mobile chairs – counting out the mixed tempo of film and live repeating; instead I finally realized the actors were changing their positions to match the changing angle of the camera. Look back at the screen, calculate, move the chair, scoot forward, turn the profile, close-up. Swoosh the chair, move back, face audience, long or medium shot. But for the present audience the change of camera angle made sound and heightened a sense of stop and start, of hesitation and go.

Now, several years on, I am still under the sway of this past acoustic event, how profound the successive layers of echo and copying became in the production, how live actors performed as the pipes whose stops are played by actors now dead in a performance filmed with the intent of giving the 1960s audience the experience of something live. The motion on film casts freedom out onto the technically controlled stage: Burton swoops through the part; Polonius fulfils his wooden-is as wooden-speaks as wooden-does role; Claudius matches bloated language with heavy acting, angry and burdened at the same time. The Wooster Group actors, Shepherd, Roy Faudree and Ari Flinkos, speak and move on stage in performed proof that one is always copying, always in imitation of a sound gone, of a motion made. Yet the experience of receiving feels like the experience of being in an echo chamber; the more the sound and motion bounce off each other, the more the language of the play and its myriad, over-copious meanings seem to fill, to fulfill the space we are in, improvised from something seemingly past and gone.

Something seemingly past and gone: the sound of Cleopatra's power-filled breathlessness, the interanimation of *Hamlet* as text, of *Hamlet* as video production of live theatre, of *Hamlet* revisited sonically and aurally through the practice of the Wooster Group and the practice of their audiences. The power of the re-said, the re-staged, the re-heard to remind us that past and gone allows for future and coming:

> a certain phenomenon remains ... perhaps best described precisely as the phenomenon of the remainder as such or, better yet, as the mark of the totality that 'everything' (that which is in Shakespeare and Baraka and their 'objects') can never capture [raising] certain questions that trouble the distinctions between the object of sight and the events of seeing, the heard voice and the event of hearing ... the recording is a determination that is also an improvisation, one that extends, emanates, holds a trace that moves out of the tragedy the blues holds.
>
> Perhaps it is this: that the dark lady improvises through the blues and all that it implies from within its form and in the fixity of the recording. Perhaps it is this: that the tragic-erotic end that the blues seems always to foreshadow is supplemented not only by the transformative effect of improvisation, but the ghostly emanation of those last records, the sound that extends beyond the end of which it tells. Perhaps it is this: that the sonic image of a death foretold contains not only the trace of its early and generative beauty but the promise of a new beauty.
>
> (Moten 119–20)

These sentences, this powerful example of the inseparability of thinking and feeling, of thinking as a process done out loud through forms of orality, become forms of philosophy created by Moten in order to convey to the reader the percussive doubled duty of seeing and hearing. Moten's meditations offer a rich ending for this chapter, an ending that indeed prompts future work for the sonic, the improvised, the recorded (in every sense) and the generative nature of the practice of Shakespeare as sounding explorer across those years Wooster evokes, stopping the chapter *in media vox*, accepting the verdict of temporary silence and the demands of printed duration. All the last words, Antony's and Cleopatra's, the dead dead and the newly dead after the live perform-ance of Hamlet, echo something like the intimate whispers the Wooster actors' voices became as they were miked, speaking *sotto voce* instruc-tions for motion as their bodies move, not unlike the reverberation of 'swear' that lingers beyond the dead father's voice into the next genera-tion and the next, amplified unnaturally in the past and in the future, once by a ghost and now echoed endlessly by the ghostly machine. So the walls we clambered up on top of to 'hear' early modern sound now seem to disintegrate in these impossible relations between smoky clubs and Danish sea coasts, between biers lifted towards the heavens and the simple quiet of a queen relinquishing the pleasures of noise buried with her lover and with her own voice. Until the next time.

12
Silence

Robert Shaughnessy

I

On 29 August 1952, a concert hall in Woodstock, New York, hosted
the premiere of a new work by the 39-year-old composer John Cage.
It was one that he had worked on for longer than any other of his
compositions (nearly four years). Cage was already established as one
of America's most adventurous and original musical thinkers, but few,
if any, in the original audience settling down for *4′33″* could have
anticipated what they were about to experience. At the beginning of
the performance, the renowned pianist David Tudor walked on to the
concert platform, sat at the piano and closed the keyboard lid. After 30
seconds (timed with a stopwatch), Tudor signalled the end of the first
movement, during which he had played not a single note, by briefly
lifting the lid. For the second movement, which lasted just short of two
and a half minutes, Tudor remained motionless while the wind stirred
the trees outside. The third and final movement, lasting one minute
and forty seconds, and in which, as before, the pianist made no sound,
completed the piece. Four minutes and thirty-three seconds: *4′33″*.

The composition has become legendary, and to this day continues
both to delight and intrigue those who would rank it, with Cage himself, as his definitive work, and to outrage those who regard the very
idea of it as an assault on musicality. At the premiere, Cage recalled, the
audience 'began whispering to one another, and some people began to
walk out'; far from finding it amusing, or, as he hoped, an opportunity
for contemplation, 'they were irritated when they realized nothing was
going to happen, and they haven't forgotten it 30 years later: they're
still angry' (Kostelanetz 65–6).

199

This twentieth-century musical turning point belonged to a moment in which the framing of absence and nothingness was already reconnecting the artwork, the participant, and everyday experience was already finding expression in a variety of forms and media, which notably included the acknowledged influence on Cage's work, Robert Rauschenberg's *White Paintings* (made in 1951 and exhibited in 1953; these consisted of panels of blank canvas upon which viewers were enticed to imaginatively project their own perceptions of light, shade, colour and shape). At the time, it angered listeners because it engaged conventions and expectations of musical performance only to refuse them but also because, by doing so, it flouted the basic rules of commodity art production and consumption, violating the terms of the performance transaction by seemingly offering nothing in return for the audience's investment in the performers, the work, and the event. Silence? To commit time, and possibly money – to *this*?

My topic in this chapter is the use and significance of silence in Shakespearean performance; I begin with Cage partly for the obvious reason that the premiere of *4'33"*, not coincidentally, belongs to a moment of cultural history when silence in the performing arts generally, and the theatre especially, began to be used in new ways, but also because it presents in exquisitely distilled form questions underpinning the discussion that follows: what is it we hear when silence falls on stage, and how and why do we hear it? And why, more often than not, does the sound of silence make us tense, or anxious, or even angry?

II

A point of departure is provided by another summer performance, this time a Shakespearean one, mounted two years before Cage's composition, in Stratford-upon-Avon. The play was *Measure for Measure*, and the director was Peter Brook. The production, which succeeded in placing a play which during the first half of the twentieth century had been afforded few revivals firmly on the theatrical map, was notable in several respects, among them John Gielgud as Angelo and Brook's own scenic designs, which vividly rendered the murky Viennese underworld as one of Hogarthian squalor and violence. Most notable of all, however, for our purposes, were the pauses that interspersed the dialogue, culminating in what Richard David described as the 'breathtaking' moment when Barbara Jefford's Isabella was urged by Mariana to kneel to plead for Angelo's life (5.1.435). 'The pause that followed', wrote David, 'must have been among the longest in theatre history'

(137); for Kenneth Tynan, the 'thirty-five seconds of dead silence ... were a long prickly moment of doubt which had every heart in the theatre thudding' (151). This was no ordinary pause; as Brook later explained, Isabella's silence lay at the heart of a production of a play which, as he saw it, 'almost schematically' contained the simultaneously opposing and coexistent worlds of Rough and Holy Theatre; it was 'a silence in which all the invisible elements of the evening came together, a silence in which the abstract notion of mercy became concrete for that moment to those present'. This was the first time (but certainly by no means the last) that this moment would be freighted in this way, and on this occasion Brook used it to test the limits of the audience's tolerance: he instructed Jefford 'to pause each night until she felt the audience could take it no longer', with the result, on occasions, of it producing 'to a two-minute stopping of the play' (1972: 99–100). Its force is registered in the occult terminology that Brook applies to the device (it 'became a voodoo pole', he records), and in the physiological acuteness of David's and Tynan's response (the caught breath, the thudding of the heart); both suggest that not only the stress of emotional complicity with Isabella's plight was in excess of what might be considered normal or even reasonable, but that Isabella's extended silence seemed to harbour within it the threat that something had gone or might go horribly wrong. The longer the silence, the more (imaginatively, if not actually) possible it seemed that the next line (and with it capitulation, and closure) might never materialize. No wonder the unease was so keenly felt.

Nicholas Ridout has recently drawn our attention to what he has identified as theatre's constitutive wrongness, of which both the embarrassment and anxiety which is endemic to spectatorship and theatrical representation's propensity to unmake or undo themselves are symptomatic. Acknowledging a propensity for failure that is endemic to all performance, he attaches particular significance, especially within the modern theatrical avant-garde, to work that 'puts the question of theatrical undoing squarely on the table' (7). The silence of Brook's and Jefford's Isabella might be accounted an instance where this question at least implicitly is at issue; and in this respect it offered a brief, prescient engagement with the kinds of dramaturgical vocabularies that would, in the course of the decade that followed Brook's production, proceed to position theatrical silence as central to the acts of theatrical doing and undoing, making and unmaking. In itself, theatrical silence – especially within the realist tradition – was hardly a novelty. Stanislavsky, for one, saw the art of the pause as one of the actor's most powerful instruments.

He distinguished the 'logical' pause, which acts as a form of natural, relatively unobtrusive punctuation from the lengthier and more charged 'psychological' pause, which manifests subtext, signifying intense emotion, dilemma or crisis. He wrote of the 'exalted position' of the latter, which he saw as 'not subject to any laws', with 'all laws of speech, without exception ... subject to it' (139). Stanislavsky found his most eloquent silences in the work of Chekhov; but the 1950s avant-garde was dealing in silences of a very different order, duration and intensity. The first and most obvious manifestation of this was, of course, in the work of Samuel Beckett, beginning for the English theatre with the premiere of *Waiting for Godot* at the Arts Theatre in 1955, in which, under the direction of Peter Hall, the orchestration of silences 'lengthened to the point of embarrassment before being broken' provoked its first audiences to worry that the cast had lost their lines (Knowlson 414; see also Cohn). The response was entirely apposite: as Hall recognized, the play's dialectics of expectation and failure are experiential as well as thematic; trapped in their seats waiting for answers that might never arrive (and that in any case provided no solutions even when they did), many among *Godot*'s audiences in London in 1955 were no less riled than those on the other side of the Atlantic who, three years earlier, had sat through 4′33″.

Godot's excruciating lacunae affronted theatrical sensibilities by conjecturing the scenario not just of a breakdown in communication, and abandonment of narrative progression and closure, but of a systemic failure of the apparatus of theatrical representation itself; the drama that followed in its wake (and that to a large extent it made possible) presented the Shakespearean theatre of the 1960s with a more amenably domesticated variant of the poetics of the unsaid, and one that played a substantial and lasting part in shaping the new forms of Shakespearean acting. The key figure here, in addition to Beckett, is Harold Pinter, particularly as directed by Hall in the RSC productions of the mid-1960s.[1] For Hall, writing in 1964, Pinter was simply 'the most significant new English poetic dramatist and one very relevant to Shakespeare', partly as one of a number of contemporary writers whose sensibilities enabled Hall and his contemporaries to access Shakespeare's modernity, but, more importantly, as one whose writing 'has the balance, the inevitability, and the precision of poetry' (1964: 46).

---

[1] For a discussion of the Pinter–Shakespeare connection with particular reference to Hal's silences in *1 Henry IV*, see Shaughnessy.

Pinter's pauses are, of course, legendarily regarded as the defining feature of his work; and it was certainly what seemed to many his extensive use of the pause (with regard to both frequency and duration) that recommended, and discommended, him to his first (and subsequent) critics: as W.B. Worthen summarizes, 'the history of Pinter criticism' suggests that 'what's *in* the *Pause* – if anything – remains a key interpretive controversy both for literary critics and performers' (2005: 82–3). For Hall in the early 1960s, the task in hand when directing Pinter was less a matter of speculating about what was 'in' the silences than of identifying their functionality as intervals in the context of a mode of reading and production that envisaged the script as verbal score. For Hall, the notation is as precise and specific as the marking of musical rests:

> If there is a pause in the proceedings, for a small pause he puts three dots; for a large pause he puts 'Pause'; for a very, very long pause he puts 'Silence' ... Harold writes in silence as much as he does in words; he defines silence by the noise on either side of it and the literal communication on either side of it.
>
> (1974: 16)

Inevitably, there is an immediate connection with Shakespeare. Recounting the experience of conducting a 'dot and pause rehearsal' for his landmark 1965 RSC production of *The Homecoming*, Hall confessed that (understandably enough) it 'drove the actors absolutely mad', and claimed that it revealed the extent to which the performers neglected to 'remember the phrases'. It was, he said, '[e]xactly as if an actor in Shakespeare had learned his text without knowing where the ends of the lines are, which is the whole phrasing unit. If you run the line on in Shakespeare, which you must once in ten, you still must *know* where the end of the line is' (1974: 16–17). In a separate conversation, Hall directly parallels Pinter's methods of phrasing and punctuation with Shakespeare's; referring to the 'organic rhythm and shape about his prose, which has to be observed', he presses the point that, '[i]n exactly the same way, you cannot ignore the ends of the lines of Shakespeare, the commas of Shakespeare, the full stops, the rhythmic regularities and irregularities' (Marowitz 153).

The view that the punctuation of Shakespeare's texts provides a guide to speech rhythms may be dubious on historical grounds (it is in most cases more likely to be compositorial rather than authorial), as is the widespread supposition that phrasing is a matter of the logical and psychological rather than the oratorical. Nonetheless, it is one that carries considerable weight within the profession. Hall's remarks define not only his own directorial position but an approach to Shakespearean verbal delivery and characterization that, largely initiated, codified and formalized by Hall and his RSC colleagues in the 1960s (and subjected to periodic readjustment since), continues to mark the parameters of mainstream practice both within the RSC and beyond. Shakespeare's text is equated with Pinter's in the sense that both are simultaneously highly formalized and realist; the challenge for the actor and the director is one of striking the appropriate balance between conveying the shape of the verse and sounding like a real person speaking, or, as John Barton put it, 'simply ... to marry the two traditions of heightened language and naturalistic acting' (20). Hall's position would subsequently harden considerably, to the extent that he came to believe that text should be treated as 'a piece of writing containing its voicing and staging in precise rhythms through precise codes, so that plays are viewed as being as complete containers of directions for their performance as an opera's musical score contains all the notes the singers and orchestra will need to perform' (Holland 2008: 143). Hall now notoriously describes himself as an 'iambic fundamentalist'; during the formative period of the early 1960s, however, the relationship between the iambic and the demotic was still a relatively ecumenical one. In this context, the application of the Pinteresque metrics of silence to Shakespearean speech offered a means of regulating and structuring the pauses that were an increasingly indispensable component of the actor's repertoire of techniques.

To assess the history and significance of the pause in Shakespearean performance since the early 1960s (and in England alone) would be, to put it mildly, a considerable task; however, given the fact that both the RSC and the National Theatre have from their inception comprehensively documented their work in the form of audio recordings (held, in the former case, in the British Library's Sound Archive), it is one for which an immense amount of documentation is available.[2] Such an exercise is not without precedent: what have been described as

---

[2] A small but intriguing sample of this archive is provided by the RSC-produced double-CD set *The Essential Shakespeare Live: The Royal Shakespeare Company in Performance* (2005), which features excerpts ranging from Laurence Olivier's mesmerizing Coriolanus of 1959 to Judi Dench's Countess in the 2003 *All's Well that Ends Well*.

Shakespeare's 'open' silences have also been the focus of a full-length investigation dating from the classic phase of stage-centred criticism, in Philip C. McGuire's *Speechless Dialect* (1985), a work which offers a series of subtle and intricate close readings of the ways in which actors have chosen to inhabit and animate textual silences which modern performance has increasingly found troubling, enigmatic or ambiguous: Hippolyta in the first scene of *A Midsummer Night's Dream*, Antonio and Isabella at, respectively, the ends of *Twelfth Night* and *Measure for Measure*. For the purposes of this chapter, however, a preliminary mapping of the contours of this vast soundscape, which affords some sense both of the scale of the enterprise and of the rich variety of uses to which silences and pauses have been put, is provided by listening to the testimony of those whose task it has been to preserve and to summarize what has been noteworthy, memorable and innovative about Shakespearean performance during the period.

Let us begin by considering the annual accounts published in *Shakespeare Quarterly* and *Shakespeare Survey*, which have kept close eyes and ears on the work of the RSC (and in the latter case, especially more recently, the National and other regional companies) from the outset. In the course of five decades of Shakespearean performance history, the annals yield just over fifty instances where the reviewer thought it worth documenting, and sometimes commenting upon, a pause or a silence. The record begins in 1960, with the RSC's first-season *Merchant of Venice*, which was notable for a rhymed pair of silences: Antonio's, as he was left isolated at the end of the play, and that of Shylock, who at the end of the trial scene faced up to Portia before departing, 'the point of the moment', according to John Russell Brown, being 'to show that all had been done, that the two were irreconcilable' (135). It ends in 2007 with the RSC's *Coriolanus*, in which the most powerful and eloquent silent moment was not when Coriolanus took his mother by the hand (5.4.183), but an interpolated pause that augmented her non-speaking processional appearance in the subsequent scene. Staging the women's return to Rome to the cheers of the crowd, director Gregory Doran suddenly had them 'fall unexpectedly silent' as Janet Suzman's Volumnia reached the centre of the stage. 'She pauses,' writes Michael Dobson, 'and looks up, and takes a breath, about to make a speech in response; but suddenly, already too keenly aware that the effect of her intercession can only be to condemn her son to death, she cannot utter a word, almost cries, looks to the floor, hurries away' (Dobson 2008: 326). Two mute exits, separated by half a century. Between them (to cite but only the most memorable highlights): the long, agonizing pause as

David Warner's Prince went eyeball-to eyeball with Brewster Mason's Claudius at the end of *The Mousetrap* in Hall's 1965 *Hamlet*; Paul Scofield's intricate and extensive use of caesuras in his Hall-directed Macbeth of two years later, which, by transforming key lines into interrogatives, delivered the most introspective and speculative Thanes ever seen at Stratford; the silence in the penultimate scene of John Barton's 1973 *Richard II*, in which Ian Richardson and Richard Pasco, alternating the roles of Richard and Bolingbroke, came face to face in the king's prison cell; the exquisite pacing of Judi Dench's invitation, as Beatrice, to Donald Sinden's Benedick in Barton's 1976 *Much Ado*, 'Against my will (*pause*) I am sent (*pause; glower; then very emphatically*) to bid you (*then very fast, very loud*) come in to dinner' (Warren 1977: 172); Ian McKellen's rendering, in Hall's 1984 National Theatre production, of *Coriolanus* 5.3.183, by seizing Volumnia's hand 'as she was about to storm away', and holding her 'by force amid a prolonged, tense, electric silence' (Warren 1986: 119); the 'truly astonishing moment' in Adrian Noble's 1985 *As You Like It*, where, Orlando having issued his threat to kill 'He ... that touches any of this fruit / Till I and my affairs are answerèd', Alan Rickman's sardonic Jaques silently 'walked steadily from downstage to the table, and, on "If you will not be answer'd with reason, I must die", picked up an apple and bit it' (Shrimpton 202); another moment in the same director's 1986 *Macbeth* when Jonathan Pryce entered at the beginning of 3.1, discovered Fleance sitting on his throne, and dropped the crown on the boy's head, hailing him as 'our chief guest' (3.1.11); the silence that descended after the courtiers had taken the oath during the first scene of Terry Hands's 1990 *Love's Labour's Lost*, as the hapless quartet 'realized they could think of nothing to do' (Holland, 1992: 125); the interminable pause that, in the same season's *Two Gentlemen of Verona* at the Swan interceded between Proteus' 'My shame and guilt confounds me' (5.4.73) and his appeal to Valentine for forgiveness; the complex choreography of departures, glimpses of reconciliation, hesitations and exchanged gazes – variously amazed and uncertain, elated and anxious – that transformed the mass exodus of the final scene of Tim Supple's 1996 *The Comedy of Errors* into as comprehensive a compendium of open endings, half-resolved issues and unanswered questions as a production of this play could ever hope to accommodate; the breathtaking hold during the trial scene of Trevor Nunn's 1999 National Theatre *Measure for Measure*, as Henry Goodman's Shylock poised with his knife over Antonio's bared chest; the desolate gaps that punctuated the horrible, desperate and futile attempts by Alex Jennings's Leontes, in Nicholas Hytner's 2001 *The Winter's Tale* at the

National, to enforce a reconciliation in the statue scene; and, finally, the silence that was experienced, in all its awkwardness, *before the play had even begun* in Doran's 2006 *Antony and Cleopatra* at the Swan: in which, as we waited and fretted, impatient for the show to start, and for Patrick Stewart and Harriet Walter to make the entrance, that for reasons unknown had been delayed well past the scheduled start time, we found ourselves, in our own anxieties about a pre-emptive unravelling, embroiled in Philo's exasperation.

As this broadly representative set of examples indicates, the exercise of the art of silence in modern Shakespearean performance is on the one hand as varied and specific as the narrative, generic, situational and character contexts in which it operates, and, on the other, noticeably consistent in its operating principles, applications and effects. Though the foregoing overview offers a generic as well as historic spread, a closer look at the record reveals not only that certain plays, and genres, attract more attention as occasions for than others, but that instances of the silent treatment tend to cluster around a noticeably limited set of incidents and character moments. Here the synoptic and summative nature of the chronicles proves their usefulness as a means of arriving at a preliminary mapping. Since it is partly the task of the *Shakespeare Survey* or *Shakespeare Quarterly* reviewer to highlight the unusual, exceptional and the innovative as much as, if not more than, the perennial manoeuvres of performance tradition, the records tend to dwell not upon instances where a silence has come to be expected but upon those where an unexpected, or strategically well-placed, pause somehow encapsulates an actor's conception of a part or a particular directorial take on the play. According the testimony of those entrusted since 1960 by these two journals with the task of preserving for posterity what was salient, novel or memorable in Shakespearean performance, the pointed pause or weighted silence has been substantially more the preserve of performances of the Comedies than the Tragedies (some thirty reported instances versus around twenty). Of these, the Isabella dilemma has, understandably, been the most frequent, with more than half a dozen mentions, the majority of which occur between 1970 (Barton's production) and 1981 (at the National Theatre, directed by Michael Rudman). Brook had in 1950 instigated a silence prior to Isabella's capitulation to Mariana's plea for her to intercede to save Angelo's life; 20 years later, Barton extended the zone of recalcitrance by directing Estelle Kohler to ignore the Duke's offer of marriage; as the decade proceeded and actors, directors and audiences began to attend to the play with ears at least partially attuned to feminism, and what Isabella did not say in this scene, and how she didn't say it, became increasingly as significant as what she did. Philip McGuire cites both moments as instances of Shakespeare's 'open silences': points where the audience's entire response to the play is decisively subject to the 'nonverbal, extratextual' components of the theatrical event that are manifestly beyond the remit of the words on the page, that can vary drastically from one production to the next, and yet can be crucial determinants of its outcome (xix–xxiii).

The way McGuire sees it, and the way most performers have played it, Isabella's speechlessness is a *character* opportunity; the extent to which she pauses, or does not pause, before responding to Mariana, the reaction that she makes, or does not make, to the Duke's marriage offer, both acting as crucial indices of what is thought and felt but unsaid, and perhaps unsayable. 'The longer Isabella pauses ... that is, the more sustained her silence,' writes McGuire, 'the greater will be the audience's sense of the anguish and bereavement she must struggle to overcome' (xv). Now although his seems to me a fair description of how this moment usually works in modern performance, there are a number of tacit assumptions at work here that require a little unpacking. The first is that, whether it is allowed by the script or apparently mandated by it (Barton suggests that short lines contain Shakespeare's 'hidden stage directions to the actor ... we can be pretty sure that he is indicating a pause of some sort'; 30), silence has weight because it is assumed to be both significant and active. This assumption may be grounded in the first instance in the conviction that Shakespeare is, in his mature work at least, always sufficiently in command of his craft to ensure there is no one on stage who is there without a purpose, and that therefore if a character says nothing, their silence is meaningful. This conviction is likely to be reinforced by modern actor's habitual practice of fashioning his or her Shakespearean part into a continuous and coherent whole by coordinating what the character says and does with what others say to her or about him, and by integrating the role into the play viewed as a whole. This was not, of course, the privilege of the early modern actor and many of his successors until as late as the nineteenth century, equipped as he or she was with only part and cue lines (Stern, 2004: 113–26).

For the actor playing Isabella, the 85 lines that follow 'Thoughts are no subjects / Intents but merely thoughts' (5.1.445–6) not only give her nothing to say, but give her nothing to say in response either to the revelation of the brother she thought to be dead, or to the Duke's twice-iterated marriage proposal; but rather than regarding this silencing as a failure of the text, as gap or omission, or even as a deliberate downsizing of the part that shifts the scene's focus conclusively to the Duke, most Isabella-actors treat it as a space of personal choice, and of self-definition. This is an important move: in effect, it internalizes a textual lacuna that is perhaps symptomatic of the play's narrative habit of evading its own consequences, transferring a structural impasse to the level of individual deliberation. As Paola Dionisotti (RSC 1978) put it:

> [t]he fact that Shakespeare doesn't script Isabella's answer to the Duke's proposal but just leaves him with his line, 'Give me that hand,' tells me she *doesn't* give him her hand. I think it's quite clear. Shakespeare is leaving an extremely big void there, a figure who goes completely silent and makes no commitment. She doesn't. He asks. But she doesn't' ...

For Juliet Stevenson (RSC, 1983), alternatively, '[m]aybe ... she doesn't know what to say to the Duke's proposal', and, after 'a long, long pause ... I took the Duke's hand' (Rutter 40, 52). Dionisotti and Stevenson instinctively ascribe agency of a subtextual, and very decisive, kind to Isabella at a moment where the only clues that the text affords are those that the actors have planted there themselves, but by doing so they are simply acting in manner congruent with their entire conception of the role. Stevenson's case, Jonathan Holmes contends, involved 'the placing of her performance self in textual gaps and silences' (164). My interest here is less in whether they are wrong to do so (in the sense of being naively anachronistic in their realist presumptions about Shakespearean 'character' (see Escolme, 2010) than in the means that are typically deployed to secure and sustain the impression of the real selves that are apprehended by spectators. In both instances, there is synchronicity between volition and timing, or between the placement and duration of the pause and the sense that options are being weighed and a choice being made. In Isabella's case, the longer the performer says and does nothing, the deeper the audience's investment, the more intense the subjectivity-effect – and the sharper the sense of anxiety.

The silences that have become part of the texture of *Measure for Measure*, though in some ways particular to that play, and though more notably fraught and forceful than most, are nonetheless exemplary. The examples we have been considering thus far have attracted notice in part because they are both climactic and palpable: more often than not found at a crisis point which renders the outcome of the action, at least momentarily, insecure by placing closure in jeopardy or at least in contention, the strategically positioned pause typically works to underscore the sense that a choice, a decision or a commitment is made on the part of an agent who is, in however limited a sense, purposeful, self-determining and self-aware, free to embrace certain options and to reject others. And the agent's power is the agent's vulnerability: because the pause, however infinitesimal, places text and time (and with it, perhaps, the breath of the listener) in suspension, it always harbours within it the possibility of failure, of the theatrical undoing that inheres in the possibility that the next word, the expected action, might never come. In words, deeds and silence, the making of theatrical selves, even in the most naturalistic of scenarios, remains dependent upon – perhaps we should say subject to – its simultaneous liability to unmaking. Everybody knows, of course, that Isabella has no other textual option than, sooner or later, to concede to Mariana's plea; but it is in the space between sooner and later that the agony and the ecstasy of selfhood resides.

Whether at the macro-level of the 'Big' pause, or at the micro-level of the actor's word-by-word delivery of the script, timing is everything. Big pauses, usually, cannot work in isolation, but must be prepared for, and worked up to; one of the obvious preconditions for a character to appear to be recognizably the same person in their final scene as in their first is that the rhythmic patterns of speech, silence, gesture and movement through which they define themselves exhibit at least some degree of consistency (which is not the same as uniformity) throughout. For Stanislavsky, this imperative of consistency is defined as tempo-rhythm: 'Stage action, like speech, must be musical. Movement must follow a continuous line, like a note from a stringed instrument, or, when necessary, stop short like the staccato of a coloratura soprano ... . Movements have their legato, staccato, andante, allegro, piano and forte and so on' (quoted in Benedetti 50–1). 'Tempo', as Jean Benedetti puts it, 'denotes the speed of an action or a feeling – fast, slow, medium. Rhythm, internally, indicates the *intensity* with which an emotion is experienced: externally it indicates the pattern of gestures, moves and actions which express the emotion' (50). The dominant tempo-rhythm of contemporary Shakespearean speech in action is, Bruce R. Smith proposes, that of 'ragtime', a mode that 'depends on a regular musical rhythm' that is 'open to all sorts of syncopations, all sorts of variations' (2005: 60). Among the many techniques of variation available to the actor, syncopation is, for our purposes, key. Though it is found in all musical traditions, it is the especially defining feature of modern and popular musical forms such as jazz, blues and rock: syncopation, the technique of disrupting or displacing the regularity of the beat, of asymmetric stressing, works in a wide variety of ways but in particular, by introducing gaps, hiatuses and delays in unexpected places, to generate tension, the impression of spontaneity, liveness. As a core component of improvisational technique, syncopation is the means through which a musician can creatively, or idiosyncratically, individualize a piece of music, and, as does the actor with her text, makes the notes his own.

For the contemporary Shakespearean actor, likewise, syncopating verse and prose is (*pace* Peter Hall) essential to the task of, as Peter Lichtenfels defines it, being '"on *voice*"', 'a state in which the *text* is integrated into the body, so that when actors come to perform they are able to respond in the moment to other characters as if they are hearing the others' lines for the first time and speaking their own thoughts as they think them' (Jenstad, Lichtenfels and Magnusson 13). Reflecting on his work on the title role in Noble's 1993 *Macbeth*, Derek Jacobi provides a succinct account of how this can operate in practice: stating that 'my approach to all the speeches was to make them as true as possible, and as light as possible too, so as not to impede the thought', he gives the example of the brief exchange between the Thanes at the end of 1.3:

> Macbeth says to Banquo 'Think upon what has chanced' (l. 153) and it seems as though they are about to talk to each other again in the old way. Then Macbeth says 'Till then, enough', and I tried to suggest that he was about to say something serious and confidential, then paused and instead said 'enough', implying uncertainty about sharing his thoughts with him: the process of separation has gone a little further. Even the final 'Come, friends' seemed to have a double edge: 'Come,...' – and what am I to call them? Are they friends? Yes, everyone is a friend at the moment. What *am* I worrying about?
>
> (196)

In Jacobi's hands, the commas that in most modern editions divide 'then' from 'enough' and 'Come' from 'friends' (the First Folio has 'Till then enough: / Come friends') mark pauses that are psychological as well as logical, and it is the split-second timing, the barely perceptible delay before hitting the note that makes them so. And, as Jacobi's intricate parsing of Macbeth's thought-processes demonstrates, untold emotional riches lie within even the tiniest of caesuras.

III

In order to trace the relationship between the micro- and macro-silences that collectively and cumulatively syncopate a Shakespearean part, in more detail, I want to return to a production that has already been cited as featuring one of the most extraordinary extended pauses of recent times: Trevor Nunn's *The Merchant of Venice*, staged in the National Theatre's Cottesloe Theatre, and subsequently the Olivier auditorium in 1999, and filmed for the BBC in 2001. As an outstanding example of what Roberta Barker, following Cary Mazer, terms Shakespearean emotional realism, Nunn's production reveals with exceptional clarity the interplay between speech rhythm, pacing and punctuation and character-construction. The BBC film, which, by carefully preserving the studio-scale dynamics of the performance for the small screen, serves as an invaluable adjunct to the National's archival records of the show, provides a rare opportunity for a kind of close reading that is impossible in the theatre, though feasible in the archive.[3] This is of some importance for what follows, as I shall be taking the measure of the production's silences in what might strike some readers as rather literal terms. Qualitative investigation, in this case, will be based, at least partially, on quantitative grounds.

As we heard earlier, the defining moment of this production, and of its extraordinary Shylock (Henry Goodman), was the agonizing hesitation between Shylock's 'come, prepare' and Portia's seemingly desperate improvisation, 'Tarry a little' (4.1.299–300): occupying just over a minute of stage time, it showed a Shylock, visibly backed into a corner by the Christian court, caught on the horns of a terrible dilemma, knowing full well that he is in a lose–lose situation, committed to a course of action that must and yet cannot carry through, torn between hatred for Antonio and for what Antonio represents, and a sudden, unexpected empathy with his intended victim, tortured by rage and

---

[3] My discussion draws upon the National Theatre's very full archival records of the show, which include video recordings of both the Cottesloe staging and the Olivier transfer, as well as the BBC film version. One of the primary reasons for selecting this production as a case study is the wide availability of the latter, which enables readers to test my conclusions against their own viewing. It should be borne in mind, however, that there are some significant points of difference between the timings of the stage production and the screened one: thanks to some light cutting and to rapid cutting between scenes, the latter is, at 162 minutes, about three-quarters of the length of the stage show.

grief over Jessica's betrayal; it also showed an Antonio moaning with terror as he faces what seems like the very real prospect of bloody death; it showed a Portia, who in this production had no idea how to resolve the situation, devising the 'jot of blood' clause, in panic, at the very last second.

'Never have we been so close to Shylock,' wrote Sheridan Morley, 'nor so sure that he is about to murder (albeit legally) Antonio' (*Spectator* 26 June 1999). If this sense of deadly proximity was in part an effect of density and quality of the detail that shaped and occupied that minute of near-silence, it was also due to the exactitude of its timing, in terms both of the internal rhythms of Goodman's mime and of its placement within the time frames of the scene, the play and the production. The production prompt book notates the sequence thus:

after prayers –
Shy steps towards Ant – holding out knife
The tip of the knife touches Ant's breast
Shy shakes – withdraws – steps back.
Puts apron round himself
Pause.
Steps forward to take a pound of flesh

P interrupts – stopping Shy – she x D
to SR of Ant + Shy. She has the bond in her hand.

When it comes to the details of blocking, prompt books (which are designed to serve the purposes of calling the show, rather than the needs of the theatre researcher) can be variable: this particular one is both unusually full and, I suggest, remarkably eloquent, an instance where the pencilled pages of the production bible not only notate the moves but seem imprinted with their grace and force. Whichever member of the stage-management team made this transcription, he or she had an exquisite – we might say, Pinteresque – feel for the dramaturgy of the sequence, with each move allocated a separate line, a designated – and punctuated – pause, and, at the moment of crisis, an aporetic space between Shylock's lunge forward and Portia's interruption. The video records yield the following timings: for the prayer sequence, 20 seconds; 12 seconds as Shylock takes two steps forward, places the knife, freezes; 20 seconds as he takes four steps back, wipes the blade, and gathers himself together; and less than a second for him to lunge towards Antonio again and for Portia to intervene. Beat by beat, Goodman paces out a deadly, conflicted, silent, solo tango: his, and the production's, last dance (slow, slow, quick, quick, slow; slow, slow, quick, quick, STOP).

The power of the sequence was enhanced by its placement within the architecture of both the scene and the play. Taking place exactly two-thirds of the way through the trial scene, and thus marking the transition between its second and third movements (the passage from first to second being marked by Portia's entrance at 4.1.161), Shylock's nemesis was, at 40 minutes after the interval, and two hours and 33 minutes into a total performance time that lasted three and a quarter hours (three and a half when it transferred to the Olivier auditorium), a fulcrum moment, almost exactly midway through the show's second half, turning it, on the trembling point of Shylock's blade, from tragedy to a deeply compromised, tragicomic closure. As with Brook's *Measure for Measure* half a century earlier, several of the reviewers who commented on this moment (and quite a few did) registered the intense physicality of their involvement in it: for Morley, it was 'a genuinely breath-holding moment' (*Spectator* 26 June 1999); Smallwood spoke of the 'tense, painful seconds of almost unbearable suspense' (269) and Georgina Brown of the *Mail on Sunday* recorded that 'you watch ... on the edge of your seat' (27 June 1999). Rigid with tension, breath suspended, implicated within the event by the proximities of the Cottesloe, reporters' bodies are captivated not only by the spectacle of the unthinkable (*'Oh no, he's going to kill him'*), but also by the shaping rhythms of a show that has, slowly, slowly, quick, quick, slowly been building towards it from the moment that the audience first settled into their seats.

At just before 10 in the evening (or 4.30 in the afternoon, at matinees), that might have seemed quite a while ago. A number of reviewers commented on the seemingly laboured pacing of the early scenes in particular: Morley reported that it 'starts slowly, even hesitantly', and John Gross that it 'gets off to a shaky start', citing such naturalistic embellishments as 'A frivolous 1920s setting, yawning tedium, immoderate laughter, too much Champagne, jokey home movies, cabaret turns' (*Sunday Telegraph* 20 June 1999); as Michael Coveney pithily summarized, the 'novelistic attention to detail takes time' (*Daily Mail* 1 June 1999). Nunn's location of the play within a 1920s–1930s Weimar-ish milieu, it was generally recognized, created a fairly precise and specific social and emotional context for the play, and for Shylock especially. But the practicalities of the realist *mise-en-scène* also dictated the production's basic tempo, one driven by the rhythms of striking and setting, furnishing and unfurnishing, bringing things on and carrying them off, picking up and setting down. Unfolding within a series of particularized locations (Club, Casket Room, Quayside, Terrace), this was a production whose changeovers were cinematically accompanied by mournful, slow-tempo keyboards, strings and percussion, and interspersed with the sounds of traffic, seagulls and distant dogs, which was packed with material period detail: an upright piano for Antonio to strum in the first scene, a drum kit, a microphone, café tables and chairs, cigarettes and ashtrays, a display cabinet, coffee cups and glasses of tea, cocktail shakers and champagne flutes, newspapers, notes and documents (particularized to the level of Bassanio's 'list of things to do in preparation for trip to Belmont' and Tubal's 'bills and expenses regarding … trip to Genoa to find Jessica'), caskets and court ledgers, the occasional table on which perched Shylock's precious framed photograph of his dead (and beautiful and young) wife, Portia's home cine-projector, Launcelot Gobbo's mop and bucket and Old Gobbo's yellow suitcase, a flamenco guitar to accompany the heel-clicking Prince of Aragon, weighing scales and a knife. Realism of this order 'takes time', indeed: less in the sense of its speed and duration than in its capacity to command the rhythm, pacing and articulation of verbal and psychological detail.

In a production extensively punctuated by pauses and silences, by wordless moments of reaction and reflection, interpolated encounters and face-to-face confrontations, no performer had greater command of the resources of stillness than Goodman as Shylock. Gut-wrenching as it was, the climactic business over the pound of flesh was but the third of (at least) five big silences during the trial scene. The first came when, having listened patiently to Portia's earnest, urgent, close-up delivery of the 'quality of mercy' (4.1.202), Goodman 'agonized for several seconds of almost unbearable suspense before a returning awareness of the Gratiano mob rekindled his resolve' (Smallwood 269). The second was when Portia ordered Antonio to lay bare his breast. In another of Nunn's directorial interpolations, an entry was scripted at the start of the scene for Tubal, who joined the courtroom audience as a silent witness. On Shylock's 'Nearest his heart' (l. 250), he silently rose from his chair and walked out, stopping momentarily to meet Shylock eye-to-eye and give a reproachful half-shake of his head; Shylock, as he was all too aware, was now utterly on his own. The third preceded 'I am content' (l. 389), a line that seemingly had to be torn from him; the fourth and final silence was at Shylock's exit (1.396), which saw him divest himself of his yarmulke and drop it on the scales, gaze at Antonio for one last time, and then take the long, unsteady journey across the floor of the courtroom to the door.

Shylock's silences in this scene were part of a pattern, which also included an accidental walk-on part in Launcelot Gobbo's stand-up

routine, a wordless encounter with Antonio at the end of 2.6, just
before he entered the house which Jessica has just abandoned, and, in
one of the most commented-on scenes, the shocking, heartbreaking
moment in 2.5 when, reacting with fury to Lancelot's remark about the
masquers, he struck Jessica across the face, and was then immediately
overwhelmed with remorse. These were the mute crescendos of playing
that consistently opened up spaces between words, that invited their
auditors to hear within them the broken music of a heart and a mind;
and they also typified this actor's, and the production's, enlargement
of the role to the point where the rhythms of Shylock's entrances and
exits (scripted and unscripted), speech and action actually seemed to
determine that of the production as a whole. Until his spectacular collapse in the trial scene, this show's time was largely Shylock's time; a
time that was established in – literally – the opening seconds of his first
appearance, as he responded to Bassanio:

> Three (*beat*) thousand (*beat*) ducats. (*three second pause*) Well. (*with a
> slow, ruminative nod*)
> …
> (*pitched slightly higher, interrogative*) For three months? (*four second
> pause, a light chuckle*) Well. (*clipped, staccato; Shylock suddenly performs
> a little self-mocking jig*)
> …
> Antonio (*beat*) shall become bound (*with a falling inflection. Seven-
> second pause*). We-ell. (*disyllabic, with a rising inflection on the second
> syllable*).
>
> (1.3.1–5)

The exchange is proleptic (for, in this production, Antonio will, truly,
become 'bound', and the downward glance that Goodman casts on
this line seems to foresee him pinioned in the courtroom), and it
shows Goodman's Shylock, not only very much 'on voice' but also at
his most playful: here, and throughout this, his first scene, his command of the Christians – and of the audience – is exercised through
the timing that dictates pace and duration. This, in turn, significantly
impacts upon the production's overall time frame. It takes over half
a minute to deliver these five lines; the entire scene, totalling 175
lines, lasts 12 minutes; the first (185 lines) and second (113 lines), in
comparison, take just under 8 and 5 minutes, respectively). In effect,
1.3 takes almost 30 per cent longer overall than the length of the text
on its own would appear to suggest it should, not because the verbal

delivery is any slower than is usual, but because of its intricate, yet never obtrusive, pointing.

This expansionary technique was operative throughout. It was no surprise that the trial scene commandeered more than half of the show post-interval; but the extent of Nunn's foregrounding of Shylock's role through silent augmentation really becomes apparent when we take into account the timings of the scenes in which he is scripted to appear as well as the production's interpolations during the production's first half. The additions included an exchange in Yiddish with Jessica at the beginning of 2.3, and the father and daughter's shared singing of 'Eshes Chayil' in 2.5, an addition which contributed to the extension of a scene of 55 lines to 6 minutes. The interval was placed after 3.1, a scene of 170 lines lasting 11 minutes; and the scene ended, splendidly, with 'If I can catch him on the hip / Cursèd be my tribe If I forgive him', transposed from 1.3.41, 46–7, and sound effects of scavenging gulls and an ominous ship's foghorn. The text assigns Shylock 224 (that is, about 18 per cent) of the 1,229 lines of the play to this point; Goodman was on stage for over a third of the first half. Shylock's silences significantly augmented the stage time he is allocated by the text.

It was, then, by presenting a stage presence that was constituted in significant measure by verbal absence that Goodman fashioned a Shylock that seemed so much more than the sum of his words. Though in some ways exceptional, Goodman's manipulation and inhabitation of both textual and paratextual silences is, I suggest, not at all untypical of contemporary Shakespearean performance technique. But if the timing of the pause, large or small, is crucial to the work of rendering heightened text as words that are plausibly those of a speaking subject, it is far from the only kind of silence that Shakespeare, and our own theatre, have to offer. Theatre practitioners have been particularly adept, as we have seen, in devising gaps that audiences have invested with desire, longing, anticipation and anxiety; and it is in the crucible of these discontents that theatrical persons are forged. But silences can be, and often are, political as well as personal. It is no accident that *The Merchant of Venice* is second only to *Measure for Measure* as the play most cited by the chroniclers of the journals *Shakespeare Quarterly* and *Shakespeare Survey* to have been subjected to extensive and significant interpolated pausing; if Isabella's silences have internalized her play's problem status as personal crisis, the anguished gaps that have opened up in *The Merchant of Venice* on the post-Holocaust stage have spoken even more eloquently of the anger and shame that it continues to provoke, of our ongoing difficulties with it, and of the contradictions of our engagements with its racial politics.

Though it was not a 'political' production, the setting of Nunn's *The Merchant of Venice* worked to position the play in relation to twentieth-century history; and in this respect, its most haunting absent presence was that of its play-world's future. It was, perhaps, in this spirit of grim retrospection that Alastair Macauley noted that the production contained silences in which the audience could find themselves genuinely, and painfully, implicated; responding to Shylock's enforced conversion to Christianity, he recorded that 'the silence in the audience, as Shylock and others take in the news, really does seem one of outrage' (*Financial Times* 10 July 1999). Here, even if for a moment only, it is the audience's own silence, its passivity, its complicity with what is most troubling about the play, about the world the production has constructed, and about the world we have inherited and constructed ourselves, that is at stake. It is a moment that bears comparison with an even more confrontational, and much more directly political, use of silence in an earlier production of a problem comedy: Michael Bogdanov's *The Taming of the Shrew*, which he directed for the RSC in 1978. This came at the end of 4.1, at the close of Petruccio's 'Thus have I politicly begun my reign' monologue (4.1.169–92), and at the start of the final phase of a modern-dress production that had seen a taming plot staged with unremitting, near-psychotic brutality. Taunting the audience with the final couplet, 'He that knows better how to tame a shrew / Now let him speak. 'Tis charity to show', Jonathan Pryce then stopped, lit up, and, calmly smoking, dared a reply. What followed, the prompt book records, was a pause which 'can be as long as 1½ Minutes'. Enough said, I think.

If these examples serve as reminders that theatrical silence is public as well as private property, and that what happens in it is as much, and possibly more, the responsibility of the spectator as it is that of the performer, they might also remind us of an even more important truth: that there is, in actuality, no such thing as silence, in the theatre or anywhere else. And if even the briefest of Shakespearean pauses rings with the amplified clamour of our own hopes and fears, it is also suffused with the sub-threshold sounds of the beating of our hearts, the intake of breath and the shuffling, fidgeting, coughing, swallowing, rustling and all the other voluntary and involuntary sonic emissions of an audience in shared space. Should that space not be an enclosed one, as anyone who has experienced Shakespeare in the open air will immediately recognize, the acoustic landscape widens still further, to incorporate the ambient and often obtrusive sounds of the city or countryside: the noise of construction, transit and law enforcement, of the wind and the rain, and of passers-by, barking dogs and birdsong. Although this is often experienced as outdoor performance's biggest drawback (the mood of, say, *As You Like It* is generally not enhanced by the accompaniment of sirens and pneumatic drilling), the muzak of modernity can, just occasionally, serve to its advantage. I recently spent a warm May afternoon at a performance of *Macbeth* at Shakespeare's Globe, during which a play whose atmospherics are sculpted by invocations of flight of various kinds, whether natural, sacred or diabolic, and which is flocked with images of winged creatures, was accompanied by a sometimes distant (and sometimes not so distant) chorus of jet engines and helicopter blades: far from breaking the spell, the sounds of powered flight uncannily reinforced the claims of the play upon a century in which mass slaughter has so often been airborne.

It will be said, perhaps, that this was down to chance. But that – returning by way of coda to the place where we started – is precisely the point: for John Cage, the achievement of *4′33″* resided in its capacity to frame the random beauty of the everyday, and of the unexpected and unplanned patterns and juxtapositions which would be utterly different every time, and in every place, that the piece was performed. By framing silence as an object of aesthetic contemplation, Cage hoped that his listeners might 'feel that the sounds of their environment constitute a music which is more interesting than the music which they would hear if they went to a concert hall' (Kostelanetz 66). Listening more attentively to the unquiet silences that surround and shape Shakespeare's text, we hear the noises of nature and of culture, of physiology and of history, that are as vital a part of its strange musicality as the sound of the words.

Afterword

John Russell Brown

The way ahead for the study of Shakespeare in performance

During the last few decades, the study of Shakespeare's plays has made convincing progress. From a close examination of individual texts, their use of language and rhetoric, their intellectual origins and contexts, and the mirror they hold up to nature, scholarly attention has moved on to consider the dramaturgical qualities of those texts, what has been made of them in performance and what might become of them in future. No resting place is here because no agreed way has been found to describe and evaluate individual productions of a play, either in the past or present, either actual or imaginary. Clearly not all productions are equally profitable for study or suitable for every purpose, but how can a critic make a choice between them? Nor are descriptions by reviewers and critics equally open-minded or well and truly observed.

Questions arise at every hand and raise major issues. How can time and space, essential elements of all theatrical experiences, be given appropriate and sufficient attention? How can the stage presence of individual performers be taken into account, or their skills, strengths and weaknesses? How does a performance reach its conclusion, and what satisfaction does that bring? Is this significantly different with each repetition and, if so, to what effect? Description tends to freeze and stall what is happening or developing on stage and, in doing so, simplifies it and takes immediate sensations out of the reckoning. What constancy or authority does a particular theatrical effect possess? Does stage business contravene obvious features of the text and say less about the play than about the skills and intentions of director, producer and actors? Records of what happened on stage will need careful harvesting, sorting and evaluating, especially many years after its last performance. Audiences must also be described and assessed: what words and techniques are best suited to considering or predicting the reactions of an audience? The gate to the wide field of performance studies has been swung open, but it will not readily yield its full crop of relevant information; few scholars interested in theatre production have entered.

As studies of literary texts require an understanding of their contexts and origins, which are the source of much of their value, so do studies of theatrical events, but with one very important difference. Play-texts do not hold all the relevant information: practical processes, physical realities and the personal skills and qualities of everyone involved must also be taken into account. How, why and by whom was each element produced? When and where did this happen, for what purpose and to what effect? Much is likely to escape attention, especially small physical details, personal circumstances and the strengths and weaknesses of the individuals involved, the accidents that occurred and, not least – though often difficult to discover – the time and finance that were available for doing everything necessary. Study of any theatrical event calls for an encyclopaedic mind, a strong and accurate memory, historical perspective, comparative judgement, careful observation and analysis, a strong and disciplined imagination – the qualities of all good scholarship but, because of the variety of evidence to be handled, more demanding here than in other branches of study.

Who is able to undertake such a wide and comprehensive view? Almost certainly no single person but, rather, a team working with common purpose and the means to share the results of each line of investigation as it proceeds to a conclusion. Numerous collections of essays on related themes have been published, but each contribution stands alone and serves its own purpose. Some anthologies publish papers originally written for a conference on a prescribed theme but without an overall view or assessment; the journal *Connotations*, published in Munich, is exceptional in encouraging comments and replies in successive issues. Even this falls short of a publication that would reproduce a debate and argument between contributors in which individual scholars would accommodate or oppose the views of others and work towards a shared perspective and judgement. However sensitive and knowledgeable participants may be, in studying the making of theatre attention must be paid to more than ascertainable facts and responsible thought; imagination is also needed, personal engagement and a foresight that is able to look beyond the time and place of any one performance. Such a group exercise should recognize that everything that can be said about a theatrical event will be incomplete and, consequently, is often unsatisfactory or wrong when seen in a wider context.

A sensible policy would be to pay less attention to single plays and their production and more to comparisons between plays or productions that could reveal what is most original in any one, and so be better able to estimate its worth. Many difficulties will have to be overcome. Study of a theatrical event must be both personal and detached, and yet personal preferences and experience will limit the reach of research. Although necessary, actual and immediate reactions cannot take the place of cool critical judgement because they are too dependent on individual talents, interests, experiences and presuppositions. Looking at similar scenes in a number of plays would allow a range of styles and content to be compared before setting out on intensive study of whole plays.

A search for meanings and consequences will yield positive results, but is liable to give too much importance to words and too little to narrative, action, dramatic structure and physical performance: a play offers sensations to an audience to which attention is due, as well as the ideas and meanings implicit in its words. Perhaps the greatest critical challenge is to find words and questions that are able to register feelings, suggestions, processes and progress, as well as a play's more manageable verbal statements, debates, arguments and conclusions.

Despite all these difficulties, attention paid to the making of theatre offers the best hope of discovering the hold that theatre can exert over an audience and its attraction for individuals who wish to understand themselves and the society in which they live. That raises another difficulty, because to understand the power of theatre is to be aware of the society to which and for which theatre is made: it should be seen as a special branch of social studies and be able to use the techniques developed, and still being developed, for that large and vigorous branch of academic endeavour.

Because a number of differently qualified and practised individuals come together to make a performance, it is not surprising that study of a theatrical event is a group and usually a corporate achievement. Individuals are bound to be limited in background and knowledge, and will come together with different intentions, but if they are to study theatre they must be ready to subordinate individual interests to what may grow to fulfilment between them. Because theatre holds a mirror up to human nature and society, at its best it becomes a lively microcosm of the society that it serves and entertains. Many individuals contribute to making a performance and many more will travel to see it, pay for the opportunity and express their response by applauding, showing disapproval, clamouring for encores or leaving before the end of the play.

Because performances are often repeated and audiences are able to express their pleasure, disapproval or boredom, actors are best suited to know how successful they have been and, in that process, learn how best they can make theatre. An acting company never stays unchanged but is committed to its future and renewal; if it is not, the weight of disapproval will settle upon all it does, no energy remains and very soon that company will die. While specific theatrical events should form the basis of any study of how theatre is made, they are also the most appropriate focus for viewing the entire phenomenon of theatre. While the making of theatre will always be difficult to study, a determined attempt to do so could be a significant influence on theatre's future in our changing world.

Bibliography

Unless otherwise indicated, all references to Shakespeare's works are from *The Norton Shakespeare: Based on the Oxford Shakespeare*. Ed. Stephen Greenblatt et al., London: Norton, 1997.

Aebischer, Pascale. *Shakespeare's Violated Bodies*. Cambridge: Cambridge University Press, 2004.

Allerston, Patricia. 'Consuming Problems: Worldly Goods in Renaissance Venice.' In *The Material Renaissance*. Eds Michelle O'Malley and Evelyn Welch. Manchester: Manchester University Press, 2007: 11–46.

Anon. *The Two Noble Ladies*. Ed. Rebecca G. Rhoads. London: Malone Society Reprints, 1930.

——. *The Taming of A Shrew*. Eds Graham Holderness and Bryan Loughrey. Hemel Hempstead: Harvester Wheatsheaf, 1992.

Appadurai, Arjun. 'Introduction: Commodities and the Politics of Value.' *The Social Life of Things: Commodities in Cultural Perspective*. Ed. Arjun Appadurai. Cambridge: Cambridge University Press, 1986: 3–63.

Archer, Ian W. 'Material Londoners?' In *Material London ca. 1600*. Ed. Lena Cowen Orlin. Philadelphia: University of Pennsylvania Press, 2000: 174–92.

Barker, Roberta. 'Inner Monologues: Realist Acting and/as Shakespearian Performance Text.' *Shakespeare Survey 62*. Ed. Peter Holland. Cambridge: Cambridge University Press, 2009: 249–60.

Barton, John. *Playing Shakespeare*. London: Methuen, 1984.

Baskervill, Charles. *The Elizabethan Jig and Related Song Drama*. Chicago: University of Chicago Press, 1929.

Bate, Jonathan, ed. *Titus Andronicus*. The Arden Shakespeare (3rd Series). London and New York: Routledge, 1995.

——, and Eric Rasmussen, eds. *The RSC Shakespeare: The Complete Works*. Basingstoke: Palgrave Macmillan, 2007.

Beckerman, Bernard. *Shakespeare at the Globe, 1599–1609*. London: Macmillan, 1962.

Benedetti, Jean. *Stanislavski: An Introduction*. London: Methuen, 1982.

Bennett, Susan. *Theatre Audiences: A Theory of Production and Reception*. 2nd edn. London: Routledge, 1996.

Berger, Harry, Jr. 'Impertinent Trifling: Desdemona's Handkerchief.' *Shakespeare Quarterly* 47.3 (Autumn 1996): 235–50.

Berry, Herbert. 'The Bell Savage Inn and Playhouse in London.' *Medieval and Renaissance Drama in England* 19 (2006): 121–43.

Bessell, Jaq. 'The 2000 Globe Season. The White Company. *Hamlet.' Research Bulletin* 17 (March 2001). http://globeeducation.org/files/Hamlet_2000.pdf [accessed November 2010].

Bevington, David, ed. *Antony and Cleopatra*. The New Cambridge Shakespeare. Cambridge: Cambridge University Press, 1990.

Billing, Christian M. Review of *The Roman Tragedies*. *Shakespeare Quarterly* 61.3 (2010): 415–39.

Blau, Herbert. *The Audience*. Baltimore, MD: Johns Hopkins University Press, 1990.

Bloom, Gina. *Voice in Motion: Shaping Gender, Shaping Sound in Early Modern England*. Philadelphia: University of Pennsylvania Press, 2007.

Bristol, Michael. *Carnival and Theatre: Plebeian Culture and the Structure of Authority in Renaissance England*. London and New York: Routledge, 1985.

Brook, Peter. 'Style in Shakespearean Production.' In *The Modern Theatre: Readings and Documents*. Ed. Daniel Seltzer. Boston: Little, Brown, 1967: 248–56. Originally published in *Orpheus* 1 (1948): 139–46.

——. *The Empty Space*. Harmondsworth: Penguin, 1972.

Brotton, Jerry. 'Who is Othello?' Globe Programme Notes: *Othello* (2007): 5–7.

Brown, John Russell. 'Three Directors: A Review of Recent Productions.' *Shakespeare Survey 14*. Ed. Allardyce Nicoll. Cambridge: Cambridge University Press, 1961: 129–37.

Bruzzi, Stella. *Undressing Cinema: Clothing and Identity in the Movies*. London and New York: Routledge, 1997.

Bulman, James C. 'Bringing Cheek by Jowl's *As You like It* Out of the Closet: The Politics of Gay Theater.' *Shakespeare Bulletin* 22.3 (2004): 31–46.

——. 'Queering the Audience: All-Male Casts in Recent Productions of Shakespeare.' In Hodgdon and Worthen 2005: 564–87.

Callaghan, Dymphna. 'Representing Cleopatra in the Post-Colonial Moment.' In *Antony and Cleopatra: Theory in Practice Series*. Ed. N. Wood. Berkshire: Open University Press, 1996: 40–65.

Carson, Christie. 'Shakespeare's Audiences as Imaginative Communities.' In Dymkowski and Carson 2010: 277–92.

——. 'The Quarto of *King Lear* – Representing the Early Stage History of the Play?' www.bl.uk/treasures/shakespeare/lear.html [accessed May 2011].

—— and Farah Karim-Cooper, eds. *Shakespeare's Globe: A Theatrical Experiment*. Cambridge University Press, 2008.

Cartwright, Kent. *Shakespearean Tragedy and Its Double: The Rhythms of Audience Response*. University Park: Pennsylvania State University Press, 1991.

Chinoy, Helen Krich. 'The Emergence of the Director.' In *Directors on Directing: A Source Book of the Modern Theatre*. Ed. Toby Cole and Helen Krich Chinoy. London: Macmillan, 1963: 1–78.

Chion, Michel. 'Wasted Words.' In *Sound Theory, Sound Practice*. Ed. Ric Altman. London and New York: Routledge, 1992: 104–12.

Choondal, Chummar. *Towards Performance*. Keralam: Kerala Folk Academy, 1988.

Clayton, Thomas. '"Is this the promis'd end?" Revision in the Role of the King.' In *The Division of the Kingdoms: Shakespeare's Two Versions of King Lear*. Ed. Gary Taylor and Michael Warren. Oxford: Clarendon Press, 1983: 121–41.

——. 'Theatrical Shakespearegresses at the Guthrie and Elsewhere: Notes on "Legitimate Production."' *New Literary History* 17.3 (1986): 511–38.

——. '"Balancing at Work": (R)evoking the Script in Performance and Criticism.' In *Shakespeare and the Sense of Performance: Essays in the Tradition of Performance Criticism in Honor of Bernard Beckerman*. Ed. Marvin Thompson and Ruth Thompson. Newark: University of Delaware Press, 1989: 228–49.

Clegg, Roger and P. Thomson. '"He's for a jig or a tale of bawdry—": Notes on the English Dramatic Jig.' *Studies in Theatre and Performance* 29:1: 67–83.

Cohen, Ralph Alan. 'Directing at the Globe and the Blackfriars: Six Big Rules for Contemporary Directors.' In Carson and Karim-Cooper 2008: 211–25.

Cohn, Ruby. 'Growing (Up?) with *Godot*.' In *Beckett at 80/Beckett in Context*. Ed. Enoch Brater. Oxford: Oxford University Press, 1986: 3–24.

David, Richard. 'Shakespeare's Comedies and the Modern Stage.' *Shakespeare Survey 4*. Ed. Allardyce Nicoll. Cambridge: Cambridge University Press, 1951: 129–38.

Dawson, Anthony B. and Paul Yachnin. *The Culture of Playgoing in Shakespeare's England*. Cambridge: Cambridge University Press, 2001.

De Marinis, Marco. *The Semiotics of Performance*. Trans. Áine O'Healey. Bloomington: Indiana University Press, 1993.

Dening, Greg. *Performances*. Chicago: University of Chicago Press, 1996.

Derrida, Jacques. *Spectres of Marx: The State of the Debt, the Work of Mourning, and the New International*. Trans. Peggy Kamuf. London and New York: Routledge, 1994.

Dessen, Alan C. *Elizabethan Stage Conventions and Modern Interpreters*. Cambridge: Cambridge University Press, 1986.

——. 'Exploring the Script: Shakespearean Pay-offs in 1987.' *Shakespeare Quarterly* 39:2 (1988), 217–26.

—— and Leslie Thomson. *A Dictionary of Stage Directions in English Drama 1580–1642*. Cambridge: Cambridge University Press, 1999.

Diamond, Elin. *Unmaking Mimesis: Essays on Feminism and Theatre*. London and New York: Routledge, 1997.

Dobson, Michael. 'Writing about [Shakespearian] Performance.' *Shakespeare Survey 58*. Ed. Peter Holland. Cambridge: Cambridge University Press, 2005: 160–8.

——. 'Shakespeare Performances in England, 2006.' *Shakespeare Survey 60*. Ed. Peter Holland. Cambridge: Cambridge University Press, 2007: 284–319.

——. 'Shakespeare Performances in England, 2007.' *Shakespeare Survey 61*. Ed. Peter Holland. Cambridge: Cambridge University Press, 2008: 318–50.

Donno, Elizabeth Story and Penny Gay, eds. *Twelfth Night*. The New Cambridge Shakespeare. Cambridge: Cambridge University Press, 1985.

Dorsch, T.S., ed. *The Comedy of Errors*. The New Cambridge Shakespeare. Updated edition. Cambridge: Cambridge University Press, 2004. Originally published 1988.

Ducklin, Keith and John Waller. *Sword Fighting: A Manual for Actors and Directors*. London: Robert Hale, 2001.

Dymkowski, Christine, ed. *The Tempest*. Shakespeare in Production. Cambridge: Cambridge University Press, 2000.

—— and Christie Carson, eds. *Shakespeare in Stages: New Theatre Histories*. Cambridge: Cambridge University Press, 2010.

Edelman, Charles. *Brawl Ridiculous: Sword-Fighting in Shakespeare's Plays*. Manchester: Manchester University Press, 1992.

Elam, Kier. *The Semiotics of Theatre and Drama*. London and New York: Routledge, 1980.

Escolme, Bridget. *Talking to the Audience: Shakespeare, Performance, Self*. London and New York: Routledge, 2005.

——. 'Living Monuments: The Spatial Politics of Shakespeare's Rome on the Contemporary Stage.' *Shakespeare Survey 60*. Ed. Peter Holland. Cambridge: Cambridge University Press, 2007: 170–83.

——. 'Being Good: Actors' Testimonies as Archive and the Cultural Condition of Success in Performance.' *Shakespeare Bulletin* 28.1 (2010): 77–91.

Evans, G. Blakemore, et al., eds. *The Riverside Shakespeare*. 2nd edn. Boston: Houghton Mifflin, 1997.

Fisher, Will. *Materializing Gender in Early Modern English Literature and Culture*. Cambridge: Cambridge University Press, 2006.

Fitzpatrick, Tim. 'Shakespeare's Exploitation of a Two-Door Stage: *Macbeth*.' *Theatre Research International* 20.3 (1995): 207–30.

——. 'Stage Management, Dramaturgy and Spatial Semiotics in Shakespeare's Dialogue.' *Theatre Research International* 24.1 (1999): 1–23.

——. 'Playwrights with Foresight: Staging Resources in the Elizabethan Playhouses.' *Theatre Notebook* 56.2 (2002): 85–116.

—— and Daniel Johnston. 'Spaces, Doors and Places in Early Modern English Staging.' *Theatre Notebook* 63.1 (2009): 2–19.

—— and Wendy Millyard. 'Hangings, Doors and Discoveries: Conflicting Evidence or Problematic Assumptions?' *Theatre Notebook* 54.1 (2000): 2–23.

Foakes, R.A. 'Performance Theory and Textual Theory: A Retort Courteous.' *Shakespeare* 2.1 (2006): 47–58.

—— and R.T. Rickert, eds. *Henslowe's Diary*. Cambridge: Cambridge University Press, 1961.

Folkerth, Wes. *The Sound of Shakespeare*. London and New York: Routledge, 2002.

Foucault, Michel. *Discipline and Punish: The Birth of the Prison*. Trans. Alan Sheridan. Harmondsworth: Penguin, 1991.

Freshwater, Helen. *Theatre & Audience*. Basingstoke: Palgrave Macmillan, 2009.

Friedman, Michael D. 'In Defence of Authenticity.' *Studies in Philology* 99.1 (2002): 33–56.

Frye, Roland Mushat. *The Renaissance Hamlet: Issues and Responses in 1600*. Princeton: Princeton University Press, 1984.

Goodman, Nelson. *Languages of Art: An Approach to a Theory of Symbols*. 2nd ed. Indianapolis: Hackett, 1976.

Griffin, Eric. 'Un-Sainting James: Or, Othello and the "Spanish Spirits" of Shakespeare's Globe.' *Representations* 62 (Spring 1998): 58–99.

Grotowski, Jerzy. *Towards a Poor Theatre*. Ed. Eugenio Barba. London and New York: Routledge, 1968.

Gurr, Andrew. '*The Tempest*'s Tempest at Blackfriars.' *Shakespeare Survey 41*. Ed. Stanley Wells. Cambridge: Cambridge University Press, 1989: 91–102.

——. *The Shakespearean Stage 1574–1642*. 3rd ed. Cambridge: Cambridge University Press, 1992.

——. 'Stage Doors at the Globe.' *Theatre Notebook* 53.1 (1999): 8–18.

——. 'Doors at the Globe: The Gulf between Page and Stage.' *Theatre Notebook* 55.2 (2001): 59–71.

—— and Mariko Ichikawa. *Staging in Shakespeare's Theatres*. Oxford: Oxford University Press, 2000.

Halio, Jay L. *Understanding Shakespeare's Plays in Performance*. Manchester: Manchester University Press, 1988.

——, ed. *The Tragedy of King Lear*. The New Cambridge Shakespeare. Cambridge: Cambridge University Press, 1992.

Hall, Peter. 'Shakespeare and the Modern Director.' In *Royal Shakespeare Company 1960–63*. Ed. John Goodwin. London: Max Reinhardt, 1964: 41–8.

——. 'A Director's Approach: An Interview with Peter Hall.' In *A Casebook on Harold Pinter's The Homecoming*. Ed. John Lahr and Anthea Lahr. London: Davis-Poynter, 1974: 9–26.

Hammond, Antony. 'Encounters of the Third Kind in Stage-Directions in Elizabethan and Jacobean Drama.' *Studies in Philology* 89.1 (1992): 71–99.

Hampton-Reeves, Stuart and Carol Chillington Rutter. *Shakespeare in Performance: The Henry VI Plays*. Manchester: Manchester University Press, 2006.

Hannaford, Stephen. 'Symbols, Emblems, Tokens.' *Theatre Journal* 33.4 (December 1981): 467–76.

Harris, Bernard. 'A Portrait of a Moor.' *Shakespeare Survey 11*. Ed. Allardyce Nicoll. Cambridge: Cambridge University Press, 1958: 89–97.

Harris, Jonathan Gil and Natasha Korda, eds. *Staged Properties in Early Modern English Drama*. Cambridge: Cambridge University Press, 2002.

Hartley, Andrew James. 'Page and Stage Again: Rethinking Renaissance Character Phenomenologically.' In *New Directions in Renaissance Drama and Performance Studies*. Ed. Sarah Werner. Basingstoke: Palgrave Macmillan, 2010: 77–93.

Hobbs, William. *Fight Direction: For Stage and Screen*. London: A.&C. Black, 1995. (Originally published as *Stage Combat*. London: Barrie & Jenkins, 1980.)

Hodgdon, Barbara. 'Gaining a Father: The Role of Egeus in the Quarto and the Folio.' *Review of English Studies* 37.148 (1986): 534–42.

——. 'New Collaborations with Old Plays: The (Textual) Politics of Performance Commentary.' In *Textual Performances*. Ed. Lukas Erne and Margaret Jane Kidnie. Cambridge: Cambridge University Press, 2004: 210–23.

——, ed. *The Taming of the Shrew*. The Arden Shakespeare (3rd Series). London: A.&C. Black, 2010.

—— and W. B. Worthen, eds. *A Companion to Shakespeare and Performance*. Oxford: Blackwell, 2005.

Hodges, C.W. *Enter the Whole Army: A Pictorial Study of Shakespearean Staging, 1576–1616*. Cambridge: Cambridge University Press, 1999.

Holland, Peter. 'Shakespeare Performances in England, 1990–1.' *Shakespeare Survey 45*. Ed. Stanley Wells. Cambridge: Cambridge University Press, 1992: 115–44.

——. 'Shakespeare in the Twentieth Century Theatre.' In *The Cambridge Companion to Shakespeare*. Ed. Margreta de Grazia and Stanley Wells. Cambridge: Cambridge University Press, 2001: 199–216.

——. 'Peter Hall.' In *The Routledge Guide to Directors' Shakespeare*. Ed. John Russell Brown. London and New York: Routledge, 2008: 140–59.

Holmes, Jonathan. *Merely Players? Actors Accounts of Performing Shakespeare*. London: Routledge, 2004.

Holmes, Martin. *Shakespeare and his Players*. London: John Murray, 1972.

Huang, Ya-Hui. 'Shakespeare in Taiwan.' Ph.D. thesis. Preston: University of Central Lancashire, 2012.

Hughes, Alan, ed. *Titus Andronicus*. The New Cambridge Shakespeare. Updated ed. Cambridge: Cambridge University Press, 2006.

Hunter, G.K. 'Rhetoric and Renaissance Drama'. In Mack 1994: 103–18.

Ichikawa, Mariko. *Shakespearean Entrances*. Basingstoke: Palgrave Macmillan, 2002.

——. 'Were the Doors Open or Closed?: The Use of Stage Doors in the Shakespearean Theatre.' *Theatre Notebook* 60.1 (2006): 5–29.

Jacobi, Derek. 'Macbeth.' In *Players of Shakespeare 4*. Ed. Robert Smallwood. Cambridge: Cambridge University Press, 1998: 193–210.

Jenstad, Janelle, Peter Lichtenfels and Lynne Magnusson. 'Text and Voice.' In *Shakespeare, Language and the Stage*. Ed. Lynette Hunter and Peter Lichtenfels. London: Arden Shakespeare, 2005.

Johnson, Samuel. *Johnson on Shakespeare*. Ed. Arthur Sherbo. Vols. VII and VIII of the Yale Edition of the *Works of Samuel Johnson*. New Haven and London: Yale University Press, 1968.

Jones, Emrys. *Scenic Form in Shakespeare*. Oxford: Clarendon Press, 1985.

Jonson, Ben. *Timber: or, Discoveries Made Vpon Men and Matter: As they have flow'd out of his daily Readings; or had their refluxe to his peculiar Notion of the Times*. In *The Workes of Benjamin Jonson. The Second Volume*. London, 1640.

Jowett, John. 'New Created Creatures: Ralph Crane and the Stage Directions in *The Tempest*.' *Shakespeare Survey 36*. Ed. Stanley Wells. Cambridge: Cambridge University Press, 1983: 107–20.

Karim-Cooper, Farah. 'Cosmetics and the Globe Stage.' In Carson and Karim-Cooper 2008: 66–76.

——. 'Performing Beauty on the Renaissance Stage.' In Dymkowski and Carson 2010: 93–106.

Kennedy, Dennis. *Looking At Shakespeare*. Cambridge: Cambridge University Press, 1993.

——. *The Spectator and the Spectacle: Audiences in Modernity and Postmodernity*. Cambridge: Cambridge University Press, 2009.

Kidnie, Margaret Jane. *Shakespeare and the Problem of Adaptation*. London and New York: Routledge, 2009.

King, T.J. *Shakespearean Staging, 1599–1642*. Cambridge, MA: Harvard University Press, 1971.

Kirwan, Peter. Review of *As You Like It*. In *Bardathon*, 2009. http://blogs.warwick.ac.uk/pkirwan/entry/as_you_like_1_2_3/ [accessed 10 August 2010].

Knowles, Ric. *Reading the Material Theatre*. Cambridge: Cambridge University Press, 2005.

Knowlson, James. *Damned to Fame: The Life of Samuel Beckett*. London: Bloomsbury, 1996.

Kostelanetz, Richard. *Conversing with Cage*. New York: Limelight, 1989.

Kott, Jan. *Shakespeare Our Contemporary*. Trans. Boleslaw Taborski. London: Methuen, 1964.

Lane, Richard. *Swashbuckling: A Step-by-Step Guide to the Art of Stage Combat and Theatrical Sword-Play*. London: Nick Hern, 1999.

Levin, Richard. 'Refuting Shakespeare's Endings.' *Modern Philology* 72.4 (1977): 337–49.

——. 'The Opening of *All's Well That Ends Well*.' *Connotations* 7.1 (1997–98): 18–32.

Mack, Peter, ed. *Renaissance Rhetoric*. London: Macmillan, 1994.

Madelaine, Richard, ed., *Antony and Cleopatra*. Shakespeare in Production. Cambridge: Cambridge University Press, 1998.

Mahood, M.M. 'Shakespeare's Sense of Direction.' In *Shakespeare Performed: Essays in Honor of R.A. Foakes*. Ed. Grace Ioppolo. Newark: University of Delaware Press, 2000: 33–55.

Marcus, Leah. 'The Two Texts of *Othello* and Early Modern Constructions of Race.' In *Textual Performances: The Modern Reproduction of Shakespeare's Drama*. Ed. Lukas Erne and Margaret Jane Kidnie. Cambridge: Cambridge University Press, 2004: 21–36.

Markham, Gervase. *The Famous Whore, or Noble Curtizan: conteining the lamentable complaint of Paulina, the famour Roman Curtizan, sometimes mes unto the great Cardinall Hypolito of Est*. London, 1609.

Marowitz, Charles. 'The Director and the Permanent Company.' In *Theatre at Work: Playwrights and Productions in the Modern British Theatre*. Ed. Charles Marowitz and Simon Trussler. New York: Hill & Wang, 1968: 148–59.

Maurer, Margaret. 'Constering Bianca: *The Taming of the Shrew* and *The Woman's Prize, or The Tamer Tamed*.' *Medieval and Renaissance Drama in England* 14 (2001): 186–206.

——. 'The Rowe editions of 1709/1714 and 3.1 of *The Taming of the Shrew*.' In *Reading Readings: Essays on Shakespeare Editing in the Eighteenth Century*. Ed. Joanna Gondris. Cranbury: Associated University Presses, 1998: 244–67.

—— and Barry Gaines. 'Putting the Silent Woman Back into the Shakespearean Shrew.' In *Gender and Power in Shrew-Taming Narratives, 1500–1700*. Ed. David Wootton and Graham Holderness. Basingstoke: Palgrave Macmillan, 2010: 101–22.

McAuley, Gay. *Space in Performance: Making Meaning in the Theatre*. Ann Arbor: University of Michigan Press, 1999.

McCandless, David. *Gender and Performance in Shakespeare's Problem Comedies*. Bloomington and Indianapolis: Indiana University Press, 1997.

McGuire, Philip C. *Speechless Dialect: Shakespeare's Open Silences*. Berkeley: University of California Press, 1985.

McKellen, Ian and Richard Loncraine, eds. *William Shakespeare's Richard III: A Screenplay*. New York: Doubleday, 1996.

Meek, Richard. 'The Promise of Satisfaction: Shakespeare's Oral Endings'. *English* 56.216 (2007): 247–63.

Melrose, Susan. '"Constitutive Ambiguities": Writing Professional or Expert Performance Practices, and the Théâtre du Soleil, Paris.' In *Contemporary Theatres in Europe*. Eds Joe Kelleher and Nicholas Ridout. London and New York: Routledge, 206: 120–35.

Metz, G. Harold. *Shakespeare's Earliest Tragedy: Studies in Titus Andronicus*. Madison: Fairleigh Dickinson University Press, 1996: 233–43.

Monks, Aoife. *The Actor in Costume*. Basingstoke: Palgrave Macmillan, 2010.

Moten, Fred. *In the Break: the Aesthetics of the Black Radical Tradition*. Minneapolis: University of Minnesota Press, 2003.

Mowat, Barbara A. and Paul Werstine, eds. *Hamlet*. Folger Shakespeare Library. New York: Washington Square Press, 1992.

Nashe, Thomas. *Pierce Penniless, his Supplication to the Divell (1592). The Works of Thomas Nashe*. Ed. Ronald B. McKerrow, rev. F.P. Wilson. 5 vols. Oxford: Blackwell, 1958, 1:212.

Nochimson, Richard L. 'The Establishment of Tragic and Untragic Patterns in the Opening Scenes of *Hamlet, Macbeth, Antony and Cleopatra* and *Troilus and Cressida*.' In Willson 1995: 75–94.

Nuttall, A.D. 'Some Shakespearean Openings: *Hamlet, Twelfth Night, The Tempest.*' In *The Arts of Performance in Elizabethan and Early Stuart Drama*. Ed. Murray Biggs. Edinburgh: Edinburgh University Press, 1991: 84–95.

Osborn, Keith. *Something Written in the State of Denmark: An Actor's Year with the Royal Shakespeare Company*. London: Oberon, 2010.

Parker, Patricia. 'Barbers, Infidels and Renegades: *Antony and Cleopatra.*' In *Centre or Margin: Revisions of the English Renaissance in Honour of Leeds Barroll*. Eds Lena Cowen Orlin and John Leeds Barroll. Cranbury: Associated University Press, 2006: 54–88.

Phelan, Peggy. *Unmarked: The Politics of Performance*. London and New York: Routledge, 1993.

Plasse, Marie A. 'Corporeality and the Opening of *Richard III.*' In Willson 1995: 11–25.

Prescott, Paul. 'Inheriting the Globe: The Reception of Shakespearean Space and Audience in Contemporary Reviewing.' In Hodgdon and Worthen 2005: 359–75.

Raffield, Paul. *Shakespeare's Imaginary Constitution: Late-Elizabethan Politics and the Theatre of Law*. Oxford: Hart, 2010.

Raleigh, Walter. *The History of the World*. London, 1614.

Rayner, Alice. *Ghosts: Death's Double and the Phenomena of Theatre*. Minneapolis: University of Minnesota Press, 2006.

Ridout, Nicholas. *Stage Fright, Animals, and Other Theatrical Problems*. Cambridge: Cambridge University Press, 2006.

Riley, Jo. *Chinese Theatre and the Actor in Performance*. Cambridge: Cambridge University Press, 1997.

Ripley, John. *Coriolanus on Stage in England and America, 1609–1994*. London: Associated University Presses, 1998.

Robinson, Jenefer. 'Languages of Art at the Turn of the Century.' *Journal of Aesthetics and Art Criticism* 58.3 (2000): 213–18.

Rocklin, Edward L. 'Shakespeare's Script as a Cue for Pedagogic Invention.' *Shakespeare Quarterly* 46.2 (1995): 135–44.

Rogers, Jami. 'Deborah Warner's *Titus* 1.1 notes.' Private correspondence, 2005.

Rokison, Abigail. 'Authenticity in the Twenty-first Century: Propeller and Shakespeare's Globe.' In Dymkowski and Carson 2010: 71–90.

Royal National Theatre. 'The Chorus.' www.stagework.org.uk/webdav/harmonise@Page%252F@id=6007&Section%252F@id=359.html [accessed 9 March 2010].

Rutter, Carol. *Clamorous Voices: Shakespeare's Women Today*. Ed. Faith Evans. London: The Women's Press, 1988.

Ryan, Jessica, *Shakespeare's Globe Research Bulletin*, issue 26, July 2002: Twelfth Night, http://globe-education.org/discovery-space/resource-library/document/782/research-bulletin-twelfth-night-2002

Rylance, Mark. 'Research, Materials, Craft: Principles of Performance at Shakespeare's Globe.' In Carson and Karim-Cooper 2008: 103–14.

Schafer, Elizabeth, ed. *The Taming of the Shrew*. Shakespeare in Production. Cambridge: Cambridge University Press, 2002.

Schechner, Richard. *Between Theatre and Anthropology*. Philadelphia: University of Pennsylvania Press, 1985.

——. *Performance Theory*. 2nd ed. London and New York: Routledge, 1988.

Schuleter, June. 'Rereading the Peacham Drawing.' *Shakespeare Quarterly* 50.2 (1999): 171–84.

Seneca. *The Works of L.A. Seneca both Morall and Naturall*. Trans. Thomas Lodge. London, 1620.

Shaughnessy, Robert. '"I do, I will": Hal, Falstaff and the Performative.' In *Alternative Shakespeares 3*. Ed. Diana E. Henderson. London and New York: Routledge, 2008: 14–33.

Shaw, George Bernard. *Geneva, Cymbeline Refinished, & Good King Charles*. London: Constable & Co., 1946.

Sher, Antony. *Beside Myself*. London: Arrow Books, 2002.

Shrimpton, Nicholas. 'Shakespeare Performances in London and Stratford-upon-Avon, 1984–5.' *Shakespeare Survey 39*. Ed. Stanley Wells. Cambridge: Cambridge University Press, 1986: 191–206.

Sidney, Sir Philip. 'The Defence of Poesy'. In *Renaissance Literature: An Anthology*. Eds Michael Payne and John Hunter. Oxford: Blackwell, 2003: 501–27.

Silver, George. *The Works of George Silver*. Ed. Cyril G.R. Matthey. London: George Bell & Sons, 1898.

Sinden, Donald. 'Malvolio in *Twelfth Night*.' In *Players of Shakespeare 1*. Ed. Philip Brockbank. Cambridge: Cambridge University Press, 1989: 41–66.

Skantze, P.A. *Stillness in Motion in the Seventeenth-Century Theatre*. London and New York: Routledge, 2003.

Smallwood, Robert. 'Shakespeare Performances in England, 1999.' *Shakespeare Survey 53*. Ed. Peter Holland. Cambridge: Cambridge University Press, 2000: 244–73.

Smith, Bruce R. *The Acoustic World of Early Modern England*. Chicago: University of Chicago Press, 1999.

——. 'Ragging *Twelfth Night*: 1602, 1996, 2002–3.' In Hodgdon and Worthen 2005: 57–78.

Smith, Emma, ed. *Henry V*. Shakespeare in Production. Cambridge: Cambridge University Press, 2002.

Snyder, Susan and Deborah T. Curren-Aquino, eds. *The Winter's Tale*. The New Cambridge Shakespeare. Cambridge: Cambridge University Press, 2007.

Sofer, Andrew. *The Stage Life of Props*. Ann Arbor: University of Michigan Press, 2003.

Stanislavski, Constantin. *Building a Character*. Trans. Elizabeth Hapgood Reynolds. London: Methuen, 1979.

Stern, Tiffany. *Rehearsal from Shakespeare to Sheridan*. Oxford: Oxford University Press, 2000.

——. *Making Shakespeare: From Page to Stage*. London and New York: Routledge, 2004.

Sterne, Jonathan. *The Audible Past: Cultural Origins of Sound Reproduction*. Chapel Hill: Duke University Press, 2003.

Stirling, Edward. *Old Drury Lane: Fifty Years' Recollections of Author, Actor, and Manager*. 2 vols. London: Chatto & Windus, 1881.

Styan, J.L. 'The Opening of *All's Well That Ends Well*: A Performance Approach.' In Willson 1995: 155–68.

Theobald, Lewis, ed. *The Works of Shakespeare*. Vol. 8. 1740.

Thomson, Leslie. 'The Meaning of Thunder and Lightning: Stage Directions and Audience Expectations.' *Early Theatre* 2.1 (1999): 11–24.

Tiramani, Jenny. 'Exploring Early Modern Stage and Costume Design.' In Carson and Karim Cooper, 2008: 57–65.

Traub, Valerie. 'The Homoerotics of Shakespearean Comedy'. In *Shakespeare, Feminism and Gender*. Ed. Kate Chedgzoy. Basingstoke: Palgrave Macmillan, 2001: 135–60.

Trewin, J.C. *Five and Eighty Hamlets*. London: Hutchinson, 1987.

Turner, Victor. *From Ritual to Theatre: The Human Seriousness of Play*. New York: PAJ Books, 1982.

Tynan, Kenneth. *He That Plays the King*. London: Longmans, Green & Co., 1950.

Vaughan, Virginia Mason and Alden T. Vaughan, eds. *The Tempest*. The Arden Shakespeare (3rd Series). London: Cengage Learning, 1999.

Vickers, Brian, ed. *Shakespeare: The Critical Heritage Vol 2: 1693–1733*. London and New York: Routledge, 1974.

——. *Shakespeare, Co-Author: A Historical Study of Five Collaborative Plays*. Oxford: Oxford University Press, 2002.

Waith, Eugene M., ed. *Titus Andronicus*. The Oxford Shakespeare. Oxford: Clarendon Press, 1984.

Warren, Roger. 'Theory and Practice: Stratford 1976.' *Shakespeare Survey 30*. Ed. Kenneth Muir. Cambridge: Cambridge University Press, 1977: 169–79.

——. 'Shakespeare in Britain, 1985.' *Shakespeare Quarterly* 37.1 (1986): 114–20.

Weimann, Robert. *Shakespeare and the Popular Tradition in the Theatre: Studies in the Social Dimension of Dramatic Form and Function*. Trans. and ed. R. Schwartz. Baltimore and London: Johns Hopkins University Press, 1978.

——. 'Thresholds to Memory and Commodity in Shakespeare's Endings.' *Representations* 53 (Winter 1996): 1–20.

——. *Author's Pen and Actor's Voice: Playing and Writing in Shakespeare's Theatre*. Cambridge: Cambridge University Press, 2000.

Wells, Stanley. 'Editorial Treatment of Foul-Paper Texts: *Much Ado about Nothing* as Test Case.' *Review of English Studies* 31.121 (1980): 1–16.

—— and Gary Taylor, with John Jowett and William Montgomery. *William Shakespeare: A Textual Companion*. Oxford: Oxford University Press, 1987.

Werstine, Paul. 'The Textual Mystery of *Hamlet*.' *Shakespeare Quarterly* 39 (1988): 1–26.

Whetstone, George. '*Promos and Cassandra*.' *Narrative and Dramatic Sources for Shakespeare Volume 2, The Comedies*. Ed. Geoffrey Bullough. London and New York: Routledge, 1958.

Willson, Robert F., Jr, ed. *Entering the Maze*. New York: Peter Lang, 1995.

Worthen, W.B. *Shakespeare and the Authority of Performance*. Cambridge: Cambridge University Press, 1997.

——. *Print and the Poetics of Modern Drama*. Cambridge: Cambridge University Press, 2005.

——. 'Texts, Tools, and Technologies of Performance: A Quip Modest, in Response to R.A. Foakes.' *Shakespeare* 2.2 (2006): 208–19.

Zarrilli, Phillip B. 'What Does It Mean to "Become the Character": Power, Presence, and Transcendence in Asian In-Body Disciplines of Practice.' In *By Means of Performance*. Eds Richard Schechner and Willa Appel. Cambridge: Cambridge University Press, 1990: 131–48.

——. *When the Body Becomes All Eyes: Paradigms, Discourses and Practices of Power in Kalarippayattu, a South Indian Martial Art*. Oxford: Oxford University Press, 1998.

Zimmerman, Susan. *The Early Modern Corpse and Shakespeare's Theatre*. Edinburgh: Edinburgh University Press, 2005.

Index

Plays

All plays by Shakespeare except where noted.

Productions

Productions are sorted by company and then year. The Royal Shakespeare Company (RSC), the Royal National Theatre (NT) and Shakespeare's Globe Theatre (Globe) are all abbreviated.